D0934923

Teaching and Learning in Higher Education

Teaching and Learning in Higher Education

Studies of Three Student Development Programs

Beatrice L. Bridglall

LEXINGTON BOOKS
Lanham • Boulder • New York • Toronto • Plymouth, UK

Published by Lexington Books
A wholly owned subsidiary of The Rowman & Littlefield Publishing Group, Inc.
4501 Forbes Boulevard, Suite 200, Lanham, Maryland 20706
www.rowman.com

10 Thornbury Road, Plymouth PL6 7PP, United Kingdom

British Library Cataloguing in Publication Information Available

Library of Congress Cataloging-in-Publication Data

Bridglall, Beatrice L.
Teaching and learning in higher education : studies of three student development programs / Beatrice
L. Bridglall.
p. cm.
Includes bibliographical references
ISBN 978-0-7391-7733-4 (cloth : alk. paper)—ISBN 978-0-7391-7734-1 (electronic)
1. College student development programs—United States—Case studies. I. Title.
LB2343.4.B75 2013
378.1'98—dc23
2013016865

Printed in the United States of America

For A. and V.,
Always

Contents

Foreword

The power of ideas and the commitment of dedicated educators and university leadership to the moral and practical goals of equity and excellence all find resonance in three remarkable student development programs featured in *Teaching and Learning In Higher Education: Studies of Three Student Development Programs*. Indeed, the crux of these ideas, namely that students can excel if exposed to both opportunities and supports to learn, is one of the hallmarks of the Meyerhoff Scholars Program at the University of Maryland, Baltimore County; the Opportunity Programs (OP) at Skidmore College, Saratoga Springs, New York; and the Premedical Program at Xavier University in New Orleans.

At a time when the field is debating the importance of bringing faculty, students and the community together to nurture and improve teaching, learning and scholarship, these three programs continue to engage in these practices in dynamic and remarkable ways. They have not, however, limited themselves to employing the curriculum in this endeavor but are actively engaged in building and maintaining partnerships and outreach to faculty, staff, students and the community. Thus, the ideas of curricular engagement, and community partnerships and outreach, long championed by the Carnegie Foundation for the Advancement of Teaching, are increasingly regarded as avenues for not only increasing student performance but also the effectiveness of school reform strategies.

Undergirding these ideas as well are sophisticated understandings of how students learn. Indeed, Dr. Bridglall's analysis of these three programs suggest that they espouse John Dewey's ideas that education needs to (1) recognize and build on students' experiences both in and out of school, and (2) cultivate the kind of creative thinking that can promote solutions to pressing issues in education and social policy. Thus, it is not a surprise that these three programs mesh both a short- and long- term perspective with respect to academically and socially preparing their students to take their place as responsible, contributing citizens who are life-long learners.

In this respect, there is not a tension between traditional and progressive education in these programs but rather a concern for exposing students to disciplined study that is rigorous and holistic; not fragmented. This focus thus on providing students with rigorous opportunities and relevant supports reflects the importance of continuity and interaction between and among faculty, staff and students. This is particularly important because the success of these three programs appear to be at the nexus of research and practice. That is, these programs continue to evolve and succeed in strategic ways based on empirical research and the dedication of university leadership, faculty, staff and students. This tri-directional approach (research, praxis and utility) is especially salient in light of the need for stronger connections between researchers and practitioners.

Dr. Bridglall's analysis of three of the most noteworthy programs in higher education strengthens the knowledge base on strategies that can be distilled, adapted and employed to improve student learning. Her policy recommendations are also relevant at a time when we need to assume more responsibility for improving local schools and building, maintaining and strengthening the ties between universities/colleges and schools and communities. Understanding and adapting the strategies that undergird the success of these three programs will enable us to not only improve student performance in the short term, but also reduce related expenditures on health care, crime and welfare in the long term. Indeed, we now know that the costs are enormous when students do not do well in their course of study. Henry Levin and Clive Belfield's recent work on the importance of investing in education remind us that even a one percent increase in the high school graduation rates for males in the United States, would yield an estimated1.4 billion in reduced crime. These scholars conclude that "A society that provides fairer access to opportunities, is more productive, and has higher employment, better health and less crime, is a better society in itself." Dr. Bridglall's timely work provides a blueprint for some of the more successful strategies in higher education that can also be parlayed into strengthening our K-12 systems. So too does it reinforce that we need to design research and interventions from interdisciplinary, multicultural and global perspectives. This approach recognizes the potential of our young people and the responsibility of those charged with caring for the nurturance and expansion of that potential.

Robert H. Koff
Professor & Director, Center for Advanced Learning
Washington University in St. Louis, Missouri
Former Senior Vice President, The Danforth Foundation

Acknowledgments

I would like to recognize Emeritus Professor Edmund W. Gordon, who initiated and supported the study of the Meyerhoff Scholars Program at the University of Maryland, Baltimore County. In the course of examining the Meyerhoff Program, we added the premedical program at Xavier University in New Orleans, to the list. Subsequent conversations with L. Scott Miller led to his suggestion to examine the Opportunity Programs at Skidmore College in Saratoga Springs, New York. Informative conversations with Drs. Robert Koff, Robert Sternberg and Alan Schoenfeld, also led to the shaping and refinement of this study. Dr. Robert Koff's steadfast support and guidance is also gratefully acknowledged. I continued this research as a faculty member at Queens College, City University of New York with encouragement and support from Deans Francine Peterman and Richard Bodnar. Additionally, this book would not have been possible without the unwavering support of the leadership, faculty, staff and students at the University of Maryland, Baltimore County (including Drs. Freeman Hrabowski and Kenneth Maton, Mr. Keith Harmon and the late Director of the Meyerhoff Program, Mr. La Mont Toliver); Skidmore College (Drs. Susan Layden and Sheldon Solomon, Ms. Terri Kindl, Dr. Lewis Rosengarten, Mr. George McNally, Ms. Kate Dudley-Perry, Ms. Alice Buesing and Ms. Carrie Fonda), and Xavier University (Dr. J.W. Carmichael and his colleagues, including Ms. QuoVadis Webster, Sister Grace Mary Flickenger, and Dr. Ann Privet). Thank you all for your friendship and collaborative spirit.

Organization of the Book

INTRODUCTION

One of the more complicated findings to emerge from the accumulated analysis of student grade point average (GPA), standardized test scores and class rank, is that African American, Hispanic and Native American students at all socio-economic status (SES) levels and throughout all levels of the educational system are underrepresented among the nation's high achieving students (College Board 1999; Miller 1995, 2005). This chronic underachievement results in relatively few bachelor's degree recipients who are competitively credentialed (Cota-Robles 2003) for admissions to selective professional schools and graduate programs in the natural and physical sciences, engineering, mathematics, computer science, economics, law, biology and medicine. These issues are particularly sobering when we consider their implications for efforts to not only *diversify* but also *integrate* our nation's professional and leadership class (Bowen and Levin 2003; College Board 2009; Shapiro 2005). That is, goals of diversity increases the numbers but integration requires a consistent distribution of academic performance; issues researchers are currently exploring in the context of increased time to degree and low attainment rates in higher education (Arum and Roksa 2011; Bowen, Chingos and McPherson 2009; Kuglemass and Ready 2011).

There are several underlying issues that hinge on both institutional and personal responsibility for these persistent and pervasive (but not intractable, Bowen et al. 2009) trends in underachievement. On the institutional side, there are few programs or strategies with robust empirical evidence demonstrating consistently high achievement from students in underrepresented groups. We can attribute this dearth in interventions to a prevailing focus on merely retaining and graduating these students (Kuglemass and Ready 2011).

Despite this, there are several empirically grounded models available from which we can distill a set of strategies for enabling student learning and high achievement. This book examines three such models in higher education – the Meyerhoff Scholars Program at the University of Maryland, Baltimore County, the Opportunity Programs at Skidmore College in Saratoga Springs, New York, and the premedical program at Xavier University in New Orleans.

Notwithstanding a focus on different populations of students and disciplines, each of the three programs, examined vis-à-vis multi- and inter- disciplinary perspectives, seek to diversify and integrate certain professions; operating thus under the assumption that we cannot begin to seriously integrate underrepresented students unless their academic performance improves considerably. And of course, even for these programs there are caveats; including the considerable expense in identifying, developing, testing, and evaluating a range of strategies; actual implementation of interventions; recruitment and training of a cadre of professionals for program implementation; and meaningful leadership with an emphasis on increasing the pool of high achieving students from underrepresented groups.

This brings us to a discussion of taking personal responsibility for achievement, which necessarily raises some thorny issues. It may be argued that before students can become agentic, that is, intentional, self-regulated, and motivated, they need both formal and informal opportunities to learn. For example, students need exposure to rigorous curriculum in a non-threatening, supportive environment (Aronson, Fried and Good 2002; Aronson and McGlone 2009). The programs noted above are implicitly structured as a defense against negative psychology. It can also be argued that students with a good sense of object permanency; have a secure base from which to explore, become disciplined, mature and resilient (Bowlby 1988). However we may rationalize the importance of one perspective over the other, there is not a tension between them because they share the same foundations, which is purposeful and consistent social, emotional and cognitive support from parents, program staff, faculty and others in positions of influence.

Thus, the purpose of this book is to explore the three undergraduate programs indicated above relative to their institutional responsibilities *to* their students and their active and consistent nurturance of a sense of personal and social responsibility *in* their students. It is written from the perspective of both *diversifying* and *integrating* real distributions of high academic achievement within highly competitive areas. (As noted above, there is under-representation even for those who go forward.) In this vein, this study focuses on investigating (1) the manner in which several selective institutions and a historically black college conceptualize student persistence and retention (and related supports to enable these outcomes); (2) the particular emphasis of their retention efforts; and (3) both individual and institutional outcomes.

This imperative becomes especially urgent in the STEM fields when we consider several dynamics, including the uncertain nature of our future science and engineering workforce and current demographic shifts in American society. With regard to the former, the changing "stay" or participation rates for international students who have obtained their doctorates in these fields in the United States emphasize the uncertainty of depending on non-U.S. citizens for our sciences and engineering workforce (Finn 2010). This dynamic becomes complicated when we consider that approximately two-thirds of Asian-American students and 44 percent of white American students ages eighteen to twenty-four, are currently enrolled in college, while just a third of African-American students in the same age group are enrolled, a figure that drops to 25 percent for this age group of Hispanic and Native American students. We are now confronted not only with issues and challenges concerning college enrollment but also how to effectively support student academic socialization within STEM disciplines. These parallel concerns will assume increased saliency since a majority of American public school students are members of what we now consider "minority" groups (www.census.gov/newsroom/releases/archives/population/cb12=90/html: accessed May 30, 2012).

SCOPE OF THE BOOK

Divided into three main sections, the first section explores several facets of this national dilemma, including the underrepresentation of minority students among the most academically able undergraduates enrolled in the nation's selective colleges and universities. This is done through a discussion, in chapter one, of increases in time-to-degree and declines in attainment rates for many low income students and underrepresented students enrolled in the nation's community and public and private colleges and universities (Berkner, He and Cataldi 2002; Bowen, Chingos and McPherson 2009; Planty, Kena and Hannes 2009) and recent findings that more than a third of college students evinced no noticeable improvement in critical thinking, writing, and complex reasoning skills after four years as an undergraduate (Arum and Roksa 2011). These findings suggest that while a focus on access to and participation in the nation's colleges and universities still remain a prominent goal, it is no longer sufficient given persistent disparities in post secondary student learning. That is, the perspective from which a large of body of research in higher education was conducted hinged on the idea of educational equity, understood primarily in terms of access and participation. Notwithstanding progress on these fronts however, recent studies indicate that college *attendance* and *completion* rates remain low for many Hispanic and African American students regardless of where they are in their higher education trajectory (ETS 2008; Provasnik and Planty 2008).

Chapter 2 explores the converging themes/findings that are common to and characteristic of each program. These themes/findings are discussed in the context of Tinto's theory on retention. Additional theoretical pperspectives; drawn broadly from the fields of sociology and cognitive, social and developmental psychology (including social capital, perceived self-efficacy and self regulation/effortful control), are examined in a continuing effort to understand how UMBC, XU, and Skidmore College perceive their commitment to student education and the particular kinds of resources that characterize this commitment.

Section 2 presents case studies of three undergraduate programs (the Meyerhoff Scholars Program at the University of Maryland, Baltimore County; the Opportunity Programs at Skidmore College in Saratoga Springs, New York; and the Premedical Program at Xavier University in New Orleans), which provide concrete information concerning the manner in which student persistence and retention is conceptualized; the particular emphasis of retention efforts; and the outcomes of targeted and comprehensive supports for students. These cases detail how salient aspects of social capital for example, pervades institutional leadership and program implementation. Equally important, they illustrate how information, norms of obligations, expectations, and support is conceptualized and acted upon to create sustainable learning communities/environments that ultimately enable students, including women and underrepresented students, to excel in competitive fields, including STEM and the social sciences.

Given the different foci of the three programs, a brief (but by no means exhaustive), historical/research context are also provided for each (and located before each chapter). That is, the broader context denoting historical, educational, economic, social and other challenges influencing the conceptualization of each of the three programs suggest their multifaceted and complex role in student learning, persistence and completion in higher education. It reinforces, as such, the significance of clearly understanding context in efforts to craft relevant and appropriate policy, particularly as it relates to access and equity. It recognizes as well, the salience of not only allocating specific resources, but also carefully arranging these resources, to contribute to the aims of social justice, increasingly a national imperative. The exploration of the three programs, within the context of their particular (and overlapping) challenges, can facilitate and refine our understanding of those aspects of settings that are not only the most salient with regard to student achievement, but also whether and how they succeed or fail (Granger et al. 2007).

Section 3 concludes with a discussion of the common policies and practices prevalent in each program with a view to informing institutional program design, implementation and iterative evaluation efforts that emphasize student learning and development vis-à-vis their students' academic and social integration; knowledge and skill development; support and motivation; and monitoring and advisement in higher education. An evolving understanding of these dynamics can contribute to important reconceptualizations of policy, research and practice in the social sciences and STEM disciplines, for example. It can also help to shape how colleges and universities sustain and institutionalize their efforts, particularly given competing priorities.

In this vein, this study seeks to inform continuing efforts on many fronts, including institutional leadership, faculty involvement and bridge programs that can markedly shape student motivation, confidence and self-efficacy and contribute to their academic and social integration, knowledge and skill development, support, motivation, monitoring and advisement in the STEM disciplines. In the main, the examination of three discrete programs with both distinct and common foci, addresses converging consensus and inherent concerns with understanding how particular social processes and by extension, the range and arrangement of resources (Granger 2010), eventually affect student learning and achievement; important points of departures for conceptualizing further research, policy and practice.

The insights gained from this research are also relevant at a time when we need to assume more responsibility for improving local institutions, including schools, colleges and universities, and building, maintaining and strengthening the ties between universities/colleges and schools and communities. These are important goals, especially when we consider the economic disadvantages stemming from long-standing gaps in academic achievement in the United States (McKinsey 2009). These gaps include those in knowledge and skills between (1) many underrepresented students and their white and Asian peers; (2) low-income and affluent students; and (3) comparable students in different systems or geographic regions. There is also an achievement gap between the United States and other nations in the Organisation for Economic Co-operation and Development. The McKinsey report (2009) and others (Levin and Belfield 2003; Hanushek and Woessman 2008) suggest that the chronic underperformance of many students in the United States comes at a great cost. On an individual level, many students who exhibit low achievement often earn less, are less healthy, and are more likely to be incarcerated (Currie 2005; Moretti 2007).

To give us a sense of the scale of these economic consequences, McKinsey (2009) calculated that U.S. Gross Domestic Product (GDP) could have increased from 1.3 trillion to 2.3 trillion in 2008 if achievement gaps in the United States and high-achieving countries such as Finland and Korea were narrowed. On a national level, U.S. GDP would have increased 2 to 4 percent or between 310 billion to 525 billion in 2008 if there were increases in black and Latino student performance. Moreover, McKinsey indicated, the economic impact of black and Latino underperformance on the nation's GDP is likely to increase as these groups increase in proportion relative to the population and the nation's workforce. On an income level, McKinsey (2009) found that GDP would have increased from 3 to 5 percent or 400 billion to 670 billion in 2008 if achievement gaps between low-income and affluent students were smaller. On a geographic level, GDP would have increased from 3 to 5 percent or 425 billion to 700 billion in 2008 were gaps between low- and high- achieving states narrowed.

Taken together, McKinsey (2009, 5) asserted that "the persistence of these educational achievement gaps imposes on the United States the economic equivalent of a **permanent national recession**" (McKinsey's emphasis). On an international level, "the recurring annual economic cost of the international achievement gap is substantially larger than the deep recession the United States is currently experiencing" (McKinsey 2009, 5). Implicit in McKinsey's analysis is growing concern for equitable human development, increasingly recognized as a prerequisite for individual, national and global prosperity. Clearly, the importance of investing in education on many fronts cannot be underestimated.

This study, which builds and expands on those current and past; provides a blueprint for some of the more effective strategies employed by successful institutions in higher education. It also reinforces that we need to design research and interventions from inter-disciplinary, multicultural and global perspectives, particularly since a decade into the twenty-first century, we are still confronted with chronic academic underperformance in the United States and abroad. Socio-economic status (a composite of parent education, income and occupational prestige) still remains the largest determinant of a students' academic trajectory. Yet, on many levels and regardless of family background, our students will increasingly have to think creatively, analytically, practically and regeneratively in efforts to address recurring issues and challenges associated with poverty, poor health, gender inequality, human mobility – both voluntary and involuntary, bioengineering, evolving technology, drought and income polarization that occur on local, national and global scales. These concerns have implications for how we educate today's students and how we prepare teachers/faculty to teach in a diverse and complex world in which habits of perspective, inquiry, imagination, empathy, commitment, humility, integrity and judgment increasingly resonate in importance. This approach recognizes the limitless potential of our young people and the responsibility of all to enable meaningful and substantive movement toward that potential.

I

Persistent Underperformance & Underrepresentation

Chapter One

Current Issues and Trends in Higher Education

INTRODUCTION

How we educate students is an enduring issue that has become particularly salient in higher education. This is evident in growing concerns over increases in time-to-degree and declines in attainment rates for many underrepresented students enrolled in the nation's community and public and private colleges and universities (Berkner, He and Cataldi 2002; Bowen, Chingos and McPherson 2009; Planty, Kena and Hannes 2009), and recent findings that more than a third of college students evinced no noticeable improvement in critical thinking, writing, and complex reasoning skills after four years as an undergraduate (Arum and Roksa 2011). These findings suggest that while a focus on access to and participation in the nation's colleges and universities for many low income students and students of color still remain a prominent goal, it is no longer sufficient given persistent disparities in post secondary student learning (Kuglemass and Ready 2011).

These dynamics, which inform a national emphasis on increasing student attainment rates *and* academic performance across demographic and socioeconomic status categories in the United States, particularly in the sciences, engineering and mathematics (Bowen, Chingos and McPherson 2009; National Research Council 2010), suggest the importance of a focus on *talent development* (Astin 1985, 1993) or *promoting access to knowledge, strategy and dispositions* (Prawat 1989) when considering the mechanisms for enabling these outcomes.

This perspective has gained increasing salience as scholars have debated the increasing commercialization of higher education, research and intercollegiate sports (Bowen and Levin 2003; Shapiro 2005). Indeed, recent

3

research by Arum and Roksa (2011) articulate concerns that, in the main, institutional cultures and practices do not focus on improving instruction or demonstrating gains in undergraduate student learning. Shapiro (2005), Bowen and Levin (2003), and a recent College Board (2009) report, *Coming to Our Senses*, suggest that this dynamic runs counter to the academic and moral obligations of colleges and universities, which includes the cultivation of a campus culture in which every student admitted is expected to graduate and in which every effort will be made to ascertain the issues and challenges undergirding why students underachieve and/or leave before completing their degree requirements. In this vein, the higher education community is urged to reaffirm its obligation to understand the educational needs of low-income, first-generation and underrepresented students and to take relevant and appropriate steps to mitigate the challenges faced by this population of students. In this vein, this chapter explores the returns from higher education; concerns with student access and attainment; student learning and institutional characteristics/contexts; and institutional and individual factors influencing disparities in higher education (including campus climate; students' pre-college and first year academic experience; financial/work related issues; discrepancies between students' academic needs and their family, community and/or cultural expectations or needs; waiting/being embarrassed to ask for help; and not getting into one's major of choice).

THE RETURNS FROM HIGHER EDUCATION

Although there is some discrepancy as to whether the individual or society benefits more (Moretti 2002), the literature demonstrates that the return from access to and participation in higher education is considerable (Pascarella and Terenzini 2005; Thelin 2004). The economic benefits to individuals include high wages and earnings that may be partially attributed to the gains seniors evince (.50 of a standard deviation/19 percentile points) in critical thinking skills when compared with incoming students (Pascarella and Terenzini 2005). (Pascarella and Terenzini (2005) note however, that this figure is markedly lower than their 1991 estimate of one standard deviation/34 percentile points—a finding discussed in the context of more recent studies). Similarly, the senior advantage in the *disposition* to think critically, an emerging research strand, was also .50 of a standard deviation/19 percentile points. Seniors' advantage with regard to their ability to reason effectively was .90 of a standard deviation (32 percentile points) and their "epistemological sophistication and maturity" was approximately 2 standard deviations (48 percentile points) (these figures are similar to Pascarella and Terenzini's 1991 analysis) (Pascarella and Terenzini, 2005).

The accumulation of human capital, including the knowledge, skills, abilities and dispositions an individual attains vis-à-vis training and educational experiences, informs interactions and work on organizational and societal levels through the sharing of knowledge and skills that can enable innovation, creativity, collaboration and competition (Bourdieu 1986; Friedman 2006; Moretti 2002). Other benefits include the ability of informed citizens to not only deliberate policy options but to make considered choices that can support economic prosperity (Friedman 1962). We are reminded also of an intergenerational effect, for example, of parents' access to higher education, on their children's acquisition of the knowledge, skills and dispositions necessary for achievement in reading comprehension, mathematics and the sciences (Martinez 2000). Despite the noted returns to higher education however, efforts to increase student access, particularly for diverse students and women, emerged only in the early nineteenth century although the nations' college building efforts began in the early seventeenth century (Thelin 2004).

CONCERNS WITH STUDENT ACCESS AND ATTAINMENT

Decades of progress notwithstanding, college *attendance* rates for African American and Hispanic students are low in comparison to their white and Asian American peers (Planty, Kena and Hannes 2009). Similarly, a number of studies and national reports in the past several decades have noted disparate college *completion* rates between majority and Asian American students and their minority peers (Berkner, He and Cataldi 2002; Bowen and Bok 1998). For example, Bowen, Chingos and McPherson's (2009) book, *Crossing the Finish Line: Completing College at America's Public Universities,* confirms increases in time-to-degree and declines in attainment rates for many underrepresented students enrolled in the nation's public universities and colleges. These trends are countered by countries abroad, where students are educated to more advanced levels and post-secondary graduation rates are higher than those in the United States (U.S. Department of Education, *A Test of Leadership: Charting the Future of U.S. Higher Education* 2006, 7). The United States now ranks seventh in the educational *attainment* of an Associate's degree or higher for young adults ages 25-34 years old (Organisation of Economic Co-operation and Development 2003) and sixteenth among twenty-seven countries compared, in the proportion of 18 to 24 year old students who *complete* college or certification programs (Callan 2006). Goldin and Katz (2008) remind us however, that these low levels of human capital development, documented since 1975, have not always been the case. Indeed, from 1900 to 1975, the increase in students who attended high school and the evolution of higher education into a universal system resulted in significant educational progress for the United States

One of the more interesting questions researchers are trying to sort through is why, despite wage premiums earned by college graduates, educational attainment rates in the United States have flattened considerably (Bowen, Chingos and McPherson 2009; Goldin and Katz 2008). Bowen and his colleague's (2009) analysis of freshman students who entered twenty-one flagship universities nationwide and all forty-seven four-year public universities in Maryland, North Carolina, Ohio and Virginia in 1999, attempted to shed some light. Not surprisingly, discrepancies in graduation rates and the amount of time it takes for students to earn a degree is significantly associated with students' race, ethnicity and socio-economic status. In the aggregate, only 49 percent of 94,316 (less than half) entering freshman students in 1999 graduated in four years from the flagship campuses nationwide. An additional 28 percent graduated several years later, bringing the six year graduation rate to 77 percent. When regard to income, 83 percent of students in the top half of the income distribution graduated within six years as opposed to 68 percent of their peers in the bottom half. Additionally, 57 percent of students in the top half of the income distribution graduated in four years while only 38 percent of their peers in the bottom half did so.

In the four state systems Bowen and colleagues (2009) examined, less than 40 percent of students graduated in four years; the number of those who did graduate in five or six years surpassed that of four-year graduates. Additionally, across the four states studied, the higher the tuition, the lower the graduation/completion rate for low-income students. Interestingly, Bowen and colleagues found that an unexpectedly large number of African-American, Hispanic and low-income students undermatch. That is, although these students are capable of attending a more demanding or selective college, they either do not enroll in college or when they do, it is in less-demanding four- or two- year colleges/universities. In this instance, data from North Carolina indicate that 59 percent of students in the bottom quartile of family income undermatch; whereas, only 27 percent in the top quartile did so. These findings closely parallel those for parental education (also derived from North Carolina data), i.e., 64 percent of students whose parents did not have a college education undermatch. The figures for students with parents with college degrees and graduate degrees are 41 percent and 31 percent respectively. This phenomenon has important implications given the relationship between the rates at which students complete their bachelor's degree requirements and the selectivity of the institution. That is, the likelihood of *comparably qualified students* graduating with a bachelor's degree depends on whether or not they attend a more or less selective institution; students are thus more likely to graduate with a credential if they attended a selective institution. Additionally, students with the intention of attaining a bachelor's degree are less likely to do so if they enrolled at a two-year institution (Bowen, Chingos and McPherson 2009).

In addition to undermatching, Bowen and colleagues found that close to half of all students who withdrew from the flagship universities did so *after* their freshman year, not during their first or second semester as widely assumed. This finding has important implications for the timing and duration of interventions, which may need further reframing given the finding that disparities in college preparation only explained a small portion of the differences in graduation rates and time to degree between majority and minority groups.

With regard to admission practices, universities "sorted" applicants through an over reliance on standardized tests. Bowen and colleagues reinforce however, that while they are not against the idea of testing, student's test scores do need to be used judiciously. For example, scores from standardized tests in tandem with students' high school grades tend to predict graduation rates at more selective institutions; high school grades however, tend to be more reliable predictors of graduation rates for less selective institutions. Exam scores from Advanced Placement tests were also found to be good predictors. Given this, an emphasis on a combination of high school grades and achievement test scores may yield insights of more than cognitive competence; that is, they may also provide evidence of coping and time-management skills, which Bowen and his colleagues suggest, also influence students' graduation rates.

STUDENT LEARNING AND INSTITUTIONAL CHARACTERISTICS/CONTEXTS

At the undergraduate level, documented racial/ethnic disparities in students' grade point averages, completion rates and GRE scores suggest the importance of also determining the nature and magnitude of post-secondary academic progress (ETS 2008; Planty, Kena and Hannes 2009). Pascarella and Terenzini's (2005) longitudinal study of 1,600 freshman and junior students in eighteen institutions who were given (in the mid-1990s) a multiple choice exam (the Collegiate Assessment of Academic Proficiency) comprised of reading, math, writing and critical thinking questions, found, after accounting for a number of student and institutional factors, that African American students were at a modest disadvantage in terms of gains in critical thinking (ES [effect size] = -0.21; Flowers and Pascarella 2003).

More recent research of differences in cognitive growth by race and ethnicity, appear to corroborate this finding (Arum and Roksa 2008). Arum and Roksa (2008) administered the Collegiate Learning Assessment (CLA) to a sample of 2300 students at twenty-four four-year colleges and universities in the fall of their freshman year (2005) and the spring of their sophomore year (2007). They found that, on average, disparities in cognitive skills between majority and African American students actually increased in the first two years of college. Their analysis also indicated that African American students did not make significant gains on the CLA during this time. However, after controlling for other socio-demographic factors, Arum and Roksa (2008), found that the differences in cognitive progress between African American students and their majority peers declined by 22 percent. With regard to Hispanic students, they found that this population of students learned at similar rates, statistically, with majority students despite entering college with considerable differences in achievement. Arum and Roksa's findings suggest that substantial disparities in achievement between Hispanic and African American students and their majority peers at college entry remained during their college trajectory. Additionally, further analysis demonstrated that *between* college differences accounted for approximately a third of the gap, implying that institutional contexts contributed to student learning (or the lack thereof) over time.

Given the salience of institutional characteristics and contexts in student learning, Kuglemass and Ready (2011) employed a national sample of 35,000 college seniors from 250 diverse institutions to examine the role of institutional characteristics, if any, in enabling not only students' cognitive development but also the distribution of these cognitive gains vis-à-vis students' race/ethnicity. With regard to student learning, Kuglemass and Ready's (2011) findings from the Collegiate Learning Assessment (mirroring that of Arum and Roksa, 2008), indicated that (1) initial academic gaps between African American students and their white peers increased during students' time in college, and (2), Hispanic students attained comparable gains relative to their white peers despite academic differences at college entry. A significant contribution of Kuglemass and Ready's study however, lies in the finding that particular aspects of institutions influence racial/ethnic disparities in students' intellectual growth. For example, the disparities between African American and Hispanic students and their white peers were somewhat smaller at colleges with larger proportions of underrepresented students. Additionally, both underrepresented students and their white peers attending selective institutions, (which in the aggregate, tend to enroll higher achieving students), demonstrated larger cognitive gains and a narrowing of achievement gaps (Kuglemass and Ready 2011). This dynamic is thought to be a function of benefits derived from interacting with high achieving peers at selective institutions (Boud, Cohen and Sampson 1999; Falchikov 2001; Gurin et al. 2002).

Kuglemass and Ready (2011, 343) also found that the cognitive gains of students in selective institutions may be a function of "how intentionally resources are directed, not simply how much is spent." That is, the resources allocated to academic support, in the form of "faculty development, teaching and learning centers, and academic support staff," is directly associated with student learning. This finding parallels Tinto's (1993) research, which demonstrates that successful student learning stems from an engaged faculty and the institutional will and ability to create learning communities/environments that enable student learning. Thus, it is the act of educating students, not merely retaining them; that is at the crux of effective institutions.

Another important finding, which parallels Arum and Roksa's (2011), is that although larger differences in student learning were found within institutions, there were also significant differences between institutions. However, while Kuglemass and Ready (2011) suggest that institutional effectiveness may explain the variance between institutions, they also posit that factors other than standardized test scores, may account for between institutional effects. Bowen and colleagues (2009) also addressed this issue and suggest that students' cognitive gains can be a function of students' time on task, study habits and time management, for example.

Arum and Roksa (2011) continued this strand of research with a recent longitudinal study which sought to determine the amount of studying and learning that occurred once students enrolled in college. Studying over 2,300 students at the undergraduate level in twenty-four colleges and universities vis-à-vis the Collegiate Learning Assessment (CLA; a standardized exam comprised of essay-based and open-ended questions), these researchers found that 45 percent of their sample did not demonstrate notable gains in critical thinking, reasoning and writing by the end of their second year in college. (The reader may recall Pascarella and Terenzini's finding of decreases in estimates of critical thinking skills among undergraduate seniors.) At the end of four years of college, Arum and Roksa (2011) indicated that 36 percent of their sample did not evince significant improvement in learning. These researchers' analysis suggests that the low level of rigor of students' courses may contribute to the lack of student learning. That is, 32 percent of their sample did not enroll in courses that required more than 40 pages of reading per week.

Additionally, 50 percent of their sample did not enroll in a course in which they wrote more than twenty pages during the course of the semester. Arum and Roksa suggest that this lack of academic progress, as evidenced by the CLA, is associated with the low levels of time students allocate to their academic work. That is, students sampled indicated that they allocated over 50 percent of their time during the week to extracurricular activities or socializing (suggesting a primary focus on social rather than academic development). Another contributing factor may be that students' interactions with faculty out of the classroom, was practically non-existent. These findings corroborate those from the National Survey of Student Engagement, which found, after sampling (for more than a decade), over several million students at more than one thousand colleges and universities, that many students allocated little time to writing or studying.

INSTITUTIONAL FACTORS INFLUENCING DISPARITIES IN HIGHER EDUCATION

In addition to the role of reduced time on academic work, the literature suggests the salience of contextual/environmental/institutional factors in student underperformance. Of direct relevance for this study however, is the impact of campus climate, and pre-college and first-year academic experiences (Fries-Britt 1998; Hurtado 1998, 1999) on noted disparities between underrepresented students and their majority peers.

Campus Climate

Hurtado and colleagues (1998; 1999) suggest that the properties of campus climate are structural, behavioral and psychological. The structural aspect includes the presence (or lack thereof), of not only a critical mass of underrepresented students on campus, but also administrative leadership on issues affecting underrepresented students, faculty and the curriculum (Castellanos and Gloria 2007; Chi et al. 2007). The behavioral aspect speaks to the presence or absence of curriculum that includes the experiences of underrepresented populations; students' lack of access to and/or participation in academically supportive peer networks; students' unawareness of the need for strong study habits and tutoring; students' unawareness of how to prevent or regulate the influence of emerging academic or personal problems; their lack of contact with faculty outside of the classroom; and their lack of mentoring relationships with faculty (including minority faculty) (Chronicle of Higher Education 2007; Fischer 2007; Fries-Britt and Turner 2002; Kennedy and Sheckley 2000).

The psychological aspect includes both subtle and overt messages that underrepresented students do not belong on campus; low faculty expectations for minority student success; and faculty/departmental unawareness that the uneven and inadequate monitoring and advisement to which underrepresented students may be exposed can result in misinformation concerning coursework and may eventually lead to students' unpreparedness for the next level of study; (Espinoza-Herold and Gonzalez 2007; Heiman 2006; Maldonado, Rhoads and Buenavista 2005; Smith and Peterson 2007). A phenomenon called racial microaggression, defined as underrepresented students' need to weigh and interpret behaviors, words and interactions also characterizes the psychological aspect of campus climate (Solorzano 2000; Sue et al. 2007). Additionally, an unwelcoming campus climate can amplify other influences on these students' decisions to leave (Fries-Britt 2000; Pascarella and Terenzini 2005). A student's major, for example, can also influence whether or not student persist in college. Underrepresented students who major in the sciences, engineering, mathematics and other technical fields have a greater likelihood of becoming academically and socially isolated on majority White campuses than do their white or Asian American peers (Heiman 2006; Milner 2002; Redden 2002).

Pre-college and First-year Academic Experience

A large body of research suggests that students' overall high school academic experience and their freshman year GPA are related to whether they persist in college or eventually leave (Feldman 2005; Swail, Redd and Perna 2003; Warburton, Bugarin and Nunez 2001). These findings are further substantiated in recent research demonstrating considerable differences in first-year college GPA between retained and non-retained students (Beyer, Gilmore and Fisher 2007). Specifically, students who left the University of Washington had steeper declines in GPA between high school and their freshman year than their retained peers. Beyer and colleagues (2007, v) also found large GPA gaps for Native American students (an average of 1.93 GPA points), Black students (average gap: 1.93), Asian American students (average gap: 1.41), and Latino students (average gap: 1.35) who left (or stopped out of) the university in their freshman year (the average gap for White students were 1.00). Additionally, although students who left after their second year demonstrated sharp declines in grades between high school and their first year of college (when compared with retained students), the gaps between different racial/ethnic groups were not considerable. (Beyer and colleagues [2007] use the phrase "stop out" rather than "drop out," because it is less negative and recognizes that while students may leave one university, they may continue their academic or other aspirations elsewhere or at another time.)

There are several reasons for these declines in grade point average (GPA), including the possibility that students from under-funded high schools may have had different experiences from those whose schools were more adequately resourced (Orfield and Eaton 1996; Orfield and Frankenberg 2007). In particular, Beyer and colleagues (2007) found considerably wider GPA gaps among students who attended high schools that provided over 30 percent free or reduced price lunches than among students from higher socioeconomic status high schools. The absence of and/or student non-participation in freshman year seminars that can help to facilitate the transition from high school to college also may play a role in student attrition (Keup and Barefoot 2006). Additionally, other factors such as social class differences, campus climate or tensions between family expectations and academic demands, may be more salient in the first rather than the second year (Cooke et al. 2004; Seidman 2005).

INDIVIDUAL FACTORS AFFECTING STUDENT COMPLETION

Although there is a declining association between students' aspirations and their race or family background (Wirt et al. 2004), underrepresented students who aspire to post secondary education do not necessarily know how to operationalize their aspirations into relevant courses of action. The literature amply demonstrates that this student population is not fully aware of how to prepare for and enroll in college (Davidson and Foster-Johnson 2001; Martinez and Klopott 2005; Wallace, Abel and Ropers-Huilman 2000). Additionally, once these students arrive on campus, research suggests that they often struggle with financial/work related issues; discrepancies between their academic needs and their family, community and/or cultural expectations or needs (Beyer, Gilmore and Fisher 2007); asking for help (or not); and getting into their major of choice; all aspects of their experience strongly associated with whether they persist and/or complete their course of study (Hurtado 1998, 1999).

Financial/Work Related Issues

African American, Hispanic and Native American students consistently cite financial needs as a barrier in the achievement of their educational and career goals (Duffy and Goldberg 1998; Gansemer-Topf and Schuh 2005). Financial needs often lead some students to work longer hours than their peers. Some students also have the added responsibility of financially supporting their families (Goldrick-Rab, Harris and Trostel 2009). These pressures may compel some students to commute long distances to off-campus jobs, sometimes held since high school (Horn 1998; Mortenson 1999). Students' long commuting time appear to affect their academic work and their access to and participation in social networks and relevant academic events. Additionally, some students appear to have differing attitudes about debt and willingness to incur debt. Beyer and colleagues (2007) found that fewer minority students who left the University of Washington after their freshman year, applied for financial aid. Their analysis of financial aid data demonstrated that underrepresented students and their Asian American peers were more likely to experience greater financial need in their freshman year than White students. Not surprisingly, students who left the university in their freshman or sophomore year faced greater financial pressures than those who persisted beyond the first two years of college.

Discrepancies between Students' Academic Needs and their Families, Community and/or Cultural Expectations or Needs

For some underrepresented students, there is a tension between fulfilling the requirements of their academic courses and attending to the needs and expectations of their family, community and culture (Hrabowski, Maton and Grief, 1998; Hrabowski et al. 2002). In particular, parents may not fully grasp the commitment and time that academic success requires. This may result in their asking for financial or other assistance and inhibiting, unintentionally, their children's academic success. Further complicating this phenomenon are students' own values. That is, many underrepresented students place higher values on family and community well-being than on their own academic success. It is an intriguing finding that many of the underrepresented students Beyer and colleagues (2007, v) interviewed often regard becoming academically successful as selfish. Given this dynamic, it is not surprising that some students accommodate their family's requests for assistance regardless of whether their grades are affected. Students also feel responsible for giving back to their communities (McKinney 2002; Seider 2007). These activities include recruiting other underrepresented students, tutoring in inner-city schools, and serving on committees and in organizations geared toward assisting underrepresented people. While important, faculty and staff are concerned that these activities reduce the amount of time students can devote to their academic requirements (Astin 1993).

Waiting/Being Embarrassed to Ask for Help

Another contributing factor in why students leave college hinge on their reluctance to ask for help—and when and if they do, it is usually too late (Hermanowicz 2004; Johnson-Bailey 2004). Additionally, as a group, many freshman students are not only unwilling to ask questions in class but also unwilling to inquire about assistance outside of the classroom. This phenomenon is even more acute for underrepresented students, who report that asking for help in class spawns unwanted attention and that requesting help outside of the classroom reflects negatively on their ethnic communities (Aronson, Fried and Good 2002; Aronson and McGlone 2009).

Not Getting into Ones' Major of Choice

Students who do not get into their major of choice, or who experience delays in getting into their major, are often at greater risk of leaving the university (Daempfle 2004). This factor, when experienced with others, such as financial pressures or feeling unwelcome, can hasten these students' decision to leave the university (Pascarella and Terenzini 2005). These concrete factors not only impact whether students evince cognitive gains and progress in their postsecondary education trajectories, but also have larger implications for the U.S. economy.

CONCLUSION

Despite some student gains in selective institutions, low levels of student learning and attainment rates, meshed with longer time to degree, are indicative of unsettling trends on U.S. college and university campuses (Arum and Roksa 2011; Bowen, Chingos & McPherson 2009). These trends suggest that attempts to develop cognitive competencies must be coupled with equitable access to (1) cultural, financial, health, human, institutional, personal, and social capital, and (2), encouragement of learner behaviors such as deployment of effort, task engagement, time on task, and resource utilization, for example (Kemple and Snipes 2000; Marks 2000). This strategy reflects a strengths-based approach that seeks to understand unequal opportunities; the outcomes associated with race/ethnicity; and the variances between population groups in the acquired and culture laden cognitive, affective, and situative competencies privileged in mainstream society.

This approach also recognizes the growing role that education must play in increasing cognitive competencies for many underrepresented students at all levels in the educational enterprise (Martinez 2000). We must be reminded, however, that having realistic expectations for progress is also important, because these are complicated intergenerational advancement challenges. Halsey, Brown and Wells (1997), Martinez (2000), and Miller (1995) recognize that while the purpose of education is the cultivation of intelligence, this takes time and may not become stable in a single generation. This intergenerational issue is not just a matter of race. Some researchers indicate that most ethnic minority groups' movement into education begins with a vocational focus and slowly evolve into an academic focus usually through traditional schooling, increasingly considered the universal route (Hirschman and Wong 1984; Neidert and Farley 1985; Sandefur and Pahari 1989). European Americans and Asian Americans appear to have a longer tradition of academic success whereas the United States has engaged in educating underrepresented groups for a little more than fifty years (Miller,1995).

Finally, the sources of achievement disparities identified and discussed in this chapter are clearly not exhaustive. Patterns of underachievement associated with these sources suggest that the achievement gaps are virtually fully formed by the end of the primary grades and are sizable coming into kindergarten. This is unfortunate because most children come to school with a positive attitude—they want to learn and are eager to do so (Bowman, Donovan and Burns 2001; Miller 2008). It may well be that the orientations that Ogbu (2003) has identified and/or hypothesized emerge fairly slowly as students experience years of limited or no academic success. And, they might mean something else to many of the students—self-defensive dis-identification, for instance. This phenomenon and others, also appear to contribute to the low persistence and high attrition rates for underrepresented students at the undergraduate and graduate level. As we continue to probe deeply and use this knowledge to (1) rethink the goals and or purposes of education, and (2), devise appropriate interventions to increase achievement for underrepresented students and others, we should acknowledge the interdependent nature of our society and increasingly, the global economy/community. Indeed, we should not fail to "recognize that the restriction of educational opportunities because of race, color, and economic circumstances may mean the attenuation of [society's] chief human resource—the functioning intelligence of its citizenry" (Lorge 1945, 492 quoted in Martinez 2000, 110).

Chapter Two

Creating Effective Social and Intellectual Communities/ Environments in Higher Education

A Theoretical Perspective

INTRODUCTION

The President of Lumina Foundation, Jamie P. Merisotis (2009), suggested that while processes to improve student access are important, it is ultimately student learning that most matters. Indeed, Mr. Merisotis asserted that "learning—how to define it, how to measure it, how to nurture it in students and ensure its relevance and currency in the world—the topic that should be the central conversation about improving education, has somehow devolved to background noise." This recognition of the need to reorient higher education's priorities (Bowen and Levin 2003; Shapiro 2005) is timely given evidence of chronic disparities in student learning between underrepresented students and their Asian and white peers, particularly with regard to writing, critical thinking and complex reasoning (Arum and Roksa 2011; Bowen, Chingos and McPherson 2009). These disparities, which exist when students enter college, not only continue but also tend to increase during the course of students' postsecondary trajectories (Kuglemass and Ready 2011).

Arum and Roksa (2011) note however, that although students in general experienced only modest academic demands; they have found, in all settings investigated, students who, over the course of their study, have evinced large cognitive gains per the Collegiate Learning Assessment (CLA) assessment. Moreover, students enrolled in high achieving institutions tend to spend more time studying and were more engaged in and met rigorous reading and writing requirements; resulting thus in considerable gains in writing, critical thinking and complex reasoning when compared over time with their peers at other institutions.

The finding that students tend to fare better in selective institutions, corroborated by Bowen and colleagues (2009), raise several related questions, including what factors, perhaps in addition to, or besides, institutional support for faculty and staff development, and teaching and learning centers (Kuglemass and Ready 2011), contribute to institutional effectiveness in promoting student learning and development? This overarching question guided the studies of the Meyerhoff Scholars Program at the University of Maryland, Baltimore County, the Premedical Program at Xavier University in New Orleans, and the Opportunity Program at Skidmore College in Saratoga Springs, New York, and lead to the conclusion that although these discrete programs varied in structure and implementation, they converged in (1) how they understood the issues and challenges related to student underachievement and by extension, how they conceptualized their commitment to increasing student learning, persistence and completion; (2) the particular emphases of their retention efforts; and (3) the student outcomes they ultimately privilege (Tinto 1993). (Please see appendix A for a discussion of the study's design [participant-oriented model of evaluation] and methodology, including [1] how the programs were selected, study sample, data sources and collection; [2] analytic approach; and [3] trustworthiness of the data.)

The focus of each institution's resources and efforts revolve around their (1) institutional commitment to students; (2) educational commitment to students (which includes (a) addressing inherent challenges in teaching and (b) reconceptualizing teaching, learning and assessment); and (3) promoting a positive social and intellectual community for not only students, but also faculty and staff. These themes/findings resonate within the larger framework of Tinto's (1993) research/theory on retention, especially his link to classrooms and the challenges of teaching and learning. However, while Tinto's broad structure/theory is helpful in organizing and understanding our findings, given the complexity of the undergraduate experience for students, particularly those who are underrepresented, we examined several concepts from sociology and psychology (namely social capital, perceived self-efficacy, and self-regulation/effortful control), to further develop a more nuanced and granular understanding of this phenomenon.

This chapter examines and situates these core theoretical principles, processes and practices undergirding the institutional, environmental, and *inter*-individual origins of student change (Pascarella and Terenzini 2005); thus reinforcing Tinto's (1993) premise that the ethos of institutional commitment to *the education of students* and their academic and social integration within the college , not just their mere retention, is at the foundation of both student and institutional success.

INSTITUTIONAL COMMITMENT TO STUDENTS

Tinto (1993) reminds us that effective institutions recognize and attend to not only the interests of the institution but also the interests and needs of their students. This identifiable ethos of caring, guided by certain values is reflected in the understanding that providing equitable access, resources *and* opportunities to learn in supportive contexts, has considerable influence on the educational, career and life prospects of students in general and underrepresented students in particular (Garcia Coll and Pachter 2002; Parsons 1959).

On a conceptual level, several theoretical perspectives, drawn broadly from the fields of sociology and cognitive, social and developmental psychology (including social capital, perceived self-efficacy and self regulation/effortful control), offer an additional lens through which we can understand how the University of Maryland, Baltimore County, Xavier University and Skidmore College perceive their commitment to student education and the particular kinds of resources that characterize this commitment. These resources, including information, norms of obligations and expectations, and support that individuals can access by virtue of their relationships with others, are thought to influence students' achievement trajectories (Bourdieu 1986; Burt 1997; Coleman 1988, 1990; Lin 2001).

Norms of obligations and expectations for example, include the trustworthiness of the social environment or whether obligations will be met. An important form of support, particularly in the current economic climate, includes the provision of comprehensive needs-based financial aid (Goldrick-Rab, Harris and Trostel 2009). This is a particularly salient policy given evidence that first generation and underrepresented students who do not have adequate financial aid are hampered in their efforts to devote the necessary amount of time studying because they must either work on or off-campus (Dowd and Coury 2004; Field 2009; Gansemer-Topf and Schuh 2005) The literature further suggests that the time not available for studying negatively affects student retention, achievement and completion (Gross, Hossler and Ziskin 2007).

In addition to the importance of providing financial aid, it is equally important for colleges and universities to establish the *structures* (Coleman 1988; Granger 2010; Tseng and Seidman 2007) that will facilitate goals of effectively guiding and supporting women and underrepresented students to pursue and excel in the humanities, social sciences and STEM fields (Aronson, Fried and Good 2002; Good, Aronson and Harder 2008; Treisman 1990; 1992). The conceptual underpinnings of these structures are thus be reflective of the idea that students' ability alone is not a guarantee of academic success; rather, their ability, effort, perceived self-efficacy, self-regulation and motivation must be strengthened by a deliberate and purposeful system of academic, social and personal support (Bandura 1997; Duckworth and

Seligman 2006; Greenberg et al. 2003; Maton, Hrabowski and Schmitt 2000; Resnick 2000).

The significance of effort, self-efficacy, effortful control/self regulation in promoting student confidence in and motivation for continued pursuit of STEM and other social science majors suggest that beyond important considerations of access and opportunity, students, particularly those who are underrepresented, struggle with issues and challenges that are distinctly psychosocial (Chemers, Hu and Garcia 2001; Hurtado et al. 1999). That is, underrepresented students often have to navigate complex psychological terrain as they evolve in their identity as physicians, scientists or engineers (Hurtado 2008). In this vein, interventions that not only emphasize the integration of student effort, efficacy and self regulation beliefs but also provide the mechanisms through which students can exercise these attributes are more likely to increase student persistence and completion in STEM and other fields given their particular understanding of these psychological dynamics (National Research Council 2010).

EDUCATIONAL COMMITMENT TO STUDENTS

Implicit in the above discussion is the idea that institutional commitment to student welfare overlaps with institutional concerns with the actual education of students (Tinto 1993). That is, successful institutions recognize that sustained emphasis on students' cognitive and social development, not simply their mere retention, is foundational to their learning, persistence and completion. Thus, high achieving institutions do not leave learning to chance but actively engage in conceptualizing, implementing and evaluating activities that promote student learning. This can take the form of assessing students' skills in particular domains (i.e., mathematics, writing); placing them in appropriate course(s); and providing assistance that enables them to learn and develop, including offering constructive feedback and monitoring their progress, particularly in their freshman year. Additionally, successful institutions not only assess, on a continuing basis, the impact of their teaching practices on student learning, but also the skill set faculty need to cultivate for effective teaching (Kuh et al. 2010).

Addressing Challenges in Teaching

In targeted efforts to support meaningful and effective student learning, these steps include reconceptualizing how faculty engage students, including students from diverse racial/ethnic and socioeconomic backgrounds, in the science and art of learning increasingly complex material while simultaneously developing a broader range of competencies (Darling-Hammond and Bransford 2005). This is not a simple task, as various efforts in this regard; often guided by competing philosophies, reflect different conceptions of the purpose of education, knowledge, teaching and learning, and the role of faculty (Laboree 1997). For example, the idea of educational equity recognizes that students' race/ethnicity and socio-economic backgrounds often influence whether the benefits associated with schooling are equitably distributed (Mehan 1996). As noted above, faculty have considerable influence on low income and underrepresented students' educational, career and life prospects, which implies thus a moral and ethical responsibility to teach fairly and equitably (Turner, 1960; Villegas, 2007), particularly when we consider the increase in student diversity across the educational continuum.

Tinto (1993) reminds us that higher education faculty, are the only ones not trained to teach students. Recognizing this dynamic, successful institutions enable their faculty to develop knowledge and skills in (1) creating a vision not only for their teaching but also their continued growth and development; (2) developing core understanding about teaching, learning and the processes in young adult development; (3) developing the habits of mind or dispositions that enable the use and reflection of relevant knowledge; (4) developing practices that enable them to enact their intentions and beliefs; and (5) cultivating appropriate tools that can effectively support their practice (Darling-Hammond and Bransford 2005; Cochran-Smith and Lytle 1999a; Feiman-Nemser 2001b; Shulman and Shulman 2004).

Faculty development in these areas can begin to address several pervasive issues and challenges in teaching, including the apprenticeship of observation; inadequate support for enactment; and managing the complexity of teaching and learning (Kennedy 1999; Lampert 2001; Lortie 1975; McDonald 1992). With regard to the *apprenticeship of observation,* Lortie (1975) suggests that faculty's observations of those who have taught them and the pre-conceptions that arise from these experiences influence what and how they learn. More often than not however, faculty's long apprenticeship of observing their own teachers result in erroneous beliefs about teaching (Lortie 1975), including the notion that *teaching is easy.* This idea stems from faculty's unawareness of the fundamental knowledge, skills, and dispositions that enable planning; the selection and implementation of appropriate curricula; and the range of pedagogical approaches teachers employ to support learning for students at different levels (Munby, Russell and Martin 2001). Researchers suggest that if these preconceptions are not engaged and explored, it is very difficult for faculty to evolve in their identity as effective teachers (Richardson and Placier 2001), further resulting in issues of *enactment* (Kennedy 1999). That is, without an identity grounded in the knowledge of teaching, faculty can find it difficult to translate their intentions into action.

These dynamics have important implications for student learning and development because faculty are required to engage in many tasks simultaneously. These tasks include cultivating a poised and respected presence in the classroom; observing and understanding student behavior patterns; assisting student effort vis-à-vis explaining, questioning, and feedback; and managing the classroom efficiently. Additionally, it is important that faculty develop the ability to evaluate and respond appropriately to challenging situations; sense when they have to make mid-course changes in their lesson plans; and respond appropriately to students. However, the information necessary to engage in these and other tasks, including probing the ideas students may have about a concept or area of study; whether they conceptually understand the lessons' content; and being aware of students' learning styles, tend to surface in the context of teaching (Schon 1983); underscoring thus the complexity of teaching and learning and the importance of constant reflection and appropriate planning for meaningful instruction.

This discussion suggests that teaching is a challenging endeavor (Lampert 2001; McDonald 1992) that requires faculty, staff and administrators to not only recognize the inherent complexities in their profession but also to monitor, understand and adapt their thinking and performances in the context of these complexities (Brown et al. 1983; Bransford, Brown and Cocking 2000). Cultivating these habits of perspective and inquiry, for example, requires high levels of metacognitive awareness, which prompts frequent self-appraisal of thoughts and actions and if necessary, subsequent changes in particular assumptions and actions (Bandura 2001; Flavell 1979). Thus, it is especially important to assist faculty in developing metacognitive awareness, which will enable them to accurately reflect on their teaching and learning and how to improve in weak areas. In this context, faculty need to recognize whether or not they understand how their students learn and to act appropriately on this knowledge. Additionally, they need to be able to engage in both internal and external dialogues concerning their own learning; examine assumptions that conflict with the reality of the classroom; and explore the influence of their actions and reactions to, and interactions with, their students and peers. This knowledge can promote faculty understanding of where students need to be and how they will assist them in getting there; that is, faculty need to have a vision of the curriculum (Zumwalt 1989) as well as a sense of their students' needs as young people.

Reconceptualizing teaching, learning and assessment

These related and overlapping ideas are emphasized in Bransford, Brown and Cocking's seminal report, *How People Learn* (2000). Indeed, Bransford and colleagues (2000) reinforce that the demands on faculty are now greater given the insights garnered from neuroscience and cognition. That is, recent findings about the many and complex processes involved in learning, and new information from various branches of science have considerably improved our understanding of what it means to acquire knowledge: from the neural processes that occur during learning to the influence of culture on what people perceive and absorb. Given these dynamics, faculty, for example, now need a substantial knowledge base in a variety of disciplines; familiarity with the process of inquiry; an understanding of the relationship between information and the concepts that help organize it in a discipline; and a grasp of the processes in students' conceptual development. Conscious work in this direction can enable Schoenfeld (2010), Prawat (1989) and Bransford and colleagues' (2000) concern for the importance of learning for transfer, increasingly regarded as one of the fundamental goals of education.

Given the stated intentions and practices of these programs in intellectually and socially preparing students for the next step in their education trajectories, including application to and acceptance into graduate school, students are expected to demonstrate deep conceptual understanding of subject matter in their areas of study and the ability to apply this knowledge appropriately (Bransford, Brown and Cocking 2000). The idea of *learning with understanding* is thus concerned with knowledge (i.e., subject matter); how it is organized; why it is taught (to enable understanding and eventual application); and what competence or mastery looks like. Mastery, or expertise, requires well-organized knowledge that supports understanding. Learning with understanding is thus important for the development of expertise because it makes new learning easier (i.e., it supports the transfer of knowledge to different situations). Learning with understanding is also harder and more time-consuming than simply memorizing. Many curricula fail to support learning with understanding because they present an array of disconnected facts in a short period of time. Similarly, tests often reinforce memorizing rather than understanding. A knowledge-centered environment however, provides the tools for in-depth study and assesses students' understanding rather than their knowledge of disconnected facts. It incorporates, furthermore, the teaching of metacognitive strategies that facilitate future learning.

The importance of structuring knowledge and by extension the curriculum, however, needs to be meaningfully integrated with assessment tasks. In the HPL framework, Bransford and colleagues (2000) reinforce the importance of implementing formative assessments that are designed to make students' thinking visible to both teachers and students. In this vein, formative assessments provide the impetus for teachers and students to monitor progress and equally important, they enable teachers to ascertain their students' preconceptions and recognize where each student is along the continuum from informal to formal thinking; leading thus to evolving curriculum and instruction. Formative assessments are also more learner-friendly; that is, rather than placing importance on how well students can memorize information for exams resulting in grades that rank them relative to their classmates, these assessments provide students with opportunities to revise and improve their thinking (Vye et al. 1998), enable them to gauge their own progress over the course of their studies, and assist teachers in identifying potential issues in students' critical literacy and comprehension that may need attention. This strategy thus guards against the narrow focus of norm-referenced assessments in that it enables teachers to measure students' growth and development over time and to provide targeted support to increase student mastery of concepts in weak domains.

Additionally, although students' interest or engagement in a task is important, it does not guarantee that students will acquire the various types of knowledge that will support new learning. Thus, knowledge-centered environments considers other factors besides engagement as the primary index of successful teaching (Prawaf et al. 1992) and recognizes that there are important differences between tasks and projects that "encourage hands-on doing and those that encourage doing with understanding" (Donovan, Bransford & Pelligrino 1999, 21). Greeno (1991) suggests that knowledge-centered environments emphasize the latter.

The idea of learning with understanding thus hinge on several research based principles of learning. These include: (1) structuring knowledge around the major concepts and organizing principles of a discipline; (2) employing metacognitive processes (e.g., self-monitoring, self-regulation) in efforts to acquire competencies; (3) the tasks and activities in which students engage influence what they learn; and (4) students' capacity to learn with understanding is strengthened in interactions that are academically and socially supported (Bransford, Brown and Cocking 2000).

On an operative level, the first and third principle of learning is related to curriculum and assessment, while the fourth principle speaks to the importance of learning environments in nurturing student achievement. The third principle is embedded in the others and can be construed as part of the psychological processes that enable students to self-regulate and self-appraise themselves in efforts to persist and complete a course of study, for example. These elements of schooling (curriculum, learning, assessment, and community) comprise the How People Learn (HPL) framework (Bransford, Brown and Cocking 2000).

SOCIAL AND INTELLECTUAL COMMUNITY

An essential aspect of institutional commitment to students and to their education is their focus on creating and sustaining learning communities/environments that provide students academic, social and emotional support for their individual and collective efforts.

In this vein, Bransford and colleagues (2000) suggest paying attention to the context (i.e, the community or environment) in which learning takes place. Since learning is influenced in fundamental ways by its context, promoting student achievement via their community requires the development of norms both in and out of the classroom that support and inform core learning values. In some contexts, norms may require that students build their own information base; others may encourage academic risk taking and provide opportunities for students to make mistakes, obtain feedback, and revise their thinking. Equally important, classroom and campus norms must also support students' comfort in revealing their preconceptions about a subject, their questions, and their progress toward understanding new conceptual constructs related to a subject. Toward this end, faculty and staff must design classroom and other activities that promote the kind of intellectual camaraderie and attitudes toward learning that strengthen students' sense of community and belonging (Bransford, Brown and Cocking 2000). These activities may take the form of students solving problems together by building on each other's knowledge, asking questions to clarify explanations, and suggesting differing solutions (Brown and Campione 1994). Relatedly, the research indicates that cooperation and argumentation in problem solving enhance cognitive development and are factors in promoting student achievement (Goldman 1994; Kuhn 1991; Habermas 1990; Newstead and Evans 1995). Lave and Wegner (1991) also found that a community-centered approach supports the efforts of faculty to establish a community of learners among themselves. Such a community encourages questioning and can become a model for creating new ideas that builds on the contributions of individual members and can produce in faculty a sense of ownership of new ideas which they can transfer to teaching and learning in their classroom.

The effects of Sustained Social and Intellectual Communities/ Environments in Promoting Self-Efficacy Beliefs and Self-Regulatory Skills/Practices

Implicit in the findings above is the idea that access to particular sources of information can influence or shape students' beliefs about themselves; particularly their beliefs regarding their capacity to complete a task or achieve a goal (Bandura 1997). These informational sources, including vicarious experiences and verbal persuasion, are linked with student self-efficacy and subsequent achievement and completion in STEM and other disciplines (Hutchinson et al. 2006; Lent et al. 2003; National Research Council 2010).

With regard to vicarious experiences, Bandura argued (contrary to the views of behaviorism), that it is possible to form beliefs vicariously by observing others and their experiences. The exposure thus of students, majoring in the social sciences and STEM disciplines, to the choices, experiences and performances of mentors and capable peers, for example, can help students to not only form positive beliefs about their own abilities but also to increase their knowledge of future possible selves (Cooper 2007; Markus and Nurius 1986). Additionally, students' access to and participation in research with faculty can contribute to deepening students' interest and competence in, and identification with, the sciences and engineering, for example (Chubin and Ward 2009; Hunter, Laursen and Seymour 2007). That is, when students are afforded opportunities to engage in conceptualizing, conducting and interpreting research, they gain a sense of competence that is essential to their evolving identities in these disciplines (Edwards et al. 2011; Fries-Britt 2000; Schultz et al. 2011). Relevant strategies that support these important student attributes include meaningfully structuring research experiences during the academic year and the summer; creating a critical mass of students who motivate and support each others' interests; and socializing (vis-à-vis opportunities to participate in conferences, networking and research presentations) students to the demands and expectations of a discipline and potential profession (National Research Council 2010).

Students' self-efficacy beliefs thus shape their achievement vis-à-vis the choices they make and the goals they pursue (Bandura 1997; Bouffard-Bouchard 1990). Moreover, students with a strong sense of self-efficacy tend to employ more effective self-regulatory skills (Schunk and Ertmer 2000; Zimmerman 2002). That is, confident students not only use more cognitive and metacognitive strategies, but also put forth more effort and persevere when faced with academic challenges (Duckworth and Seligman 2006). Additionally, the quality of students' self-regulatory strategies serves to not only increase their self-efficacy but also the accuracy of their self-evaluations (Bouffard-Bouchard, Parent and Larivee 1991). The literature suggests that for students who major in the sciences and other disciplines, a sense of high self-efficacy is associated with their use of notes in learning difficult material, homework completion, and their persistence in these domains (Bembenutty 2010; Zimmerman & Kitsantas 2005).

Students' choices, goals, degree and quality of effort and resilience do not occur in a vacuum, however. An important aspect of self-efficacy is perceiving oneself as not only having membership in social and academic communities but also access to related social and other forms of education relevant capital (Bourdieu 1986; Coleman 1988). Students who do well in a course of study tend to have a strong support person and/or support system in place from which they receive advice, encouragement and other forms of assistance (Maton, Hrabowski and Schmitt 2000). While social support for majority students may include those in the education system or in their immediate family; some underrepresented students receive their support from a relative or the community. The reality however, is that many underrepresented students do not have the personal and academic support that is normally available to (and taken for granted by) majority students. Thus, underrepresented students about to enter college may not have family members or neighborhood friends who have been to college. Consequently, these students do not have ready access to information concerning the explicit (and implicit) attitudinal and behavioral demands of college (Hrabowski 2002).

These findings reinforce the influence of verbal affirmation (or verbal persuasion) on students' sense of self-efficacy (Bandura 1997). Verbal forms of support for student success in the sciences and engineering, for example, can be demonstrated by faculty encouragement of students' interest in these disciplines as opposed to employing introductory courses in these fields to "weed out" students (Hurtado et al. 2009; Maton et al. 2008). In this regard, research indicate that faculty need to be aware that introductory courses in the sciences and engineering tend not to siphon off those who are not good; but rather those who do not care for the competitive culture of science (Hurtado et al. 2009). Faculty also need to reverse the higher attrition rates of underrepresented students who are not as well prepared academically by reconceptualizing the curriculum so that the emphasis is on (1) enabling student mastery of core and advanced concepts; (2) encouraging students to both use and generate scientific and technical knowledge; (3) supporting student understanding of the importance of evidence with regard to iteratively building and sharpening models and explanations; and (4) promoting student recognition of the value of reflexive thought in producing knowledge (National Research Council 2010; Frehill, DiFabio and Hill 2008). This strategy necessitates student interaction with instructors who not only have high expectations of their students but who can also mediate their students' learning experiences (Brophy 2006; Flavell 1979; Vgotsky 1978). A focus on student mastery however, serves important purposes besides increased knowledge of the material. It enables the building of trustworthy relationships and environments as contexts that validate students' identity and enables them to take ownership of learning processes and products (Bryk and Schneider 2002; Chickering and Reisser 1993; Erickson 1968; Marcia 1966, 1980; Pascarella 1985; Weidman 1989). Gardner (1991), Greeno (2003), and Sizer (1992) underscore the internalization of the learning experience and the products of that experience as habits of mind and intellectual character.

In addition to the importance of verbal and other affirmations from faculty, it has become evident that peer study groups serve more than the purpose of helping students master the concepts in their fields; they also provide opportunities for students to receive verbal encouragement. Studying with peers who major in the sciences, social sciences and engineering disciplines for example, can promote conversations in which participants have to articulate their own ideas and listen to the ideas of others (Treisman 1992). Peer study group interactions also ensure that students make their work and thinking public and become more aware of the different perspectives and the knowledge fund of their peers (Asera 2001). As a result, students are disabused of the notion that their ability is based on sheer talent. The peer study group setting exposes students to peers who also struggle with various ideas and subject content (Bonsangue and Drew 1995; Treisman 1992; Treisman and Asera 1995). The result is that students learn quickly that excelling in a subject does not mean being able to solve problems quickly and easily but rather it means working very hard and persevering (Clewell et al. 2006; Springer, Stanne and Donovan 1999).

This shared process of working in peer study groups seems to also reduce the phenomenon of "stereotype threat" (Steele 1997; Steele and Aronson 1995). Steele and Aronson's (1995; Steele, Spencer and Aronson 2002) research demonstrates that black students' scores in mathematics may decline when they are aware that others may judge their performance in terms of their racial background, rather than in terms of their individual background. Student participation in peer study groups may reduce potential threats to stereotyping.

These norms of expectations and support and access to information (characteristics of social capital) both in and out of the classroom can greatly facilitate the institution's goals. They can also counter and/or mitigate, low faculty expectations for ethnic minority student success; students' lack of access to academically supportive peer networks; lack of supportive contact with faculty; unawareness of the need for strong study habits and tutoring; uneven and inadequate monitoring and advisement that may result in misinformation concerning coursework; students' preparedness regarding the next level of study; and unawareness of how to prevent or regulate the influence of emerging academic or personal problems (Garcia and Hu 2001; Pascarella and Terenzini 2005). As noted throughout the discussion however, progress on these fronts can benefit from concomitant reconceptualizations of curriculum, teaching and learning.

CONCLUSION

This chapter demonstrates the significance of institutional commitment to students and their education, not simply the prevention of student attrition. In this vein, successful institutions understand their purpose to include socializing students in the language, beliefs and traditions of the academy; enabling them to acquire the facts, critical thinking skills, and aesthetic awareness that will not only enable them to function in an increasingly global environment but also appreciate and engage in creative and innovative endeavors; promoting the moral courage to act with integrity, respect and personal regard to self and others; and providing transformative experiences for students so that they are actually different persons as a function of their education (S. Solomon & S, Layden, Opportunity Programs, Summer Academic Institute Lecture and Discussion, July 5 & 6 , 2011, Skidmore College).

Toward these ends, successful institutions emphasize the importance of not only understanding the issues that preclude effective teaching, but also reconceptualizing how faculty are prepared to engage students, including students from diverse racial/ethnic and socioeconomic backgrounds, in the science and art of learning increasingly complex material while simultaneously developing a broader range of domain specific and global competencies (Roberts 2007). Given these considerations, successful institutions enable faculty awareness *and* development of good teaching and learning practices (Feiman-Nemser 2001b; Shulman and Shulman 2004). Thus, a combination of content and instructional knowledge, for example, can enable faculty to reflect upon and guide their own emerging practice. The literature further suggests that faculty's access to and implementation of these strategies can further lead to their own personal and professional growth and awareness of when they need further learning (Hammerness and Darling-Hammond 2002; Hammerness et al. 2002). Given the issues and challenges in teaching and learning, namely, the apprenticeship of observation, it is crucial that faculty develop "visions of what is possible and desirable in teaching," which can serve as the basis for "their professional learning and practice" (Feiman-Nemser 2001b, 1017). Feiman-Nemser (2001b) asserts further that these visions reflect conjoined values and goals that are not only apparent in concrete classroom practices, but also in how faculty develop and assess their teaching and students' learning.

In addition to being taught how to craft a vision of teaching and learning, it is important to also provide support in efforts to enact or translate intentions into actions (Kennedy 1999). Grossman and colleagues (1999) suggest that access to and understanding of conceptual and practical tools are several ways in which to assist faculty in translating their intentions into practice. Conceptual tools include knowledge of learning theories, including Vygotsky's (1978) ideas of the development of higher psychological processes; while practical tools comprise relevant resources and pedagogical approaches and strategies that can enable the enactment of intentions into practice (Grossman, Smagorinsky and Valencia 1999).

The integration of conceptual understanding and pedagogical tools into a set of *practices*, or what Feiman-Nemser (2001b, 1018) has termed a *beginning repertoire* of classroom enactment, can include a variety of instructional activities to promote student learning, such as explaining concepts, holding discussions, designing experiments, developing simulations, planning debates, and organizing writing workshops. Faculty can benefit from access to opportunities that enable the design and implementation of unit plans and daily lessons that build understanding; developing and implementing formative and summative assessments; and offering feedback that is constructive and specific. Additionally, Feiman-Nemser (2001b) suggest that faculty should be learning not only the content of these strategies, but also when, how, where and why a particular approach can apply to their students.

Increasing foci on the above strategies and their potential effect on improving cognitive gains, particularly for diverse students, can thus be seen in the efforts of successful institutions to promote effective teaching, vis-à-vis restructured curriculum and assessments, based on principles of social justice. Although called different names in the literature: for example, Cochran-Smith's (1991) teaching against the grain; Zeichner's (1993) teaching for diversity; Nieto's (1999) multicultural education; Ladson-Billing's (1994) culturally relevant teaching; and Gay's (2002) culturally responsive teaching; this social justice perspective suggests that all students, including those who are economically and academically disadvantaged, should be prepared for full and active lives in a global context not only as employees but also as persons who are able to fulfill certain role expectations and obligations, whether as spouses, parents, employees, family members, friends, neighbors and citizens. It is also crucial for students to cultivate, toward self and others, personal regard, respect and integrity.

Similarly, it is vital that they are able to recognize and address vulnerabilities and dependencies in self and others as they navigate their life trajectories. These core qualities represent informed habits of mind that are not only practical but also creative, analytical (Sternberg, 2003) and regenerative. These habits of mind enable more than the "ability to draw on or access one's *intellectual* (emphasis mine) resources in situations where those resources may be relevant" (Prawat 1989, 1). Thus, students should not only access cognitive resources but also those that are emotional, psychological, physiological, social and spiritual. Toward this end, nurturing, training and educating students (and those who educate them) to live lives that approach these standards also warrants consideration of evolving conceptualizations of curriculum, instruction and assessments and the dynamic ends and/or goals of educational policies and practices for global education and competencies.

II

Contemporary Exemplars of Excellence

Introducing The Meyerhoff Scholars Program

Student Underrepresentation in STEM

The Meyerhoff Scholars Program's focus on preparing underrepresented students in the sciences, engineering and mathematics to enter graduate programs in these disciplines, partially stems from concerns over their underrepresentation as research scientists and professors in the academy. On a macro level, educators, policy makers and other stakeholders have been increasingly concerned about the underperformance and underrepresentation of African-American, Native American and Latino/a students in STEM fields since the 1940s (Bush 1945; National Academy of Science 2007). The National Academies' (2007) Report, *Rising above the Gathering Storm,* indicate that the primacy of the United States in the sciences and engineering has diminished when compared to the increased investment in and growth of research and education capacities in other countries. This report further suggests that the United States is now at a crossroads given this global leveling and as such, needs to place priority on investing in research, promoting innovation, and developing a competent workforce in the STEM fields.

Countering these claims of shortage however, Lowell and Salzman (2007) and others (Freeman 2008; Teitelbaum 2003), contend that the supply of STEM degrees is enough to meet the demands for STEM talent. Moreover, these researchers argue, the United States is generating more STEM-prepared students at the graduate level than there are tenure track positions available. Carnevale and colleagues (2011, 7) suggest that both the over- and under- supply perspectives are valid, "depending on which STEM workers, which education level, and which STEM competencies are being discussed."

For example, a focus on increasing STEM talent associated with research and development activities that contribute to innovations assumes a shortage in this domain. Carnevale and colleagues (2011) stress however, that STEM talent in research and development comprise a small share (21 percent) of those in STEM occupations. Thus, they caution, many aspects in the STEM debate need to be considered, including the entire STEM labor market; the range of competencies associated with STEM talent; and the growing demand for these competencies both in and out of conventional STEM occupations.

In this vein, these researchers suggest that recognizing the role that diversion plays can assist in understanding the shortage vs. supply dilemma. That is, a considerable number of "those with STEM talent or degrees divert from STEM occupations either in school or later in their careers (7)." This phenomena stems from the recognition that the core group of cognitive and noncognitive competencies associated with STEM talent and occupations, are valuable not only for STEM occupations but those that are non-STEM. Subsequently, occupations such as business, architecture and finance, may provide higher compensation; thus drawing STEM talent from traditional STEM occupations. The fulfillment of personal work values and/or job satisfaction also figure prominently in whether STEM talent consider and work in other occupations (Carnevale et al. 2011). In this vein, it appears that our system of education is not producing enough STEM-capable students to meet growing competency demands from both STEM and non-STEM occupations, particularly managerial, professional and healthcare professional occupations (Carnevale et al. 2011).

Thus, there is agreement with the recommendations from the recent National Academy Report (2007) noted above, which garnered the support of both national political parties and the executive and legislative branches of the U.S. government. Consequently, Congress sanctioned the implementation of many of the reports' recommendations with the passing of the America COMPETES Act in the summer of 2007 and provided funding through the American Recovery and Reinvestment Act of 2009 (the Stimulus Act) (National Research Council 2010). The recommendations advocated concerted efforts on several levels, including (1) improving mathematics, science and technology education for elementary and secondary students in the United States and careful training of highly qualified teachers in these domains; (2) increasing the pipeline of students who are prepared to major in and complete STEM degrees in college by growing the number of students who pass Advanced Placement (AP) and International Baccalaureate (IB) science and mathematics courses; and (3) providing supports, including financial aid, for undergraduate and graduate students to pursue study in these fields. The following section situates the importance of the third recommendation by detailing the prevalence of underachievement in STEM and declines in attainment rates despite the expression of interest in STEM fields by majority and minority groups and women.

TRACKING POSTSECONDARY STEM INTEREST AND COMPLETION: URM STUDENTS AND WOMEN

In efforts to understand the underperformance and underrepresentation of minority students in the sciences and engineering, researchers have focused on measuring these students' interest and persistence. For example, Anderson and Kim (2006) examined data collected by the National Center for Education Statistics (NCES) in the mid-1990s and found that although URM students entered college with comparable rates of interest in majoring in STEM fields as their majority and Asian American peers, the URM students not only took longer to attain their STEM degrees (six years) but also did so at lower rates. More specifically, although African American and Hispanic students persevered in these fields at similar rates as their white and Asian American peers (56 percent and 57 percent respectively) through their junior year in college (spring, 1998); they did not attain their bachelor's degrees at similar rates. That is, only 62.5 percent of URM students with majors in the STEM disciplines had attained a bachelor's degree by spring, 2001, compared with 94.8 percent of their Asian American peers and 86.7 percent of their White peers (Anderson & Kim 2006).

A more recent study by the Higher Education Research Institute (HERI) (HERI Report Brief January 2010) sampled more than 200,000 entering students across 326 four year institutions in Fall 2004 concerning their aspirations to major in and attain degrees in the STEM disciplines. HERI found that URM students attained their bachelor's degree at much lower rates than their Asian American and White peers after four (in 2008) and five (in 2009) years. That is, Latino, Black, and Native American students who entered as STEM majors in 2004 had four year STEM degree completion rates of 15.9, 13.2, and 14.0 percent respectively; and five year completion rates of 22.1, 18.4, and 18.8 percent, respectively. In comparison, White and Asian American students had four year completion rates of 24.5 and 32.4 percent respectively; and five year completion rates of 33 and 42 percent respectively. Although six year completion rates were not available for the HERI data, a comparison of this data with Anderson and Kim's (2006) suggest that disparities in STEM completion rates for URM students and their Asian American and White peers are significant and with regard to HERI's 2004 sample, seem to increase as time from matriculation elapsed. In this vein, HERI's (2010) trend analysis suggest that although there was significant volatility in student aspirations to major in STEM since 1971, the data indicates a convergence in the late 1980s and a stabilization in the early 1990s of aspirations by racial/ethnic groups.

There are also differences in completion rates between URM students who major in STEM and those who major in non-STEM disciplines. Non-STEM URM students have higher four and five year completion rates compared to their URM peers in STEM majors (Anderson & Kim 2006). There were also some differences between students who attained an undergraduate degree in a STEM field in Spring 2001, and those who did not. For example, completers tend to have at least one parent with a bachelor's degree or higher and come from households with higher incomes; whereas non-completers tend to work fifteen or more hours a week.

These studies suggest that students' preparation and motivation for STEM fields, in addition to the importance of financial support, are important ingredients for their success and completion in these high need areas. Although recent analysis of the differences between non- completers and completers are not yet available for the 2004 HERI cohort, prior research suggests the possibility of finding similar factors affecting achievement and completion rates for the 2004 HERI cohort and the 1995 NCES cohort analyzed by Anderson and Kim (2006). That is, in addition to the role of preparation and self-motivation for STEM fields, the research suggests that institutional strategies that focus on students' access to information and identification with STEM as a profession within the larger context of their academic and social integration within the institution, are important variables for consideration in efforts to increase students, particularly URM students' completion in the STEM fields (Chubin & Ward 2009).

The following chapter demonstrates how the University of Maryland, Baltimore County, has conceptualized, integrated, and implemented salient insights from the field to create a national model of student achievement in STEM, the Meyerhoff Scholars Program.

Chapter Three

Preparing Students for Research Careers

The Meyerhoff Scholars Program at the University of Maryland, Baltimore County

Beatrice L. Bridglall, Freeman A. Hrabowski, III and Kenneth Maton

INTRODUCTION

The academic underperformance and low educational attainment rates of underrepresented minority (URM) students in the sciences, technology, engineering and mathematics (STEM) has emerged as an urgent national priority (National Research Council 2010). This is the case not only with regard to our country's economic competitiveness on a global level but also our society's larger social justice agenda. This priority takes on increasing salience as the "dominance of the U.S. in these fields has lessened" even as "the rest of the world has invested in and grown their research and education capacities" in these domains (National Research Council 2010, 1). These dynamics reinforce the importance of further developing the capacities of our students, particularly those who underachieve in STEM. In 2007 for example, although URM students comprised 26.2 percent of undergraduate enrollment, they earned only 17.7 percent of the science and engineering bachelor's degrees awarded. This trend is similar in graduate school, where URM students comprise 17.7 percent of overall enrollment but earn only 14.6 percent and 5.4 percent of master's and doctoral degrees respectively, in the sciences and engineering (National Research Council 2010). These findings suggest that in addition to the importance of promoting access to higher education, successfully reducing underachievement and attainment disparities in the STEM disciplines between URM students and their White and Asian American peers requires *sustained attention to institutional contexts and their capacity to provide certain resources that enable student perseverance and completion.*

Given the considerable influence of equitable access *and* opportunities to learn in supportive contexts on underrepresented students' educational, career and life prospects, it is critical that we take a strengths based approach (Maton and Hrabowski 2004) in understanding how institutions, particularly those that are selective, promote student persistence, learning and completion on their campus. This line of inquiry is responsive to several converging strands of evidence, including Arum and Roksa's (2011) findings on the importance of improving instruction and student learning and Bowen and colleague's (2009) findings that the likelihood of *comparably qualified students* graduating with a bachelor's degree depends on whether or not they attend a more or less selective institution. That is, students are more likely to graduate with a credential if they attended a selective institution.

Thus, understanding the manner in which institutions, particularly those that are selective (1) conceptualize the supports needed for student persistence and completion; (2) emphasize student retention; and (3) focus on both individual and institutional outcomes, can contribute to important reconceptualizations of policy, research and practice in the STEM fields. This imperative becomes especially urgent when we consider several dynamics, including the uncertain nature of our future science and engineering workforce and current demographic shifts in American society. With regard to the former, the changing participation (i.e., "stay") rates for international students who have obtained their doctorates in these fields in the United States emphasize the uncertainty of depending on non-U.S. citizens for our sciences and engineering workforce (Finn, 2010).

Given the importance of systematically addressing these parallel concerns, this chapter examines the historical context that influenced the development, implementation and iterative evaluation of the Meyerhoff Scholar's Program (MSP) at the University of Maryland, Baltimore County, widely regarded as a national model for preparing students of color for careers in the sciences and engineering. This record of success is explored in the MSP's program outcomes and operationalized vis-à-vis the programs' components, which details the individual and institutional factors that influence students' persistence and completion in STEM disciplines, including a supportive campus climate; the provision of comprehensive financial aid; the synergy between student academic needs and family, community and cultural expectations; the linking of students' precollege experiences and support for their first year academic trajectories; pervasive expectations that students will engage in help-seeking behaviors; and supports and motivation as students progress in their major of choice. We conclude with a discussion of factors that predict Meyerhoff student entry into STEM doctoral programs.

THE HISTORICAL CONTEXT OF UMBC'S MEYERHOFF SCHOLARS PROGRAM

A convergence of factors influenced the University of Maryland, Baltimore County (UMBC), to launch the Meyerhoff Scholars Program in 1988 with funding from the Robert and Jane Meyerhoff Foundation. This effort was led by Freeman A. Hrabowski, III, an African American mathematician and the university's Vice Provost at the time. Shortly after Hrabowski was appointed in 1987, the campus's Black Student Union launched a protest against the institution because of what its members viewed as racist policies. In fact, the students occupied the Administration Building and remained there for several days. When Hrabowski investigated the incident, he discovered that many of the black students were not only academically and socially isolated, but also not engaged in the activities necessary for academic success at the university. He discovered that for these students, grades of "C" and "D" in such courses as organic chemistry, genetics and even introductory engineering were the norm. The practice of large numbers of African American students being "weeded out" of many disciplines, including mathematics, engineering, and the biological and physical sciences, was considered normal (Hurtado et al. 2009; Maton et al. 2008). Further compounding these problems was the fact that faculty in these disciplines had seen so few of these underrepresented minority students excelling. The few high-achieving black students in these disciplines were usually students from other countries, often having been educated in a French or British educational system.

The university responded to the frustration of students and parents by analyzing student performance and seeking resources to invest in a support infrastructure that would focus on high academic achievement and not simply remediation (National Educational Research Policy and Priorities Board 1999). While seeking funds, Hrabowski was fortunate to be introduced by the President of The Abell Foundation to Baltimore philanthropist Robert Meyerhoff, an MIT-trained engineer who was particularly concerned about the status of black males in America, a group he viewed as the nation's most disadvantaged. Similarly, Hrabowski and his UMBC colleagues were concerned about the poor academic performance of African American students in the sciences, technology, engineering, and mathematics (STEM). To that end, the Meyerhoff Scholars Program was launched to increase the number of African American males who excelled in STEM disciplines, and after the first year of the program, the number of African American students, in general, who excelled. In developing the program, Hrabowski and other university administrators initiated discussions with faculty, staff, and students regarding the nature of students' preparation in STEM fields and in relationship to their performance at the university. These discussions resulted in the accumulation of extensive data regarding (1) students' perceptions about course content and a lack of related academic support for doing well, (2) students' sense of academic and social isolation, and (3) the need for clear guidelines involving tutorial support, access to faculty, and effective study habits (Allen 1992; Harris and Nettles 1996; Nettles 1988; Treisman 1990, 1992).

After reviewing the records of students from different backgrounds on campus, Hrabowski and his colleagues discovered that regardless of race, large numbers of students were not excelling in STEM courses. As a result, many students were failing these courses, changing their major, or leaving the university altogether. The campus decided to raise admission standards for all students, including students of color. The vision of the university then focused on producing high-achieving students from all racial groups who would eventually be included among the nation's leading researchers. In tandem with this vision, UMBC's leadership focused on strengthening exist-ing orientation programs, developing strategies for improving first-year per-formance particularly in science and engineering, and building a community of student-scholars who would support each other and therefore reduce their sense of academic and social isolation (Astin 1993; Hurtado et al. 2008; Pascarella and Terenzini 2005; Steele, Spencer and Aronson 2002; Tinto 1993).

The goals of the Meyerhoff Scholars Program include (1) increasing the number of underrepresented students who could successfully complete a course of study in STEM fields in which there were historically underrepre-sented; (2) preparing these students academically and socially to pursue PhDs or MD/PhDs in these fields; and (3) increasing the number of minority professionals in these fields and faculty in the university professoriate (thus creating much needed role models for minority students of future genera-tions).

These goals are achieved through a group of integrated program compo-nents that emphasize (1) the careful selection of students; (2) the provision of merit financial support to reduce concerns about finances (Duffy and Gold-berg 1998); (3) a mandatory summer bridge program to acclimate students to the rigors of freshman year (Strayhorn 2011; (4) peer study groups for aca-demic and social support (Asera 2001; Treisman 1992) (5) the responsibility of each Meyerhoff student to one another and to community service (Fries-Britt 1995; Tseng & Seidman 2007; Zimmerman 2000); (6) the importance of taking advice; (7) meaningful and sustained interaction with faculty and mentors, including strong and ongoing involvement in research activities (Chubin and Ward 2009); (8) the importance of continued family involve-ment (Hrabowski, Maton Grief 1998; Hrabowski et al. 2002); (9) the centrality of academic excellence and scholarship (Hrabowski 1999; Maton et al. 2000); and (10) the significance of rigorously and systematically documenting and evaluating program outcomes (Granger et al. 2007). The MSP operates on the assumption that every student selected has the ability to excel in engineering and the sciences if they are provided with appropriate challenges, resources, and opportunities (Resnick 2000).

PROGRAM OUTCOMES

The MSP has proved very successful in enhancing the success of African American students in the sciences and is widely viewed as a national model. Indeed, UMBC is now among the top U.S. institutions, and is the top producer among predominantly white institutions, for preparing African American students who pursue and complete doctorates in the natural sciences and engineering between 2002 and 2006 (National Research Council 2010).

The 487 African-American Meyerhoff students from the first seventeen entering classes (Fall 1989–Fall 2005) with full study data constituted the Meyerhoff sample for the current outcome analyses. The "Declined" comparison sample consisted of 210 African-American male students with full study data who were offered admission to the Meyerhoff Program between 1989 and 2005 and declined the offer. In the vast majority of cases these students attended other institutions, mostly selective or highly selective universities. Only students who (1) had declared a science major or (2) enrolled in four or more STEM courses (or twelve or more STEM credits) during their freshman year of college – thus viewed as likely pursuing a STEM major – were retained in the sample. A preliminary analysis of the comparability of the African American Meyerhoff and Declined samples on pre-college academic characteristics indicated that the Declined sample had higher SAT math scores and a higher high school GPA (see table 1). The two groups did not differ on Verbal SAT.

Table 3.1. Pre-College Academic Characteristics for African-American Meyerhoff and Declined Comparison Sample Students: 1989–2005

	Meyerhoff	Declined
Math SAT	645	658*
Verbal SAT	633	626
High School GPA	3.7	3.8*
*p < .001	N = 487	N = 210

In terms of STEM PhD outcomes, the 1989–2005 African-American Meyer-hoff students were five times more likely to enter STEM PhD programs than their Declined sample counterparts (40 percent vs. 7.9 percent) (see table 2). Although less than one-quarter of the Meyerhoff students in the overall sample did not attend graduate or professional school (22.8 percent), fully two-fifths (40.5 percent) of the Declined sample did not attend graduate or professional school following college. Logistic regression analysis, controlling for sat scores, high school GPA, gender, and year of entry (cohort), revealed that Meyerhoff students were significantly more likely than Declined students to attend STEM PhD programs than to attend medical school, MS/allied health programs, or to not attend graduate or professional school.

Table 3.2.   Graduate Outcomes for African-American Meyerhoff and Declined Comparison Sample Students: 1989–2005

	Meyerhoff	Declined	Odds Ratio[a]
STEM PhD	40.0% (193)	7.9% (17)	
ALL OTHER	60.9% (289)	92.1% (198)	8.8*
MD	17.0% (82)	29.3% (63)	9.0*
MS/Allied Health	20.1% (97)	22.3% (48)	7.1*
MD	22.8% (110)	40.5% (87)	9.1*
*p < .01			

[a] Covariates: Math SAT, Verbal SAT, High school GPA, Gender, Cohort.

PROGRAM COMPONENTS

In examining the reasons for the program's success, results from the analyses of student process evaluation survey data and interviews conducted periodically over the years are integrated with those from non-participatory observations, interviews with the university leadership, program staff and faculty, and document analyses. There appears to be considerable agreement or triangulation in this case study (Lincoln and Guba 1985; Strauss and Corbin 1998; Creswell and Plano-Clark 2007), with convergence across the types of data. Several themes emerged from the data analysis; namely that the Meyerhoff program is implemented in a supportive campus climate; students' worries concerning financial aid or having to work while in a rigorous program of study are reduced; there were not any blatant discrepancies between students' academic needs and family, community and cultural expectations; students' pre-college and first year academic experience are effectively bridged; students' embarrassment and fears concerning help-seeking and/or not getting into their major of choice are effectively pre-empted through consistent monitoring, advisement, motivation and support.

The components of the Meyerhoff program are discussed under the categories noted above. For example, recruitment, faculty involvement and commitment, and institutional leadership are discussed in the context of a supportive campus climate. A discussion of comprehensive financial aid for students follows. Family involvement, community service and program values are discussed in relationship to students' academic needs as well as family, community and cultural expectations. Students' pre-college experiences, linked to support during their first academic year are examined in the context of the program's summer bridge, personal advising and counseling, and community service components. Finally, the program's emphasis on peer group study, peer motivation and teamwork, tutoring, summer research internships, mentoring and on the Minority Access to Research Careers (MARC) program is examined in the context of pervasive expectations that students will seek help throughout their academic careers.

Although the results are summarized according to these categories, the category classifications are not rigidly applied. The program's components can also be discussed under other categories, e.g., academic and social integration, knowledge and skill development, support and motivation and monitoring and advisement (Maton and Hrabowski 2004; Maton et al. 2000), or recruitment of a critical mass of highly capable underrepresented minority students interested in research careers, development of a tight-knit learning community focused on STEM excellence, and multiple high quality STEM research and academic experiences (Maton, Hrabowski and Pollard in press). This approach allows us to connect different components in distinct ways depending on a given activity's purpose, involvement of faculty, program staff, university leadership, student peers and mentors, and their explicit and implicit meanings.

A Supportive Campus Climate: MSP's Criteria for Recruitment and Admission

Recruitment is a year-round, labor-intensive activity. Information about the program is shared by program staff in high schools, higher education campuses, and with various educators, advisors and counselors. These professional networks serve as some of the most effective ways of locating potential students. This initial identification leads to recruitment visits, letters, phone calls and conversations with students and parents. The Program currently receives approximately 2000–2200 nominations and applications each year.

The initial admissions criteria were considered selective at that time. Successful candidates needed a minimum combined SAT score (before re-centering) above 1000, SAT-Math above 500 and strong high school GPAs. However, the actual mean scores of participants were considerably higher (for the 1989–91 cohorts, combined SAT math and verbal scores were 1180 and SAT Math scores were 635). The academic criteria for acceptance into this program have steadily increased. For example, average SAT Math scores and mean GPAs for the 2010-2011 freshman class (the program's twenty-second cohort) are 700 and 4.2, respectively (the GPA average is weighted). Meyerhoff candidates tend to earn As and Bs in rigorous high school science and math courses. Many students have completed a year or more of calculus in high school. The program strongly considers students who have taken advanced placement courses in math and science; provide strong references from science or math instructors; and have research experience. Advanced placement courses, however, are not part of the Meyerhoff Program's admissions requirement because not all high schools offer these courses. The admissions office at UMBC has an extensive database of high schools, their course offerings, and their graduation requirements. The Meyerhoff selection committee has access to this information and is aware of the strength of a student's high school academic program. If advanced placement courses were not available to the student, the selection committee tries to determine how far the student progressed beyond the minimum graduation requirements. For example, did the student take additional math or science courses at the local community college? However, students are not penalized for not having taken advanced placement courses although it does help their admissions applications. Additional criteria include a commitment to stay in the sciences; an interest in research and earning a terminal degree; and a desire to contribute to the community.

The top 100–150 applicants and their families are invited to one of two recruitment weekends on UMBC's campus. The first selection weekend, scheduled at the end of February, is for in-state students. The second selection weekend, held the first weekend in March, is for out-of state students. These two weekends provide an opportunity for faculty, the university leadership, program staff, and current students to meet and evaluate the applicants under both formal and informal conditions; expose prospective students to the MSP's expectations that its scholars will enroll in doctoral programs in the STEM fields; and afford these students opportunities for extensive interaction with current students, program staff, faculty, and the university leadership.

Prior to attending selection weekend, students are expected to complete a written test and math and English placement exams. The scores from these exams are used to plan course registration for the fall. Students invited for selections weekend are interviewed collectively by a faculty member (from various departments, such as mathematics, science or engineering), a senior Meyerhoff student, and an administrator. This team approach to interviewing provides the selection committee three different but related perspectives regarding the students' academic strengths and weaknesses, students' willingness to take advice, and the likelihood of students' becoming a part of the Meyerhoff community of high achievers. The program generally accepts between forty and seventy students each year depending on available funding.

The following quotes from African American Meyerhoff students underscore several aspects of the recruitment process:

> In tenth grade, UMBC was the first college or university to send me a letter and . . . an invitation to come and visit the campus.

> When I went to Selection Weekend, I just saw the caliber of students who were here, and also trying to get into the program. . . I just thought, "I want to be a part of that group."

> (During selection weekend) Dr. P (eminent researcher) made a promise that I would be able to work in his lab.

The first group of Meyerhoff Scholars included nineteen young African American men who enrolled in fall 1989. Now in its twenty-second year, the Meyerhoff Program is open to all high-achieving high school seniors who have an interest in pursuing doctoral study in the sciences or engineering and are interested in the advancement of minorities in these and related fields. The program currently has a total enrollment of 230 students, the majority of whom are African Americans. One of the unusual aspects of the MSP's selection process is its recruitment of students' families as well. The university leadership understands the central roles that families play in the lives of students of color (Hrabowski, Maton and Grief 1998; Hrabowski et al. 2002). Families are thus engaged and made to feel wanted in the recruitment process. Similarly, the MSP also understands the role of community service in these students' lives (Bridglall and Gordon 2004a, 2004b; Maton et al. 2000). Thus recruitment efforts include active consideration of community churches and their leaders, social organizations and clubs.

This systematic creation of a critical mass of academically motivated, high-achieving minority students enables prospective African American and other students of color and their families to see an atmosphere that supports their academic and social integration (Pascarella and Terenzini 2005). The National Science Foundation has determined that UMBC has one of the largest concentrations of high-achieving African American students majoring in the sciences and engineering in the United States. Specifically, in 1996, the Meyerhoff Scholars Program was recognized nationally with the Presidential Award for Excellence in Science, Mathematics and Engineering Mentoring. With approximately 13,000 students, about half of UMBC's undergraduates and 60 percent of the doctoral students pursue engineering and science degrees. UMBC's student population is approximately 16 percent African American and 21 percent Asian; Hispanic and Native American students collectively comprise 4 percent. UMBC's leadership recognize that although the university had been successful in producing a number of White and Asian students in engineering and the sciences, few African American students had succeeded in these disciplines until the creation of the Meyerhoff Scholars Program.

Faculty Involvement and Commitment

Freshmen in the MSP and in the university, at large, are taught by full-time, tenure-track faculty (Arum and Roksa 2011). Active faculty engagement with large numbers of students reflects extensive and continuing conversations among faculty in various departments, the university leadership, and other administrators regarding not just minority but all students' grades, persistence, and retention in their freshman year. These discussions were designed to produce a critical understanding of how students perform by course, section, and faculty member so that the necessary resources and supports can be channeled for effective student academic improvement (Bowen, Chingos and McPherson 2009).

Several initial conversations revealed, for example, that almost half of the students (including both majority and minority students) were struggling with below C averages in their first-semester Chemistry course. Some faculty members in this department suggested that these students underachieve because they (students): (1) work too many hours on the outside; (2) do not have the necessary preparation for doing well in the introductory course; and (3) were not serious about mastering the concepts and doing well. However, discussions and focus groups with students revealed that: (1) they clearly needed more constructive feedback in the form of graded homework, quizzes, and tutoring earlier rather than later in the semester; (2) they were preparing for exams by themselves rather than studying in groups; (3) they were not aware of the amount of study time necessary for excelling in rigorous science courses; (4) a large number of students did not use the department's tutorial center because they perceived it as a place failing students go for remediation; and (5) they were not always aware of the relationship between their homework, graded quizzes, exams and lectures (Bembenutty 2000; Schunk and Ertmer 2000; Treisman 1990, 1992; Zimmerman 2002; Zimmerman and Kitsantas 2005).

What also emerged from these discussions with faculty and students were erroneous assumptions that both students and faculty had about the students' academic performance in the classroom. In one instance, both faculty and students began the semester with the mistaken assumption that students of color were doing well if they earned a C in organic chemistry. In this example and others, continued discussions emphasize that many students of color tend to excel when they are exposed to faculty who consistently motivate them, are aware of their strengths and weaknesses, and encourage them to be involved in activities related to their majors (National Research Council 2010; Frehill, DiFabio and Hill 2008).

In consideration of both faculty and students' perspectives, this department's faculty has since collaborated in improving student performance and retention in its freshman year chemistry courses by using a team-teaching approach and by relating the course content to faculty research. These continuing discussions between the university leadership, faculty, relevant departments and administrators also resulted in a science-education faculty member observing and assessing a biology instructor's course and helping him to create strategies that encourage more substantive interaction with his students. Interactions with students allowed the instructor to (1) more accurately gauge student learning, and (2) use particular technology to increase mastery of pertinent concepts (Leggon 2006; National Research Council 2010). Additionally, students were and still are, assigned theoretical and practical problems to solve as groups and the chemistry tutorial center is perceived as a place where students who excel go for tutoring. The Chemistry department, through orientation sessions and faculty interaction with students, make the relationship between time on task and excelling in difficult courses very explicit (Summers and Hrabowski 2006). Students' courses include a lesson in which the course standards and requirements are made explicit. Students are also required to plot the number of hours needed for study in order to get an A in their coursework. Most recently, an interactive, small-group based "Discovery Center" for introductory courses in Chemistry has substantially improved student learning and grades.

During the conceptualization, design, implementation and iterative evaluation of the MSP, UMBC's leadership and faculty observed that underrepresented students needed a stronger foundation in mathematics and science (Moore 2006; Rascoe and Atwater 2005; Moore et al. 2003; Hrabowski and Pearson 1993). This recognition influenced the establishment of a first-year algebra mini-course designed to strengthen students' mathematics skills. UMBC's leadership also worked closely with faculty to re-conceptualize the relevancy of certain content in physics, chemistry, biology and engineering courses, for example. In chemistry, for instance, students are introduced to the faculty's research interests (Clewell at al. 2006; Cooper 2007). This approach relates theoretical concepts to real-world concerns. In an engineering course, students' participation in a project for the homeless enabled them to gain a realistic perspective regarding how engineers conceptualize and work toward solving certain social problems. Additionally, faculty convey strong, positive messages when they choose students of color to work with them on research projects.

The expectation that faculty will include students in their research and the requirement that students will study in groups are other strategies used to increase student understanding of conceptual material and internalization of knowledge and skills (Asera 2001). In peer study groups, for example, gaps in students' mathematical preparation are addressed in situ; that is, the fundamental concepts in algebra, for example, are reviewed and mastered within the context of working on advanced quantitative problems (Asera 2001; Treisman 1990; 1992). UMBC institutional researchers also found that this strategy is more effective mathematically and psychologically than the alternative strategy of routing students to remedial programs (Maton et al. 2000, 2008; Schmidt 1998, 2008). Additionally, given the leadership and program staffs' emphasis on succeeding at the highest levels, high achieving juniors and seniors function as an integral part of instruction as teaching assistants. They also mentor and counsel new students on what is required for academic excellence. On yet another level, the Meyerhoff Scholars have set up a test bank, where they share prior exams and notes to help each other succeed. This emphasis on addressing students' knowledge gaps in ongoing work with faculty, teaching assistants, and peers is a salient characteristic of the MSP model.

Students were asked to characterize their interactions with and perceptions of, faculty support. One of the implicit themes in student perceptions about faculty support is the idea of relational trust, recognized by Bryk and Schneider (2002) as an essential ingredient in effective schools. The following is a sample of students' responses:

> I interact with UMBC faculty and staff at the highest level of respect and integrity.

> My interactions often do reinforce the expectations of the program.

> My interactions are often motivated by my goals.

> The belief in honesty, all of the faculty and staff are especially adamant about being honest. Peers will often report each other to the teacher if there is a problem or question of honesty.

> Well, I think their honesty in everything that they do plays a big part in what is needed for me to be successful and to trust them in their advice.

> I'd never worked in a lab before. . . I had a really good mentor. She taught me different techniques. . . I got to do a lot of research.

Faculty also commented positively on the program, and their department's commitment to it, as reflected in the following quote from a faculty member:

> The overwhelming majority of the department is impressed...and in
> favor of [the Meyerhoff] program.

Process evaluation surveys administered periodically to students from 1990 to the present reveal that African American students in the program rate the helpfulness of faculty involvement in the program highly (a mean of 3.7 on a 5 point rating scale. See table 3).

Table 3.3. Perceived Benefit of Meyerhoff Program Components: African-American Meyerhoff Students, 1989–2005

	Mean	Standard Deviation	N
Financial scholarship	4.6	0.9	383
Being part of the Meyerhoff Program community	4.4	1.0	384
Summer Bridge	4.3	1.0	382
Study groups	4.1	1.1	391
Summer research	4.0	1.3	328
Staff academic advising	3.9	1.1	377
Staff personal counseling	3.9	1.3	376
Faculty involvement	3.7	1.2	375
Academic tutoring services	3.6	1.3	311
Family Involvement	3.6	1.4	379
MSP Involvement in Community	3.6	1.2	317
Cultural Activities	3.5	1.2	322
Group Discussions in Meetings	3.4	1.3	321
Baltimore/DC-area assigned mentor	2.9	1.5	302

Institutional Leadership

The Meyerhoff Program is supported at all levels of the university, including dedicated support from the President (Hrabowski 2004, 2006). Over the years, the program has generated a substantial amount of public recognition and support. Some of the sources of funding for the MSP include those from federal agencies: National Institutes of Health/National Institute of Environmental Health Sciences (NIH/NIEHS); National Institutes of Health/National

Institute of Biomedical Imaging and Bioengineering; National Security Agency (NSA); National Aeronautical and Space Administration (NASA); Howard Hughes Medical Institute (HHMI); Louis Stokes Alliance for Minority Participation; and the National Science Foundation. Gifts from private foundations to the MSP endowment/foundation account include: the Atlantic Philanthropic, Dow Chemical, Juvenile Diabetes, Star Foundation, Merck, Adam Rodgers Foundation, AT&T, Robert Deutsch Foundation, DuPont, Fullwood Foundation, Lipitz Family, and several other foundations that wish to remain anonymous. Additionally, the Meyerhoff Parents Association contributes to the MSP.

The MSP program staff has primary responsibility for recruiting, advising and registering students and creating, nurturing and sustaining this high-performance learning community (Maton et al. 2000, 2008). They are expected to closely monitor students and make sure that they are not derailed by issues such as financial aid, housing or personal concerns. By all accounts, they seem to understand their students' needs and appear to be knowledgeable about and connected to the broader campus community. Together, the university leadership, program staff and faculty serve as a safety net (Coleman 1988, 1990; College Board 2009) that prevents problems, and identifies and provides resources not only to students having academic or personal difficulties but also to those who excel.

UMBC's commitment to high academic achievement and social integration is demonstrated by the level of encumbered resources committed to this effort, the quality of the faculty teaching the courses, and the extent to which faculty are continually assessing their own expectations and instructional practices (Maton et al. 2000, 2008; Summers and Hrabowski 2006). This infrastructure appears to enable students to handle the rigor and difficulty of technical course work, influences their attitudes about their major, their willingness to take advice, their involvement in supplementary education, and the nature and level of their motivation to excel. This full complement of institutional commitment is important for students in general but crucial for students of color in particular (Hrabowski 2004, 2006).

UMBC's commitment is also reflected in professional development opportunities for MSP's program staff. These activities emphasize how to: (1) help freshman students set and maintain high expectations throughout their undergraduate career in the MSP; and (2) encourage students to become comfortable with their differences and skilled at addressing tensions that inevitably arise when learning to coexist with others from different ethnic, cultural and racial backgrounds (Bridglall 2004; Bridglall and Gordon 2004a). In their formal capacities as recruiters, counselors, academic advisors and student activities coordinators, for example, and in informal yet deliberate interactions with students on a personal level, program staff nurture students by taking a holistic approach to students' academic progress, extra-curricular and career interests and general well-being (Bridglall and Gordon 2004b).

PROVISION OF COMPREHENSIVE FINANCIAL AID

Financial support is contingent upon students maintaining a B average in their major. The Meyerhoff Program provides students with a comprehensive financial package (Gansemer-Topf and Schuh 2005) including, in many cases, tuition, books, and room and board (projected annual costs for tuition and room and board for 2010-2011 is $18,791 for in-state students and $28,728 for out-of-state students). Meyerhoff finalists receive a partial scholarship in addition to the many support services and activities the program offers. For any two consecutive semesters that students' GPA falls below 3.0, funding is taken away completely. Students regain their funding when their grades meet MSP's standards. The MSP program staff does not make any exceptions to this rule. The program director and his staff work closely with the financial aid office in posting funds to student accounts in a timely manner. A key part of the attraction of the program is the financial support provided. When asked "What made you decide to become a Meyerhoff?" many students answer: "The money and...", as indicated in the following excerpt:

> The full scholarship . . . and the fact the program is catered toward getting you to your graduate degree goal. MD/PhD, whatever it might be.

Process evaluation surveys administered periodically to students from 1990 to the present reveal that African American students in the program rate financial support as the most helpful program component (mean of 4.6 on a 5 point rating scale).

SYNERGY BETWEEN STUDENT ACADEMIC NEEDS AND FAMILY, COMMUNITY, CULTURAL EXPECTATIONS

Family Involvement

Parents of current students in the Meyerhoff Program are kept advised of their child's progress. Upon their child's enrollment, parents or guardians are asked to become part of the Meyerhoff Parents Association (MPA). For the active classes, approximately 85 percent to 100 percent of the parents participate, resulting in strong representation from each active cohort (i.e., all students in the freshman class are considered one cohort; all sophomores make up another, etc.). Currently, the active cohorts include MSP students enrolled from program year 19 to 22. Some parents of alumni students have remained with the association and assist with different functions.

The MPA plans and implements two major events in the academic year: the family reception and the reception for graduating seniors. Another of the associations' activities involve raising money for a scholarship fund (this is done through dues, donations from other parents, matching funds from employers, etc.). The MPA is also involved in both selection weekends and assists in opening and closing the summer bridge program. During selection weekend, for instance, there is a meeting Saturday evening between parents of current students and prospective parents. This meeting is informal, and none of the program staff are present. The program staff can count on the MPA to reassure both prospective parents and students. The MPA provides one of the venues for parents to talk with other parents and generate suggestions and insights from parental peers. The Parents Association meets once a month. Program staff believe that the MPA is effective even though it is a small, independent organization. UMBC's president is aware of the MPA's activities. By all accounts, the perception is that parents are vested in and supportive of the MSP. Program staff however, cannot discuss students' grades with parents unless the student gives permission.

It is unusual for a higher education intervention to advocate continued parental involvement. However, MSP's program staff and university leadership recognize that successful parenting does not end when the student leaves for college. Indeed, they believe that most Meyerhoff parents continue to care deeply about their children's academic and social development and are usually willing to work with program staff to make sure this happens. For example, in the several studies Hrabowski and his colleagues (1998, 2002) have done on raising academically successful African American young men and women, they discovered that parental emphasis is often on:

1. Child-focused, self-sacrificing love, including a deep and enduring commitment to education
2. Strong limit-setting and discipline by parents, especially in relation to the children's social life
3. Consistently high expectations, with the emphasis on the sons and daughters achieving their fullest potential, always striving to achieve and never being satisfied with low grades
4. Open, consistent, and strong communication between parents and children, so that the children feel comfortable bringing issues to their parents
5. Positive gender and racial identity focus, so that the young Black men and women felt positive about themselves

6. Parents' reliance on community resources, most notably churches and extracurricular activities (e.g., academically oriented summer camps). (Hrabowski 1999)

Hrabowski and his colleagues also discovered that apart from parents' own education level or economic or marital status, these parents' emphasis on education and academic success, in tandem with consistent messages concerning hard work and overcoming adversity, manifested itself in the following ways:

1. Reading to their daughters and sons at a young age
2. Parental perception that education is necessary and extremely valuable
3. Parents' active encouragement toward academic success
4. Close interaction between parents and their children's teachers
5. Strong parental interest in homework;
6. Frequent verbal praise
7. Parents having calm and thoughtful conversations with their sons and daughters to help them understand that even when they face prejudice or racism, they cannot afford to see themselves as victims and still succeed (Hrabowski 1999; Hrabowski, Maton and Grief 1998; Hrabowski et al. 2002).

This emphasis on the value of focused effort, working hard and earning respect and praise is not restricted to parent and child interaction but can be observed in student interactions with faculty, program staff and university leadership. The inclusion of parents within the fabric of the Meyerhoff program reflects the idea that parents need to continue as advocates for their children. In the program's view, parents should never cease to study their children, spend time with them, listen to them, and learn about their schoolwork, friends, interests and hobbies – not just in school, but also in the community. Process evaluation surveys administered periodically to students from 1990 to the present reveal that African American students in the program rate the helpfulness of family involvement in the program highly (a mean of 3.6 on a 5 point rating scale).

Community Service

Each cohort (grouped according to the year in which they entered the program), is assigned to assist a project on UMBC campus. This component helps to underscore the program value of "giving back" and expects students to focus on outreach activities and service to UMBC. Students can also provide service to the larger community (Maton 2005, 2008). For example, MSP students would sometimes tutor at a Baltimore high school, bringing their knowledge of sciences and mathematics and firsthand information about college to local students. Other activities include organizing environmental projects, collecting food for homeless shelters or participating in campus outreach activities to middle schools. In recent years, second year students have adopted an elementary school and have tutored students in groups of five. Community service helps students to put their studies and their potential for contributing to the larger world in perspective (Maton 2005, 2008). Students often characterize their commitment to community service in the following way: "To whom much is given, much is expected." Program staff and the university leadership believe that the community is at its most vital when the students take an active role in shaping their own environment. This is reflected in the following remarks by students:

> I feel that my success cannot become as it could be without the support of the community. In return, I will keep faithful to honest studying and many cultural activities/civic activities that improve the lives of the community.

> Community service is the primary way to give back to the community. Secondly, mentoring plays a large role.

> To expect social change, one must actively support it.

> I feel that ultimately my responsibility will be to reach the highest level of professional success in order to be in the personal position to help, motivate, guide and hire students like myself.

> It is important to give back so that someday, those younger will follow.
> By being a leader on campus, you encourage others to help as well.

Students' sense of community is also reflected in their participation in the arts, extra-curricular and cultural activities. Some underrepresented students in the MSP participate in ethnically oriented student clubs, choirs and even go to church with Hrabowski, for example. Spirituality appears to be an important element in this program, especially among African American students (Bryk, Lee and Holland 1993; Hilliard and Amankwatia 2003; Irvine and Foster 1996; Lantieri 2001). These cultural activities contribute to students' sense of belonging and enable a goodness of fit between the students and the campus environment. Given that some ethnic minority student groups sometimes remain by themselves, program staff and faculty deliberately create opportunities for all students to interact with others from diverse backgrounds.

Process evaluation surveys administered periodically to students from 1990 through to the present reveal that African American students in the program rate the helpfulness of the community service and cultural components of the program highly (means of 3.6 and 3.5, respectively, on a 5 point rating scale).

Program Values

UMBC faculty, university leadership, and program staff encourage high academic achievement values by reinforcing that students have to seek help from a variety of sources, academically and socially support their peers, work toward PhD attainment and the pursuit of research careers, and engage in meaningful community service. The shortage of underrepresented students with PhDs in STEM fields is discussed at the recruitment phase (Good, Halpin and Halpin 2002; Jackson 2003; National Research Council 2010). Similarly, the importance of earning a PhD is emphasized during selection weekend and throughout students' undergraduate careers in the program. Settling for an MD degree is considered a disappointment in this climate given the program's focus on producing PhD-level researchers. Given these goals, faculty support is critical for students (Arum and Roksa 2011; Bowen, Chingos and McPherson 2009). In our analysis, we discovered that, over the course of their undergraduate experience, students have internalized these programmatic values and express them in their own terms as a commitment to excellence, accountability, group success, and giving back. Sample quotes below are from African-American focus group participants.

> Commitment to excellence: I think being a Meyerhoff scholar means being the best.

> Accountability: It helps you stay on point. It's like when you have to get things done, like papers turned in. Even for our meetings. . . I always forget but then there's someone who will just be like 'Oh, we have a meeting tomorrow'. . . So now I let my apartment mates know.

> Group success: Well, like we're a family. So...if we all stand together, work together, we'll all have a bright future.

> Giving back: I think there is a large part of the program that's about giving back to those who are younger than you and to really try to be something that somebody else would look up to. And trying to help younger kids figure out what they want to do.

Additionally, personal values such as respect, dedication, honesty, communication, tolerance, and hard work surfaced often in students' responses.

LINKING STUDENTS' PRE-COLLEGE EXPERIENCES AND SUPPORTING THEIR FIRST YEAR ACADEMIC TRAJECTORIES

Summer Bridge Program

Once selected for the program, Meyerhoff students attend a mandatory pre-freshman Summer Bridge Program and take courses in math, science, African American studies and the humanities. In the African American studies course, for example, one area of emphasis is making students aware of the many contributions African Americans have made in the United States. Students are also exposed to relevant social and cultural events that encourage them to value each other's differences and commonalities (Strayhorn 2011).

A particular strength of the summer bridge program is committed faculty from different fields and program staff who explicitly prepare students for the new expectations and requirements of rigorous college courses (Swail and Perna 2002; Tierney 2002; Villalpando and Solórzano 2005). Students are also trained in how to study in peer groups and how to engage in rigorous and systematic problem solving (Personal communication, Mr. LaMont Toliver, 2009). This component was structured on Hrabowski's earlier experience with directing an Upward Bound (UB) program for students following high school graduation. UB programs are intended to prepare students for rigorous college-level courses; familiarize them with faculty expectations and provide students with opportunities to interact with peers, staff and faculty (Myers and Schirm 1999).

This aspect of the program is implemented with the expectation that intensive summer academic work, in addition to opportunities for building academic social networks, will prepare students for excelling in university-level work (Gándara 2002; Swail and Perna 2002; Tierney 2002). Academics in the summer bridge program and in the course of students' undergraduate academic career in the MSP are balanced with social opportunities and cultural events that encourage constant interaction with peers, faculty, university leadership and program staff (Bailit et al. 2005; Tierney and Hagedorn 2002). Interviews with the director and executive director suggest that they consider the summer bridge component to be one of the more crucial aspects of the program. One of the staff's guiding principles is Proverb 22:6:

Train up a child in the way he should go, And when he is old, He will not depart from it.

Program staff regard the six weeks they have with pre-freshmen as a crucial time because it gives them an opportunity to reduce and/or eliminate poor study habits or the practice of writing a paper overnight, for example. According to the director, "Aside from molding them and exposing students to the Meyerhoff way, the greatest things we can give students is compassion and empathy" (L. Toliver, personal communication). The director acknowledges that he and his staff have "unconditional faith and belief" in the Meyerhoff Scholars (L. Toliver, personal communication). He emphasized that it is important that his staff know their students' strengths and weaknesses, "who they click with, their background, their pet peeves, and their fears" (L. Toliver, personal communication). Program staff gain this information in the course of the six weeks of the summer bridge program and through the daily advising and monitoring of students. During this time and throughout students' careers in the MSP, a certain personal etiquette is also emphasized. "Meyerhoffs have to open doors, pull out chairs, not chew gum in public, and dress in a certain way—girls wear skirts a certain length below their knees, for example" (L. Toliver, personal communication). This emphasis is referred to as both "challenging the Meyerhoffs to be better persons and outfitting them to succeed" (L. Toliver, personal communication).

Process evaluation surveys administered periodically to students from 1990 to the present reveal that African American students in the program rate the summer bridge program as one of the most helpful program components (a mean of 4.3 on a 5 point rating scale).

> The idea of family is established through Summer Bridge…This idea that, you know, together we can accomplish much. And if you're doing well, you should pull your brothers and sisters along with you.

> I think it's kind of like boot camp…When you spend that much time [together]… you form bonds…transition [to] college.

In an open-ended questionnaire administered to graduating seniors, students were asked to characterize whether their interaction with program staff was formal or informal. Their responses largely reflect the authoritative/parental surrogacy roles played by the program staff:

> Formal interaction is more like mentor/mentee relationship or parent-child. Informal interaction is extremely laid back and friendly.

> I am rather friendly with the staff of the MSP. Although I am occasionally told to stop by the office more often, I still can feel the care in their tones.

> MSP staff treats you like adults but don't forget to give you support and guidance that you may need.

> The formal interaction with program staff has been fine. With some staff members, I feel that I have a personal bond.

As African American and other students adjust to their new environment during the summer bridge orientation process and throughout their career in the MSP, program staff work tirelessly to help students become academically focused and socially and emotionally comfortable. This strategy is critical given the importance of academic confidence and identification with the university in student retention (Tinto 1993). Similarly, this orientation process and continuous interaction between program staff and students are regarded as essential as students manage the social and academic challenges that may emerge in daily interactions with faculty and students from other racial/ethnic groups. In the process, students are taught how to take responsibility for their own behavior, exercise self-regulation, manage their time effectively, and cope with change and related stresses. Program staff's effectiveness in helping students to develop a sense of belonging, bond with students from different ethnic groups, and perceive themselves as valuable members of the campus community is reflected in the MSP's retention rate of 92 percent.

Observations of the program staff's interactions with students suggest that they genuinely care about how well students do. Both program staff and students openly admit that the program is intrusive. It is this characteristic they believe, that partially accounts for the program's effectiveness. However, "males have more trouble with intrusiveness than females" and they (males) "are not open to talking about what's happening to them" (L. Toliver, personal communication). Students have to check in almost daily with program staff, who are concerned about the students they do not see often. From the perspective of the program staff, they "work well together with students like a family" (L. Toliver, personal communication, UMBC). Some students however, chaffed at the constant monitoring and intrusion.

> I feel the staff interactions are all formal interactions to remind us that someone is in charge. However, I receive my encouragement and support to develop as a human being from my friends.

> Formal interaction with staff is sometimes nerve-racking and informal interaction is just about non-existent.

> Formally, mostly them chastising me for my mistakes. We have no informal relationships.

> Formal: difficult at times. Informal: sometimes enjoyable, sometimes uncomfortable.

Personal Advising and Counseling

The program employs four full-time academic advisors and other staff members who monitor and advise students regularly (Glennen, Baxley and Farren 1985). Advising includes the formal task of helping students schedule the appropriate complement of courses. Incoming freshmen are advised to avoid the pattern of scheduling five "solid" courses. The program's academic advisers work with students so that they initially register for fewer courses. This strategy enables students to focus more intensively on mastering the course content. "Passing" these foundational courses with a grade of C is considered inadequate. Earning a grade of C results in students being advised to repeat the course to achieve a grade of B or higher since the program designers' experience suggests that a grade of C does not reflect solid conceptual mastery (National Research Council 2010; Frehill, DiFabio and Hill 2008).

At the informal level, advising means constantly "checking in" with and connecting students to opportunities (summer programs, graduate school, future career opportunities and access to faculty) that will benefit students' academic careers. Additionally, academic advisors meet with freshman and sophomore students to discuss how they manage their time, apply their study skills and function in study group meetings (Astin 1993). Students are advised and expected to talk with their professors during office hours and not just after class. They are also expected to ask faculty about their professional experiences and their perception of the field/discipline's future. Thus, students are socialized on how to not only approach faculty but also on the kinds of conversations that need to occur in interactions with faculty (Pascarella 1985; Tinto 1993; Weidman 1989).

Accordingly, personal advising and counseling is what they do best and most (L. Toliver, personal communication). He regards this component (in addition to the summer bridge component, where advising and counseling effectively starts) as an integral part of the program. For example, there are two math courses in the summer bridge program: Math 290 emphasizes advanced problems in calculus and Math 150 focuses on pre-calculus. Students are placed into Math 290 or Math 150 depending on their math placement score. Students are not allowed to place out of a summer math and science course because they have taken advanced placement math and science courses in high school.

Freshmen are advised to take one math and one science course in the first semester. After freshman year, students may negotiate and must justify why they want to take certain courses. Advisors are not concerned with the number of courses a student plan to take but rather the combination of courses. For example, if the student plans to register for one math course, one science course, and an English course, this combination is viewed as complementary. But when a student plans on a combination of rigorous courses in which they may not be able to devote the necessary time and attention to excelling, advisors strongly advise them to reconsider their courseload. For students who are willing to take this advice and trust that the advisors have their interest in mind, there is a great likelihood that the student can get a 4.0 GPA in freshman year. The program director also clarified that freshman year courses are largely review. In freshman calculus for example, students are generally getting acclimated to the faculty and the course's content, requirements and expectations.

Program staff note that freshman year GPAs for those students who resist taking advice are often below 3.5. In the MSP, having a GPA of less than 3.5 is not doing well by the program's standards. According to the program director, students are "advised out of respect, not fear or coercion" (L. Toliver, personal communication).By their junior year, students need to have an advisor in their department to approve courses. Junior and senior students also consult with the program director before finally registering for courses. The director and assistant director share the duty of advising juniors and seniors with majors in the natural and life sciences and engineering and those students with double majors. The program's academic coordinator advises freshman and sophomore students.

The program director suggests that his approach to advising involves asking more questions than giving answers. For example, he will ask students to "give me a rationale for taking this course. How does it fit in the big picture?" (L. Toliver, personal communication). Advising also means getting a sense of where students see themselves in 5 or 10 years, giving them information about research opportunities and helping them to access and participate in these opportunities early and often. Students with very high GPAs are also encouraged to tutor their peers.

Students are constantly reminded of the program's commitment to them through the implementation of advising and other services. An essential part of the advising component is talking candidly with students about how they feel about the Meyerhoff program. If the student is floundering, the program director suggests that he and other members of his staff will ask the student how they have failed him/her and how they (the program staff) can change the situation. The director notes that it is often difficult for a freshman or sophomore to answer this question. Juniors and seniors are usually more comfortable verbalizing their concerns (L. Toliver, personal communication). The following three students commented positively on the value of the MSP staff.

> You can talk to staff about the problem that you're having. We feel so close to them.

> My grades began to go down. Mr. A. [Staff] was my encouragement. I could have given up completely on physics, but I didn't.

> Emailing me, calling me, 'You need to do this. You need to do that. You have a deadline to meet.

Process evaluation surveys administered periodically to students from 1990 to the present reveal that African American students in the program rate the helpfulness of staff advising and staff counseling, highly (means of 3.9 on a 5 point rating scale).

Program Community

The infrastructure supporting this component is the family-like social and academic support system available for students (Granger et al. 2007; Hoffman et al. 2002–2003). For example, all students are required to live in the same residence hall during their first year and on campus during subsequent years. Most students agreed that it is easier to study together and to "form friendships with people and have the same interests." Other advantages include:

Academic bonding with my peers.

It is easier to study because everyone is located in the same place. We also have accessibility of resources.

Not being concerned with travel and the maintenance of a home while pursuing studies.

I don't need to factor in time for traveling. I can also stay better connected with other Meyerhoff students because it is easier to coordinate study groups.

The idea of being surrounded by a group of supportive peers with the same goals seems to be especially important to many students (Allen 1992). Some students suggest however, that so much togetherness "inhibits some maturing that can go with the responsibility of living off campus." One student believed that "it is good experience to live in the dorm/same residency," although he "personally liked staying home—[he] can focus better at home since [he] had some difficulties living at the dorms." Other students suggest that living on campus is a disadvantage because:

I interact with the same group of people.

I do not have opportunities to meet new people.

I feel isolated from non-Meyerhoff scholars.

It sometimes gets too loud.

Everyone is in [my] business—there is a lack of any real privacy.

The dorm rooms are too small and the food isn't great.

A sense of community can also be observed in the continual contact students have with program staff who are highly accessible and involved in practically all aspects of student life (Coleman 1988, 1990). Additionally, the president, students, and program staff participate in large "family" meetings at the beginning and end of each semester. During these meetings, Hrabowski is present and interacts with the students. In the course of an observed family meeting for example, the president asked for students who are doing well to identify themselves. (Doing well means getting an A in physics or biochemistry, for instance.) He then asked for the students who are not doing as well to identify themselves. This question was followed up by his request of those students who are excelling (usually juniors, seniors and upper seniors), to take responsibility for tutoring their peers. The essence of these meetings reflects a dual celebration of student achievements and support for talent development (Brophy 1981, 1985). Male and female Meyerhoff scholars also have separate meetings with the president that include discussions of racial, cultural and diversity issues and challenges. These meetings are private and thus, are not available for observation.

Process evaluation surveys administered periodically to students from 1990 to the present reveal that African American students in the program rate program community as one of the most helpful program components (mean of 4.4 on a 5 point rating scale). They also perceived the group discussions at the "family meetings" to be a helpful program component (mean of 3.4).

PERVASIVE EXPECTATIONS THAT STUDENTS WILL ENGAGE IN HELP-SEEKING BEHAVIORS

Peer Group Study

Meyerhoff students are expected to engage in peer group study by the university leadership, faculty and program staff. Peer group study is perceived as an important part of succeeding in the sciences, engineering and other technical fields. One of the assumptions undergirding this idea is that regular peer group study meetings enable students to better manage their time and improve their study skills (Treisman 1990, 1992). In the MSP, peer group study starts during the summer bridge component and continues throughout students' undergraduate career in the program. Study groups include two to four student peers; groups are no larger than four students. During group work, students work with their peers in learning course content, mastering concepts and completing assignments. They talk about each homework problem, and in the process may discover a new approach to solving conceptual and practical problems (Asera 2001).

Program staff closely monitor the number of students in a peer group and how often these students meet. Students are expected to take ownership and responsibility not only for their own but also for each other's success. This is especially important in the first semester of freshman year when some students become overconfident and do not study as intensively as they should. If students get less than a grade of B in an introductory science, engineering or mathematics course, they are strongly advised to retake the course. According to program staff, students quickly learn that they have to seek help so that they can master the foundational concepts. They also note that students' help-seeking behavior result in better grades and GPAs. After freshman year, most students take the initiative to get their study groups together. Students are advised that peer study groups are one of their tools for success and expected to continue their study groups for the entire four or more years of their undergraduate career in the MSP.

Process evaluation surveys administered periodically to students from 1990 to the present reveal that African American students in the program view study group as one of the most helpful program components (mean of 4.1 on a 5 point rating scale).

Peer Motivation and Teamwork

Interviews with program staff suggest that peer study groups serve more than the purpose of helping students master the concepts in their fields; they also enable students to regard themselves as part of a high-performance learning community. Peer study groups promote conversations in which participants have to articulate their own ideas and listen to the ideas of others. These interactions also ensure that students make their work and thinking public and become more aware of the different perspectives and the knowledge fund of their peers. As a result, students are often disabused of the notion that their ability is based on sheer talent (Resnick 2000). The peer study group setting exposes students to peers who also struggle with various ideas and subject content (Treisman 1990, 1992). Students learn quickly that excelling in a subject does not mean being able to solve problems quickly and easily but rather working very hard and persevering (Clewell et al. 2006; Maton, Hrabowski and Schmitt 2000; Springer, Stanne and Donovan 1999; Resnick 2000). Some students characterized their peer group study and tutoring interactions as follows:

> [I let my peers] know how important it is to that particular person who needs to be tutored and explain how tutoring not only helps the students, but also helps the tutor. [I] encourage them to be reminded of their goals and to use that as a source of motivation.

[I] study with them, even if it's not the same subject (for moral support) and to study together if it is the same subject.

I let my peers know that being good at getting good grades is one thing but to make the knowledge one's possession is another. I strongly encourage my peers to study to make the knowledge theirs.

Seeing others going through the trials and tribulations as successfully as you are at the same time gives a source of motivation that no one else can give.

It helps me to stay focused knowing there are so many other people close by to support me.

Because we operate out of an expectation of truth; because we know each other, we know how to support, encourage, respect each other appropriately (according to who each person is).

I try to be there for my peers whenever I can, and they try to be there for me if I need them. We can count on each other.

Process evaluation surveys administered periodically to students reveal that African American students in the program rate both the academic and social interactions with peers as among the most helpful aspects of the program (means of 4.4 and 4.3, respectively, on a 5 point rating scale).

Tutoring

One of the defining characteristics of Meyerhoff students is that they are responsible not only for their own academic success but for each other's as well. They are expected and advised to seek out the resources and opportunities that will support them toward this end. The idea of tutoring and being tutored, for example, is commonly regarded on UMBC's campus as activities in which students who aspire to excel and those who are excelling, engage (Falchikov and Blythman 2001). This includes being exposed to systematic tutoring and coaching. MSP's emphasis on tutoring explicitly holds students to high standards by providing both the resources and support students need to achieve those standards. The effect of this process is evident in the high expectations students, program staff, faculty and the university leadership set for each other and themselves. Tutors are regularly identified from within and outside the program. Program staff are aware of those students who do very well in upper level courses. Usually juniors and seniors, these students are often asked to volunteer to tutor those students who need assistance. Students are usually open to requests to tutor their peers (L.Toliver, personal communication). UMBC has a campus-wide tutorial center that provides chemistry, physics, mathematics and English tutorials. Meyerhoff students are expected to use these services and volunteer as tutors in providing tutorial services to their peers.

Process evaluation surveys reveal that African American students in the program rate tutoring services as a helpful program component (mean of 3.6 on a 5 point rating scale).

SUPPORTS AND MOTIVATION AS STUDENTS PROGRESS IN THEIR MAJOR OF CHOICE

Summer Research Internships

If students are not graduating at the end of the academic year, they are required to participate in summer research internships each summer. These internships are especially important in enabling students to experience the practice of science or engineering while creating venues for mentoring relationships (Hurtado et al. 2008, 2009). Program staff emphasize that these research internships are opportunities that can be translated as strengths on a student's resume. Students are advised that the research and publications that can result from summer research internships do set them apart.

The associate director, with extensive access to an electronic list of summer research internship opportunities, works closely with each student to complete relevant applications. The MSP has special relationships with companies and certain researchers and universities where students are selected to participate. For example, more than twenty students have completed internships with Dr. Thomas Cech, the Nobel Laureate and former president of the Howard Hughes Medical Institute. The staff has approximately twenty internships they regard as high profile and are proud of their students' ongoing participation in these opportunities. Some students start their research during their summer research internships and continue throughout the school year. Several students commented on the importance and value of the summer research component:

> This summer I had a very good research experience...the give and take with the Professor... You're interacting with them as a colleague, they're helping you to formulate your plan. I really enjoyed that. It just cemented that I loved research.

> Meyerhoff provides] . . . a huge connection...to get into good summer internships. It's been a huge help.

Process evaluation surveys reveal that African American students in the program rate summer research internships as one of the most helpful program component (mean of 4.0 on a 5 point rating scale).

The director and associate director also assist graduating seniors with the graduate application process. They conduct a professional development seminar series in which they discuss topics ranging from proper etiquette to providing guidance concerning how to write personal statements, resumes and requesting recommendations from faculty. Upper-level juniors scheduled to graduate the following year receive a graduate application booklet that has information on how to write a personal statement, choosing the right graduate program and school, and how to contact organizations for more information. The director and associate director assist students in narrowing their focus from 30 schools to 1, solidifying their personal statement, deciding when to take the GREs, and learning how to read GRE scores. The coordinator meets with graduating seniors twice a month during the fall. In these meetings, there is a bi-directional flow of information in that the director and associate director are updated concerning where students are in the application and interview process, and students are coached with respect to the referenced processes. The director and associate director meets with graduating students once a month during the spring semester. Students usually obtain their results from graduate schools in mid-April or early May.

Assigned DC/Baltimore Area Mentors

Meyerhoff students are paired with mentors who are professional role models with doctorates (e.g., PhD, MD, MD/PhD) in the sciences, engineering, mathematics and other technical fields (Hunter, Laursen and Seymour 2007; Hurtado et al. 1999). Mentors are recruited from a variety of settings including universities, private laboratories, government facilities and corporations within these disciplines. The MSP matches students with mentors in their fields of study. These assignments last throughout students' undergraduate careers. Program staff advise mentors to talk with students about educational and career issues as well as topics ranging from class scheduling, internship experiences, graduate school placements, career choices and personal concerns. Mentor and mentee relationships are expressed formally by lab visits, lectures, business meetings, and a Mentors' Reception held annually by the MSP on UMBC's campus. The program staff, the Meyerhoff Parents Association, and the Meyerhoff students jointly coordinate the Mentors' Reception. During this Reception, students present an award to the mentor of the year (usually nominated and vetted by the students) and are addressed by various mentors at the top of their field. The relationship is also expressed informally through social outings, letter writing, and recreational activities. These facets of the Meyerhoff Mentoring process seem to facilitate student educational and professional growth before and after graduation.

The director notes that they can now tap into a strong alumni base who are very much committed to and want to give back to the program (L.

Toliver, personal communication). Additionally, current mentors will often-times nominate their friends and colleagues as potential mentors. Prospective mentors are provided with a Potential Mentor Packet, which includes a letter requesting them to be a mentor, information about the MSP, and a request for the Mentor's demographic information with an addressed return envelope. Currently, about 155 – 170 active mentors support the students and contribute to the program in other ways.

Process evaluation surveys reveal that African American students in the program rate the assigned mentoring component as a somewhat helpful program component (mean of 3.1 on a 5 point rating scale).

THE MARC PROGRAM

The National Institutes of Health initiated the Minority Access to Research Careers (MARC) Program in 1977 with seventy-seven students at twelve colleges/universities. (A current listing of MARC Programs can be found at www.nigms.nih.gov/Minority/MARC/PartInstUSTAR.htm.) The central goal of the MARC program, which UMBC began to offer in 1997, is to provide educational and financial support to juniors and seniors from histori-cally-underrepresented groups. Specifically, these services are set up to enable selected students to achieve terminal degrees and to enter careers in biomedical research and mathematics. The principal investigator of this National Institute of Health (NIH) MARC Program is the chair of UMBC's biology department. This program models the Meyerhoff Program in that its requirements include extensive undergraduate research with faculty mentors from the biological sciences, chemistry, mathematics, psychology and engineering departments.

Recruitment for this program targets the growing pool of academically-talented students from underrepresented groups at UMBC, including, transfer students new to UMBC; UMBC students interested in biomedical or mathematical research careers; and Meyerhoff scholars who are interested in switching to the MARC program given an interest in biomedical research. One of the ways the MARC program recruits students is by supporting the research projects of sophomores (pre-MARC students). Students accepted into the program receive full fall and spring tuition remission and assistance with academic fees; health insurance (only if the student needs it); support for extended research projects at UMBC or off-campus; National Institutes of Health (NIH)-determined stipends to cover room and board, and twice-yearly book allowances of $500; lab supplies for research; travel expenses to scientific meetings and conferences; Graduate Record Examination (GRE) Test Preparation; personal development courses for Pre-MARCs and transfer students (i.e., technical writing); special session tuition if need is demonstrated; and special tutoring as needed.

Admission to this program requires a 3.2 cumulative GPA; a minimum of sixty college credits; an interest in a research career with a major appropriate to biomedical or mathematics graduate study; letters of recommendation from faculty; SAT scores; past research experience; interest in seeking a doctorate (PhD); and an interview with a MARC panel. Students accepted to the MARC program must maintain a 3.2 cumulative GPA; have an approved major; and comply with program requirements that include an extended research project, community service, attendance at regular meetings, successful completion of program activities and an ethics course.

Program direction and participant selection are guided by the MARC Steering Committee and administered through the Meyerhoff Program by a full-time MARC coordinator and additional staff. The MARC administrative coordinator is the primary student advisor of all MARC program participants. He monitors student performance; promotes the MARC Program on and off campus; receives and organizes applications; organizes Steering Committee meetings; travels with students to meetings; coordinates orientations and student program meetings; plans the annual Research Fest; assists with the publications of materials and prepares annual grant applications. The MARC program facilitator assists with grant administration; especially the tracking of program expenses, with special emphases on ensuring that funds are spent in accordance with the program's policies. The program facilitator also assists with the sorting of applications that are competitive or otherwise; mediates contacts between students and research mentors when necessary; issues contracts and termination notices to program participants; coordinates the ethics course; and collaborates with the administrative coordinator on program administration activities, including orientation, applicant interviews and annual program events. Annual, comprehensive evaluations ensure that the program remains focused on its goals and objectives.

PREDICTORS OF STEM PHD ENTRY

We are often asked to provide a small set of "core" or "foundational" elements of the MSP (see table 4) that can guide the efforts of other universities aiming to increase the number of minority students who enter STEM PhD Programs. Broadly defined, three appear especially important:

1. Recruitment of a critical mass of highly capable underrepresented minority (URM) students interested in research careers;
2. Development of tight-knit learning community focused on STEM excellence; and

3. The provision of multiple high quality STEM research and academic experiences.

Preliminary analyses were conducted to examine predictors of STEM PhD Entry. The significant predictors that emerge appear linked, respectively, to these three foundational elements, respectively. First, students with higher MATH SAT scores, higher high school GPA, and who enter college with higher levels of research excitement (assessed on a five-point likert scale) were more likely to enter STEM PhD programs. Second, students who

Table 3.4. Significant Pre-College and College Predictors of STEM PhD Entry: African-American Meyerhoff Students, 1989–2005

Pre-College	PhD Entry (S.D)	All Others (S.D)
Math SAT	654.3* (43.5)	642.5 (42.9)
High School GPA	3.8** (0.4)	3.7 (0.3)
Research Excitement	4.3** (1.0)	3.6 (1.2)
Helpfulness of Components		
Financial Support	4.7* (0.9)	4.6 (0.8)
Summer Research Component	4.3** (1.4)	3.8 (1.1)
MSP Staff Counseling	4.1** (1.3)	3.7 (1.2)
Faculty Involvement in MSP	3.9** (1.2)	3.5 (1.2)
MSP Involvement in Community	3.8** (1.3)	3.4 (1.2)
Family Involvement in MSP	3.8** (1.5)	3.3 (1.4)
MSP Group Discussions	3.6** (1.2)	3.1 (1.3)
MSP Assigned Mentoring Component	3.1** (1.5)	2.7 (1.5)
Research Experience & GPA		
Summer Research (# summers)	2.2** (1.0)	1.6 (1.1)
On-Campus Research (% yes)	33.9%**	18.1%
Undergraduate GPA	3.5** (0.3)	3.2 (0.4)

*p ‹ .05; **p ‹ .01

entered PhD programs rated eight of the program components as more helpful than those who did not enter PhD programs: financial support, summer research, staff counseling, faculty involvement, involvement in community (component service), group discussions at program meetings, and interactions with the Baltimore/DC area assigned mentor. Finally, such students were more likely to participate in summer and academic year research, and to obtain higher GPAs.

CONCLUSION

Enhancing the academic success of underrepresented minority students in the STEM fields is a pressing national priority (National Research Council 2010). It represents both an economic necessity so that our nation can stay competitive in the global economy, and a critical part of our nation's larger social justice agenda. The outcome findings presented in this chapter suggest that the Meyerhoff Program is an effective intervention for African Americans, enhancing the number who pursue graduate education in STEM PhD programs. Furthermore, based on process evaluation findings, it appears that a combination of factors seems to influence Meyerhoff students' success: a supportive university climate; substantially reduced financial concerns; congruency between students' academic needs and family community; cultural expectations; a highly structured pre-college and freshman-year academic experience; a culture of peer support; and structured support for students in their academic work. These components appear related to three, underlying foundational elements that our nation in general, and our universities can increasingly strive for: 1) Recruitment of a critical mass of highly capable URM students interested in research careers; 2) Development of tight-knit learning community focused on STEM excellence; and 3) The provision of multiple high quality STEM research and academic experiences.

Introducing The Opportunity Programs

The Benefits of High Attainment/Completion Rates in Context

The increase in graduation rates for Opportunity Program students at Skidmore College is significant in light of data analyzed by Bowen and colleagues (2009), the Lumina Foundation and others. This data suggests that despite the more than one million students who begin four year colleges and universities each year, less than four in ten will graduate within four years and barely six in ten will graduate in six years (www.luminafoundation.org). As noted in chapter 1, academic attainment disparities between White and Asian American students and their African American, Hispanic and Native American peers have persisted for over four decades. Indeed, only 18 percent of African American and 10 percent of Latino students earn a bachelor's degree by ages 25–29 compared to 33 percent of their white peers in this age category. Kirsch and colleague's (2007, 3) report suggests that this disparity in educational attainment is a factor in divergent skill distributions, one of the forces contributing to a perfect storm in our nation. Indeed, this and other forces, including the changing economy and demographic trends, will impact our nation in myriad ways, including an emergence of "greater inequity in wages and wealth, and increasing social and political polarization" (Kirsch et al. 2007, 3).

These concerns, implicit in President Obama's recent State of the Union Address (February 13, 2013), reinforce the role of higher education in not only increasing opportunities for upward mobility but also rebuilding a stronger, more robust economy, particularly from a global vantage point. In this vein, federal and state policies that provide for scholarships, Pell Grants and student loans, for example, are vital to enabling access to and participation in higher education.

Toward this end, calls for increases in retention and completion rates for students at all levels of study in our nation's colleges and universities have resulted in laudable goals; including those proposed by close to forty states and supported by private foundations, notably the Lumina Foundation, which is actively working toward a goal of 60 percent of Americans with higher education certifications and other credentials by 2025. The returns on investing in a college education have been briefly noted in chapter 1 but cannot be overstated, particularly when we consider (1) large job losses affecting those with only a high school diploma (or less) during the recent recession; and (2) the anticipated need for and reliance on postsecondary training in future jobs. Even in this period of economic recovery, undereducated workers find themselves increasingly left behind.

Alternatively, there was some job growth (180,000 jobs), for those with a bachelor's degree or better during the recession. Carnevale and colleagues' (2012) report indicate that workers with exposure to the college experience or those with an associates degree accessed 1.6 million jobs since the economic recovery began in 2010. Similarly, those with a bachelor's degree or higher obtained an additional 2 million jobs. Those with only a high school diploma or less however, appeared to have lost about 230,000 jobs during this time. On another level, these figures impact the unemployment rates differentially for workers with or without a higher education credential. That is, the unemployment rates for recent college graduates declined from 11.1 percent in July 2011 to 6.8 percent in May 2012. In contrast, the unemployment rates for recent high school graduates declined to 24 percent in May 2012; down from a high of 30 percent in January 2012.

The graduation/attainment rates for students however has implications beyond that of their simply attaining existing/current jobs or even those emerging in our knowledge based economy (Friedman 2006). These include nurturing in our college and university graduates, the ability to adapt and adjust to the demands of changing social, cultural, demographic and global dynamics; skills and dispositions thought to drive/enable future economic growth and development. Indeed, those with the requisite technical and generalizable skills; who can think critically, analytically and regeneratively; in short, those who are equipped with the knowledge, skills and disposition to learn how to learn, will be better positioned to take advantage of potential opportunities and challenges. These dynamics are associated with and/or contribute to growing wage differentials between those with higher education credentials and those without.

In addition to the noted benefits of higher education however, we are confronted with the rising costs of attaining a degree. Issues around cost are very real considerations for many students, particularly those who are under-represented in our nation's colleges and universities, and as such, concern all responsible for their success. It is thus crucial that we envision environments and contexts in which we craft, implement and iteratively evaluate policies and interventions that serve the needs of today's students; especially when we consider the increasing integration of online learning with courses on campus; open access courseware; and experiential/project-based learning on college campuses.

These emerging conditions, more salient now in our knowledge based global economy, has increased concerns in some quarters that an ambition gap, a knowledge gap and a numbers gap exists in the United States (Friedman 2006). The growing debate about these gaps reflects the concern that the United States will be increasingly unable to meaningfully compete in the global marketplace. This possibility has also raised concerns for how today's students develop and are educated. Unlike the industrial model, which considered students as raw materials to be efficiently processed by teachers for certain ends (DeMarrais and LeCompte 1998), it is increasingly recognized that today's students need to evidence certain habits of mind and work, including understanding the current state of their knowledge, which will allow them to assess gaps in their knowledge base and make efforts to build on it and improve. In their movement from a novice to an expert, these metacognitive skills can enable them to conceptualize, make and assess decisions in often shifting conditions (McLaughlin and Talbert 1993). The Opportunity Programs at Skidmore College in Saratoga Springs, New York is an example of how the above issues, including funding from New York State, coupled with institutional and other resources can converge to bring about the outcomes with which we are concerned, including creating faculty and staff commitment that enable and expect high student achievement and completion.

Chapter Four

Creating Opportunities to Learn

*The Opportunity Programs at Skidmore College,
Saratoga Springs, New York*

Susan Layden, Beatrice L. Bridglall and Sheldon Solomon

INTRODUCTION

The academic achievement of low income, working-class, first-generation and underrepresented minority students at elite institutions of higher education has emerged as a salient issue. While there is evidence that these students are both attending college and graduating at higher rates than they have historically, gaps persist between their levels of academic achievement and that of their more affluent and academically prepared majority and Asian American peers at the same institutions (Bowen and Bok 1998; College Board 1999; Miller 1999; Bowen, Chingos and McPherson 2009). While the Black-White achievement gap narrowed between 1960 and the early 1980's, there has been a reversal in that trend since the late 1980's (Lee 2002). Bowen and Bok (1998), in a sample of 28 selective colleges and universities, found that the average graduating grade point average (GPA) for White students was 3.15 while the average graduating GPA for Black students was 2.61. Many elite colleges and universities are now confronted with the reality that they have not adequately addressed these gaps in achievement and may thus inadvertently perpetuate the inequalities of American society (Bok 2003; Richards 2002; Shireman 2003; Clayton 2003). The use of standardized tests in admission decisions for example, considered accurate predictors of academic performance for majority students, tend to both over- and under-predict the academic performances of underrepresented minority students in college and professional schools (Bok 2003). That is, measures of past performance predict higher (in the case of overprediction) or lower (in the case of underpediction) achievement than is actually achieved (Cole and Barber 2003; Miller, Oztuk and Chavez 2005).

Although varying perspectives are offered as explanations for the overprediction phenomenon, we are concerned here with the dynamic of underprediction. For example, one perspective suggests that elite colleges, including selective liberal arts colleges, may be admitting students who are both under-prepared for and less capable of succeeding in a selective college setting (Cole and Barber 2003; Espenshade and Radford 2009). An alternative perspective suggests however that the academic and psychosocial environment at many liberal arts colleges contributes to these patterns of underachievement (Oyserman and Swim 2001; Massey et al. 2003: Massey and Fischer 2005). Skidmore College subscribes to this alternative perspective, which undergirds its iterative development and implementation of a model program to promote the high academic achievement of first generation and under-represented students. As such, Skidmore College believes that institutions can and must meet the needs of all students admitted—this includes not only those who are academically prepared but also their low-income, working-class, first-generation, and underrepresented minority peers who are not. As the competitive post-graduation context is only likely to increase over the next decade, it is imperative that administrators and faculty conceptualize and design relevant interventions to maximize the academic performance of all students (Bowen, Chingos and McPherson 2009; Tinto 1993). Skidmore College's Opportunity Program (OP) is a concerted and comprehensive effort to meet these challenges.

Skidmore College, which has an enrollment of approximately 2,400 students and a student-faculty ratio of 9 to 1, offers a select group (approximately 160 to 170) of its underrepresented students a coordinated and comprehensive system of support through the auspices of its Opportunity Program (formerly, the Higher Education Opportunity Program/Academic Opportunity Programs [HEOP/AOP] and now referred to as OP). Students admitted to Skidmore College through the OP are considered "inadmissible" to the College vis-à-vis Skidmore's regular admission criteria. That is, many OP students typically have low standardized test scores and high GPAs from very weak schools while others have low GPAs from very strong schools. The OP staff assumes that upon admittance these students will necessarily need an integrated set of supports that include financial aid, a pre-freshman summer bridge program, and extensive counseling and academic support particularly in their freshman and sophomore years. Institutional data regarding the OP at Skidmore College demonstrate that for over a decade, although OP students' entering profiles underpredict their actual level of academic achievement, they achieve, are retained, and graduate at comparable rates with their non-OP peers.

In this chapter, we note the historical context that influenced the development and implementation of Skidmore's OP program via a brief history of New York States' Educational Opportunity Programs in Higher Education (of which HEOP is a part). This is followed by a discussion of the OP's processes, including recruitment and selection; funding and financial aid; the program's pedagogical evolution and pre-freshman transitional and academic supports; and student academic and other institutional outcomes.

THE HISTORICAL CONTEXT OF SKIDMORE'S OP

New York State has supported educational opportunity programs for academically and economically disadvantaged students in higher education since 1964, when it created the College Discovery program for community colleges. This was followed by the creation, in 1966, of the Search for Education, Elevation, and Knowledge (SEEK) program for the four-year colleges of The City University of New York (CUNY). The Educational Opportunity Program (EOP) was instituted in 1967 for disadvantaged students in the two- and four-year institutions of the State University of New York (SUNY). Similarly, the Higher Education Opportunity Program (HEOP) was created in 1969 for disadvantaged students in New York State's independent colleges and universities. Skidmore College was one of twenty-seven founding institutions in New York State, establishing its HEOP in 1969. In 1999, as one of the closing acts of his presidency at Skidmore College, David H. Porter added a parallel program for students who reside outside of New York State or do who not meet the strict economic eligibility guidelines established by the New York State Education Department (NYSED). The goals of this parallel program include providing both the opportunity to enroll in and support for additional students who fall just outside of NYSED mandated guidelines. As subsequent OP students demonstrated increasing levels of academic success, the College increased the number of students admitted into OP; effectively moving from an entering class of twenty to twenty-five students, to approximately 40 students. Thus, Skidmore expanded its efforts to provide opportunities for academically and economically disadvantaged students from around the country (and the world) by admitting students similar in economic and academic profile to their peers in HEOP but who were from other geographic locations or might have family incomes slightly above New York State's income eligibility requirements (see table 1). For a short period of time this combined program was referred to as HEOP/AOP, and is now referred to as the Skidmore College Opportunity Program (or OP).

Table 4.1.   New York State Education Department Guidelines: For students entering college on or after July 1, 2011

Number in household including head of household	Total annual income in preceding calendar year - Household -2 parents -one worker	Household = one worker holding down 2 or more jobs	Household = One parent family	Household = 2 workers
1	$15,590	$18,300	$21,000	$21,000
2	$21,000	$23,710	$26,410	$26,410
3	$26,420	$29,130	$31,830	$31,830
4	$31,830	$34,540	$37,240	$37,240
5	$37,240	$39,950	$42,650	$42,650
6	$42,650	$45,360	$48,060	$48,060
7	$48,060	$50,770	$53,470	$53,470
More than 7	+$5,410 for each over 7			

In 2003–04, over $53.3 million (of which $22 million was appropriated for HEOP in sixty-three programs at fifty-seven independent colleges and universities for a projected enrollment of 5,175 students), was appropriated by the State Legislature for all of the opportunity programs in New York. During the 2003–2004 academic year, independent institutions contributed $12,832 per full-time equivalent student (FTE); an increase from the $12,305 per FTE contributed in 2002–03. These contributions provide financial aid and other supports to HEOP students (HEOP Annual Report 2003–04).

HEOP's Annual Report for fiscal year 2003–04 documented that a total of 5,615 HEOP students (of whom 1463 were freshman), were enrolled full-or part-time during the 2003–04 academic year. Demographic figures indicate that almost 74 percent of entering students during the 2003–04 academic year, had gross family incomes below $21,101, and 45 percent had incomes of $13,301 or less, the lowest category of the HEOP economic eligibility scale. Forty-eight percent of freshman students entered college with a high school average below 80 or with an equivalency diploma or no diploma; approximately nine percent of the entering freshmen were from the latter two categories. Of those for whom scores on the Scholastic Assessment Test (SAT) were reported, 67 percent scored below 500 on the verbal SAT, and 61 percent scored below 500 on the math SAT. A score of 550 on either test is a typical cut-off for regular admissions to many selective institutions of higher education.

With regard to race/ethnicity, close to 34 percent of HEOP students were Black and 41.7 percent were Hispanic. (Native American students comprised

0.50 percent; Asian American students comprised 9.2 percent; White, non-Hispanic students comprised 10.40 percent and students in the other category comprised 4.6 percent). HEOP provides funds to independent colleges and universities to assist in the recruitment, screening and testing of prospective students. Once enrolled, students receive structured support services, including a pre-freshman summer program, counseling, tutoring, and remedial/developmental coursework. Students also receive financial aid toward their college expenses (http://www.heop.org).

Despite economic and academic disadvantage, HEOP students perform well academically as measured by grade-point averages, credit accumulation, and graduation rates (HEOP Annual Report 2006–2007 per James Donsbach, New York State Education Department (NYSED), personal communication, April 2011). In 2006–2007, 81 percent of HEOP students had cumulative grade-point averages above 2.0 and almost 36 percent had grades of B (3.0) or better. On average, HEOP students completed 88 percent of credits attempted. The most recent figures for the freshman class admitted in 2000–2001 at four-year institutions indicate that approximately 58 percent of that class had graduated by the end of Spring, 2007. Of the 961 students who graduated in 2006–07, 74 percent were employed directly after graduation; enrolled in graduate or professional school; or matriculated at a senior college or another institution (HEOP Annual Report 2006–2007). HEOP graduates total over 32,527 since the program started over four decades ago (Personal email communication, Mr. James Donsbach, NYSED, February 11, 2011).

SKIDMORE COLLEGE'S OPPORTUNITY PROGRAM

Student recruitment and selection

As noted earlier, students enrolled in Skidmore's OP are considered not only under-prepared for the academic demands of this selective liberal arts institution but also inadmissible compared to regularly admitted students. For more than a decade (1995–2008) however, nearly all of the students in this program persist and graduate, often with similar or higher graduating GPAs than their non-OP peers. The majority of students admitted to and enrolled in Skidmore's OP program are underrepresented students; many of whom did not have access to strong academic programs in their urban or rural high schools. It is important to note here as well that the gender distribution for enrolled OP students is approximately 50 percent male and 50 percent female (see table 2).

The program developers are aware that the students they recruit have significant gaps in knowledge and skills as demonstrated by their limited access to Advanced Placement (AP) courses and their lower scores on AP

Table 4.2. Race/Ethnicity and Gender Distribution for OP Students from 2005–2008

Race/Ethnicity	2005	2006	2007	2008
Male				
African American	3	4	8	8
Asian	8	6	9	4
Hispanic	4	3	5	4
Native American				
White		3		3
Other		1		
Non-resident alien (non-citizen)	1	3	3	2
Race/ethnicity not available	1			
Total Male	*17*	*20*	*25*	*21*
Female				
African American	2	7	6	3
Asian	4	4	2	5
Hispanic	10	3	9	6
Native American		1	1	
White	2	2	2	3
Other				
Non-resident alien (non-citizen)		2	2	
Race/ethnicity not available	3	3		
Total Female	*21*	*22*	*22*	*17*
Total Male & Female count	**38**	**42**	**47**	**38**

Source: Skidmore College Institutional Research Department, January 2009.

exams, low to average scores on the New York State. Regents subject area exams, and relatively low SAT scores (Miller et al., 2005). For example, students' SAT or ACT scores are lower than the median of the enrolled class of regularly admitted first year students at Skidmore. That is, the average combined math and verbal SAT score for non-OP freshmen in the fall of 2008 was 1240; for OP freshmen, the average was 1000. Thus, the average SAT gap between OP and non-OP students is approximately 240 points. As an institution, Skidmore College still uses math and critical reading scores primarily. When the data is disaggregated however, we find that more OP students enter with stronger math SAT scores than critical reading SAT scores (see table 3).

Table 4.3. SAT Scores for Opportunity Program Students, 2005–2010

SAT Scores	2005	2006	2007	2008	2009	2010
Verbal						
Score under 500	25	25	25	21	25	29
Score at or above 500	12	14	11	17	16	8
Score not available	1	3	11	0	0	3
Total OP students	*38*	*42*	*47*	*38*	*41*	*41*
Math						
Score under 500	8	14	15	13	19	11
Score at or above 500	29	25	22	25	21	25
Score not available	1	3	10	0	0	3
Total OP students	*38*	*42*	*47*	*38*	*41*	*41*

Source: Skidmore College Institutional Research Department, January, 2011

Thus, although SAT and ACT scores are considered in the recruitment process, the OP staff places more weight on students' high school transcripts as a more influential variable in admissions decisions. Additionally, the profile and strength of students' high school and related courses are other variables of importance in the admissions process. Other recruitment criteria include recommendations from students' teachers and counselors, and indications of students' motivation and willingness to work hard and take responsibility (derived from students' admission essays) (Layden, Knickerbocker and Minor 2004). The OP staff use the expression "strivers" in describing the students they seek to admit and enroll - students who have high GPAS and are described as hard-working and highly-motivated. Testing is intentionally devalued as an indicator of academic achievement.

Recruitment Weekend (Discovery Weekend)

Skidmore College hosts a recruitment weekend in April for students who have been accepted for the following academic year. A number of activities, including a welcoming barbeque on Friday evening; information sessions in which current students host panels to talk about their experiences at Skidmore and invite students to ask questions and share their concerns; dinners with faculty and staff; and meetings with faculty concerning course work, are in place to help prospective students make their decisions. Regularly admitted students join prospective OP students in these activities. Additionally, prospective OP students meet with OP program staff and current OP students both individually and as a group. For example, during a panel presentation by current OP students for prospective OP students, six current students discussed their courses, the expectations of their professors and the program staff regarding high quality work, their extracurricular activities, involvement in clubs and semesters abroad. At the end of a recent presentation, for example, students were asked what made them decide to attend Skidmore. They replied as follows:

> The size of the college was very important to me

> The friendliness of the people;

> You are able to balance all interests, for example, I can play ice hockey and be in the orchestra. There are also a lot of activities to do in Saratoga Springs itself.

Current students were asked how hard the college is academically and to describe a typical workload. They replied as follows:

> Different fields of study have different workloads; it is really up to the individual student to take more or less credits.

> You can expect to have 2–3 hours of homework per hour of class, for instance, if a class is 2 hours, you expect to have 4–6 hours of homework.

One of the prospective OP students asked the panel whether they get tired of being tokens. The students responded as follows:

> It is uncomfortable being the only black or Hispanic person in class but please don't get caught up in negativity but focus on your studies, which you need to balance with other interests.

> It is a culture shock coming from a diverse high school to a predominantly white institution. But how you are able to handle the competing demands on your time depends on your personality.

> Having friends make the transition to Skidmore easier. You need to make Skidmore work for you. Don't change for Skidmore unless you want to change you.

The conversation shifted toward a prolonged discussion of racism. Current OP students in the audience responded as follows:

> There is a lot of backlash against racism on campus.

> You need to step out of your comfort zone and ask for help, be it emotionally or academically.

You need to believe that you can succeed by making yourselves get out there.

Students who eventually enroll in Skidmore's OP rank in the top 10 percent of their graduating class. This recruitment process allows the OP office to create a cadre of students who can achieve at high levels at Skidmore given appropriate opportunities and supports to learn. Developing a culture of high expectations begins with the faculty and staff, but it also requires substantial work with the students, which essentially begins during the recruitment and admissions process. Prospective students are apprised of the culture of high expectations in Skidmore's OP at information sessions at their high schools, at college fairs, in interviews on Skidmore's campus, during accepted candidates' days and on other campus visits. In references to the intensity of the summer program and the first year, current students tell prospective students, "*These people aren't kidding,*" and "*They mean business.*"

OP staff members reinforce the message that selection as an OP student at Skidmore is an honor, and that with this honor comes the understanding that the staff and faculty working in the program will challenge them at every turn. Additionally, OP staff members specifically address the question of feedback by asking prospective students to talk about the kind of feedback they have received historically from their secondary teachers and the types of assignments they have completed. OP faculty and staff follow up on this inquiry by painstakingly describing the difference in feedback they will receive if they come to Skidmore through its OP. At the accepted Candidates meetings for OP students, Dr. Solomon can be heard saying, "*Don't come here if you don't want to work hard.*" What is remarkable about this strategy is that it does not discourage accepted candidates; rather, it seems to work as a marketing tool. The yield on OP admissions offers is exceptionally high.

The OP office received 425 applications from the Skidmore admissions office in the 2010 admissions process and eventually made offers of admission to fifty-six students, and enrolled a class of forty (a yield of 71 percent) (see table 4). Although the process is very competitive (only a 13 percent acceptance rate), the OP staff are not under any illusion regarding the considerable academic and personal support students will need for sustained knowledge and skill development. Consequently, students selected to and enrolled in the Opportunity Program arrive at the mandatory summer bridge program with weaker writing skills, inadequate exposure to reading and examining challenging texts, and overt disparities in their mathematics and science preparation (Miller et al. 2005).

Before prospective OP students depart for home on Sunday, they have brunch with the president of Skidmore College and his wife at the president's home. The president and his wife personally interact with every student. Faculty members and OP staff are also present and interact extensively with students. Indeed, brunch at the presidents' home has become a tradition for

Table 4.4.   Factors affecting student achievement and retention

Factor	Achievement	Retention	Citation
Academic adjustment programs	Positive	Positive	Pascarella & Terenzini, 2005
Living-learning centers	Positive		Pascarella & Terenzini, 2005; Shapiro and Levine, 1999; Barefoot, et al., 1998; Kuh, et al., 1991
Social integration and involvement		Positive	Pascarella & Terenzini, 2005
Academic student culture	Positive		Pascarella & Terenzini, 2005
Student-faculty interaction		Positive	Pascarella & Terenzini, 2005; Light, 2001
Academic Advising	Positive	Positive	Pascarella & Terenzini, 2005; Light, 2001; Astin, 1993; Tinto, 1993
Working off-campus		Negative	Pascarella & Terenzini, 2005
Academic self-efficacy	Positive		Garcia & Hu, 2001; Tatum, 1997
Optimism	Positive		Garcia & Hu, 2001
TRIO Programs	Positive		Blake, 1998
Positive view of one's own racial/ethnic group	Positive		Allen, et al., 1999
Small group learning	Positive		Springer, et al., 1999
Positive peer group influence	Positive	Positive	Feldman & Newcomb, 1973
Scaffolded learning opportunities	Positive		Vygotsky (1934/1986)
Good time- management skills		Positive	Astin, 1993
High intellectual self esteem		Positive	Astin, 1993
Lack of student community		Negative	Astin, 1993
Enrollment in honors programs		Positive	Astin, 1993
Feelings of academic inferiority	Negative	Negative	Steele et al., 2002; Massey, et al., 2003

prospective OP students. The growing levels of financial and other resources for the OP is a reflection of Skidmore's President Glotzbach support of and commitment to not only the program's sustenance but also diversity on campus.

Sources of Funding and Financial Aid

In developing a program that has as its central goal a broad effort to support the high academic achievement of under-represented students, providing comprehensive financial aid is among the top priorities. This is a particularly salient policy in light of evidence that first generation and under-represented minority students who do not have adequate financial aid are hampered in their efforts to devote the necessary amount of time studying because they must either work on or off-campus (Dowd and Coury 2004; Field 2009; Gansemer-Toph and Schuh 2005). The literature suggests that the time not available for studying negatively affects student retention, achievement and completion (Duffy and Goldberg 1998; Gross, Hossler and Ziskin 2007). Skidmore College receives a small grant (approximately $400,000) from the New York State Education Department (NYSED) to administer the HEOP portion of its Opportunity Program, and as an institution, provides the rest of the programmatic support. Each year, the college invests approximately 5.6 million to support the 160–170 students enrolled at the college through OP. A large share of this funding covers student tuition, room and board, and fees (the total cost of attendance at Skidmore is estimated at over $55,000 yearly). As these are economically disadvantaged students, in most cases they qualify for full-need packaging and are eligible for over 4 million dollars in federal, state and other outside financial aid and grants. First-year OP students also have a reduced work/study requirement and no student contribution from summer earnings. Thus, Skidmore's ability to minimize student debt burden enables students to place academic success as their primary focus the moment they arrive for the summer program. Indeed, students are told early and often that "*Success in the first year means success across all four years.*" Skidmore's OP has received several gifts to its endowment that has facilitated the expansion of the program to its current enrollment level.

Creating a Culture of High Academic Achievement

Central to Skidmore's OP is a coordinated and specialized system of academic support commencing with a transitional summer bridge program and continuing to graduation. From its inception in 1969 until 1995, the HEOP program at Skidmore was similar in structure and function to most HEOP programs in New York. That is, a summer program for incoming students consisted largely of remedial instruction in math and writing, a study skills class (primarily devoted to note-taking and time management), and a pre-college class. The pre-college class was taught by professors who chose material from courses they typically offered during the academic year (e.g., learning and memory for a psychologist; mind-body dualism for a philosopher; the basic distinctions between capitalism and communism for an economist). Although the pre-college class material had no particular connection to courses students would be taking in the fall, exposure to any college level academic discourse was thought to produce benefits that would generalize to novel settings by making students more familiar with, and comfortable in, a college environment. Following the summer program, HEOP students received the same limited academic support (primarily from the Writing Center in the English Department) as their peers at Skidmore, in addition to the psycho-social support provided by HEOP counselors.

The math and writing instruction worked tolerably well at the time; that is, greater attention was given to diagnostic assessment and the provision of a wider range of instruction to students with varying needs (including those with strengths in one area (generally math) while very weak in writing, for example). However, the pre-college and study skills components of the summer program were considered ineffective for the most part. That is, although the summer program helped HEOP students to become somewhat familiar with the college classroom, they were still academically unprepared for their freshman year. For instance, students did not recognize the distinction between high school and college instruction (i.e., teaching vs. professing), and lacked the reading, writing, critical-thinking, note-taking, exam-taking, time management, and classroom decorum skills to fare well in college courses. Additionally, they were not sufficiently aware of what education consists; how to obtain an education; the benefits of having a college degree nor how their impoverished educational and economic backgrounds (including the effects of race and class biases) undermined their chances for academic success. HEOP students consequently floundered in their courses, and had difficulty identifying academic interests and choosing their majors.

They thus became known at Skidmore for their weak skills and poor performance by faculty and students peers, and were stigmatized as a result. Faculty had low expectations of HEOP students, either because they viewed them as congenitally inferior, or hopelessly stunted by their impoverished backgrounds. Research (Clark 1965; Jussim 1986) indicates that teachers treat students differently as a function of their expectations, and students respond to such treatment in ways that confirms teachers' unfavorable impressions of them. Disadvantaged students consequently fulfill the prophecy of their teachers' low expectations (Merton 1948; Metcalf 1995; Krovetz 1999). Close to five decades ago, Clark (1965, 131), argued that students in these circumstances "do not learn because they are not being taught effectively and they are not being taught because those who are charged with the responsibility of teaching them do not believe that they can learn, do not expect that they can learn, and do not act toward them in ways which help them to learn."

HEOP students exposed to these dynamics generally internalized the negative perceptions others had of them, resulting in a sense of personal unworthiness and humiliation that further undermined their academic performance (Katz, Roberts and Robinson 1965; Steele and Aronson 1995). This phenomenon of being at risk of confirming a negative conception of one's group is referred to as stereotype threat (Steele, Spencer and Aronson 2002). For example, Black college students performed more poorly than White students on standardized tests when their race was made salient (e.g., students were asked to identify their racial background before taking the exam); however, the performance disparity was diminished or eliminated entirely when race was not emphasized (Alter et al. 2010). Caucasian American women reminded of their gender do worse on math tests, confirming the stereotype that females are bad at math (Aronson et al. 1999). Asian American women also do worse on math tests when they are reminded of their gender, but their performance improves when they are reminded that they are Asian, confirming the stereotype that Asians are good at math (Alter et al. 2010). Additional research indicate that academic performance can be undermined by the knowledge that one's behavior may be evaluated in terms of negative racial, class and gender stereotypes (Steele and Aronson 1995). Stereotype threat can also increase self-handicapping strategies such as studying less, so that poor performance can be attributed to situational factors ("I could have done better if I studied harder") rather than dispositional factors ("I'm bad at math") (Aronson and McGlone 2009). This in turn can diminish students' interest in particular subjects, and limit the range of majors and professions they choose to pursue.

Given baseline outcomes data, including GPA and graduation rates for HEOP students in the early 1980s, Layden and Solomon were convinced that an effective HEOP program would require: (1) revising the summer program curriculum; (2) modifying teaching methods and how study skills would be inculcated in the summer program; (3) making more explicit efforts to provide a stimulating academic environment to increase motivation; (4) conveying a sense of unconditional positive regard for students (i.e., that professors respect students, and consider them capable of succeeding with considerable effort on their part in tandem with high quality instruction on the part of faculty and staff); (5) fostering a culture of high expectations by professors and students (i.e., professors expect HEOP students to succeed, and HEOP students expect to succeed) to offset the adverse effects of low professorial expectations and stereotype threat; and (6) providing more structured and sustained academic support to HEOP students throughout their academic career at Skidmore (especially in their first and second years at the College).

This refinement of OP was also influenced by Skidmore's implementation (in 1985) of a new curriculum to provide all incoming students with a stronger foundation for a liberal arts education. The Liberal Studies program was designed by Skidmore faculty (from all academic disciplines) with support from the National Endowment for the Humanities. The centerpiece of the program was a core course, the Human Experience, which was taken by all incoming students in their first semester at the college. (This course has since evolved to become what is currently Human Dilemmas.) The content of this course was influenced by Allan Bloom's *The Closing of the American Mind* (1987, based on an essay published in The National Review in 1982), as well as E.D. Hirsch's *Cultural Literacy* (1987). Bloom argued that there are certain canonical ideas of which any educated individual must be in possession; specifically those articulated in the classic works of western civilization. Hirsch agreed that such canonical knowledge is necessary, but not sufficient; rather, an educated person must be conversant with prevailing intellectual and cultural constructs in a social milieu in a given time and place. Or according to Harvard historian and sociologist Orlando Patterson (1980, 72): Industrialized civilization imposes "a growing cultural and structural complexity which requires persons to have a broad grasp of what Professor Hirsch has called cultural literacy: a deep understanding of mainstream culture, which no longer has much to do with white Anglo-Saxon Protestants, but with the imperatives of industrial civilization. It is the need for cultural literacy, a profound conception of the whole civilization, which is often neglected in talk about literacy."

Accordingly, the Human Dilemmas course was designed to address classic questions about what it means to be a human being situated in the context of a western industrial civilization at the end of the twentieth century and the beginning of the twenty-first century): *How do we know? What is knowledge? Who am I? Who am I in relation to society? Who am I in relation to the natural world?*

The first section of the course, *How do we know?,* considers the nature of education, followed by a brief introduction to epistemological issues surrounding the nature of knowledge (e.g., the distinction between beliefs, facts, theories and truth) and the various ways that humans come to know themselves and the world around them (including through science, art and religion). The next section, *Who am I?,* explores human identity, starting with Darwin's theory of evolution by natural selection (to establish that humans, like all other life forms, are products of evolution by natural selection). This is followed by the study of the self as a bio-social-psychological construction (i.e., whereas some aspects of selfhood are genetically acquired, and some significant components of identity are socially constructed, individuals can still have considerable influence on their own self-development). The next section, *Who am I in relation to society?* examines the fundamental tension between the individual and society from a historical perspective (from Plato's contention in the *Crito* that individuals are necessarily subordinate to society, to John Locke's insistence in the *Second Treatise on Government* that individuals originally existed independently and formed societies by conscious choice to protect their property), with particular concern for how to foster constructive social change in response to injustice. Finally, *Who am I in relation to the natural environment?* reflect human beings' fundamental dependence on the natural environment, the effects of human activity on nature, and what (if anything) can be done to offset these effects.

Pedagogically, the Human Dilemmas course, conceived as a sequential hierarchy of multi-modal interdisciplinary recursive common experiences, serves as the foundation for subsequent academic endeavors in a liberal arts environment. Specifically, (1) the material in the course is arranged in an orderly sequence (i.e., in contrast to a topical assortment of ideas common for introductory survey courses in specific academic disciplines); (2) the course content becomes more sophisticated over time (i.e., ideas introduced in the middle and at the end of the course would not be comprehensible at the outset because they are predicated on basic concepts acquired early on); (3) traditional academic discourse (reading, writing, lectures and classroom discussion) is complemented with other kinds of experiences, including dance, music and dramatic performances, art and science exhibits, trips to farms and hikes in the Skidmore woods and in the Adirondacks, and service learning in the community; (4) faculty and course materials for the Human Dilemmas course are drawn from all academic disciplines across the College; and (5) everyone at the College (students and faculty) would share this experience.

The Human Dilemmas course is thus structured around large group common experiences followed by small group seminar meetings. For example, all students meet in a large auditorium for presentations by Skidmore professors or special guests who introduce the topic and readings for the week (e.g., in the *Who am I?* unit of the course, a biology professor introduces Darwin's theory of evolution by natural selection; a sociology professor explains how the self is socially constructed; and a psychology professor describes the psychological aspects of self-hood). Thereafter, students (in groups of fifteen to eighteen), meet in small seminar groups led by a professor with support from a peer mentor (an advanced OP student). To prepare students for future college work, there are a variety of assignments and assessments, including short papers (where students get extensive feedback on drafts and are expected to revise their work accordingly), in-class and take-home exams, and projects with oral presentations.

Given its depth and richness, the Human Dilemmas course served as the basis for the pre-college course curriculum in the OP summer program. Consequently, in 1989, the pre-college component of the OP summer program was modified to teach incoming students a condensed version of the Human

Dilemmas course. In particular, concentrated attention is devoted to the first part of the course on education, knowledge and belief, and ways of knowing. This is followed by an introduction to the *Who am I?* and *Who am I in relation to Society?*, sections of the course, with particular emphasis on how historical and social factors contribute to identity, and how the inequitable distribution of material and psychosocial resources influence poverty, ignorance, self-loathing and despair. Finally, different approaches to social justice are considered (ranging from non-violent resistance to "by any means necessary"), and students are asked to ponder the relationship between individual rights and social obligations as human beings in general, as Americans (or as individuals residing in the United States), as Skidmore College students, and as members of the Skidmore OP program.

The pre-college course was also re-structured to mirror the Human Dilemmas course required in the fall. Students were organized into small seminar groups of ten to fifteen students at the outset of the program but all students attend a common lecture/presentation in a large classroom twice a week. Following each large group presentation, students meet with their seminar groups and their instructor to discuss the lecture/presentation and the assigned readings. Additionally, the study skills component of the summer program was integrated within the pre-college Human Dilemmas course. That is, instead of teaching generic note-taking, paper-writing, and test-taking in isolation, students learn these skills vis-à-vis the reading material, lecture and discussions employed in the Human Dilemmas class. Thus, students learn effective time-management skills, appropriate classroom behavior and demeanor, and how to interact with peers and professors within the context of participation in the pre-college Human Dilemmas course.

Additional pedagogical strategies were implemented based on Vygotsky's (1978) notion of the zone of proximal development (i.e., optimal learning requires engaging students with material slightly more difficult than their current abilities) and step-wise scaffolding of course content and external support. This approach in the initial phase of the summer program focuses on supporting students to gain a competent command of concrete ideas. Early assignments are based on short readings that students are asked to accurately summarize. Faculty and staff build on these skills by helping students to learn to recognize relevant points of comparison and contrast between ideas. This strategy serves as a basic foundation for promoting critical and abstract thinking. Over the course of the summer, readings become longer and more sophisticated, and students take informed positions on specific issues and present intellectual justifications for their views (after learning that people are not entitled to opinions about ideas they cannot accurately articulate or do not yet understand). By the end of the summer program, students read an entire book (the summer reading for all incoming students in the fall) and are given opportunities for creative expression (i.e., to generate their own ideas above and beyond those in the course materials) on a final writing assignment.

Throughout the summer program, students frequently receive detailed feedback on writing assignments (papers and exams) with opportunities to revise their work accordingly. Grades are candid and accurate assessments of student's current standing in specific academic domains; consequently, most students receive D's and F's (sometimes a grade of F- is used to indicate work so poor or lacking in effort that it is not yet worthy of a thorough evaluation by instructors) on early assignments. It is critically important for students to acquire a realistic sense of their current academic weaknesses. Many OP students were honors students in their high schools and accustomed to receiving A's for producing a grammatically correct sentence or forcefully expressing an opinion about a topic of which they knew little. Thus, this type of feedback is obviously unexpected and unwelcome initially, so it is equally important to emphasize that Skidmore professors hold students accountable to the highest standards while simultaneously affirming their abilities with repeated assurances that they are quite capable of succeeding if they exert the requisite effort and avail themselves of the academic support provided by the college and the OP program in the summer and throughout their time at Skidmore.

This curriculum thus provided opportunities for students to cultivate new interests by exposing them to many academic disciplines at the college, including some they were unlikely to have encountered in high school (e.g., philosophy, art history, religion, anthropology and economics); thus giving them more options for future course selections and eventual majors. The course material and assignments were also suitable for redressing students' academic weaknesses. That is, the readings were varied (many were of an appropriate length for students to closely scrutinize) and students were exposed to a wide range of academic demands (e.g., listening to lectures, participating in seminars, writing papers and taking different kinds of exams). Finally, because they were required to take the Human Dilemmas course in the Fall, prior exposure to the course in the summer program would give OP students a psychological boost by situating them as equals with their non-OP peers instead of their usual stance as "token" representatives of minority groups in obvious need of massive remedial attention.

In continuing efforts to refine the OP, Solomon and Layden began working with key faculty and administrators at the college in 1994 to improve the academic, personal, and interpersonal outcomes achieved by OP students at Skidmore. Although the program was considered exemplary in the state of New York at the time because of its higher than average graduation/retention rates, Skidmore OP students often took more than four years to complete their degrees and their cumulative GPAs were nearly a full GPA point below the mean at the college, though above the national average for students from historically under-represented backgrounds. What was clear to the individuals committed to improving the program was that these students were capable of higher levels of academic achievement but were lacking the academic and personal support necessary to compete with their more privileged, non-OP peers.

In thinking about the changes and concomitant resources necessary to foster a culture of high academic achievement in light of relevant research (see table 5), Solomon and Layden determined that they needed to: (1) create a visible and viable academic culture among OP students; (2) provide scaffolded learning opportunities (i.e., engaging students at their current level of academic ability for a given subject and teach more sophisticated skills in a step-wise fashion building on prior accomplishments; and (3) cultivate a sense of high intellectual self-esteem, as central goals in further program improvements (Pascarella and Terenzini 2005; Vygotsky 1934/1986; Astin 1993). Additionally, they sought to create learning opportunities in which students are engaged in developing language and literacy skills in situations that underscore the reality that language is constructed, social and situated (Gee 1990; Gee et al. 1996; Donato 2004; Torres 1998). Moreover, the idea that affinity groups—in this case a community of learners—as important in the development of knowledge, is central to the work in the OP (Gutierrez 2005; 2008).

Accordingly, the Summer Bridge Program was reconfigured to place greater emphasis on critical mentoring; a scaffolded pedagogy was attached to the core course (Human Dilemmas) considered central to positive student learning outcomes; and a culture of high expectations was developed by working with faculty and staff to increase awareness concerning the difficulties encountered by first generation and underrepresented minority students in predominantly white and more privileged settings. Key to this work was the shared expectation that OP students could be among the most successful students on campus if they were provided with a stellar summer program, were given reason to believe they could be high achievers, and that staff and faculty working with the students in the program both believed this and held students to these high expectations. A decision was made to transition from the use of peer tutors during the summer program to the use of professional tutors (comprised of staff from the college and highly skilled teachers or graduate students). Additionally, academic-year supports were restructured to emphasize the provision of academic support (rather than the former emphasis on counseling), and mentoring in gateway courses, particularly during students' freshman and sophomore years. New staff positions in which successful candidates must demonstrate an ability to provide stellar academic support across the curriculum at a liberal arts college, were thus constructed when possible.

Table 4.5. OP Admissions Yield Data

Year (class of)	Referrals	Early Decision (ED) Offers	Spring Offers	Target	Acceptance Rate	Early Decision Yield	Spring Yield	Yield to Target	4 year yield average
2010 (2014)	425	6	50	40	13%	6 (100%)	35 (70%) not wait listed (WL)	103%	70%
2009 (2013)	424	9	43	40 (+1)	12%	7 (78%)	30 (69%) (WL offers =5)	75%	75%
2008 (2012)	438	6	44	4C (+1)	11%	6 (100%)	25 (57%) (WL offers =11)	77%	77%
2007 (2011)	337	5	55	40	18%	5 (100%)	45 (82%) (No WL)	113%	77%
2006 (2010)	258	6	43	40	19%	6 (100%)	38 (88%) (No WL)	95%	76%

Source: Skidmore College's OP Office. July 2011.

The strength of the academic support provided by the OP lies in the commitment of several key members of the Skidmore faculty, particularly Sheldon Solomon, professor of psychology, members of the English department and, historically, key members of the Department of Mathematics. Dr. Solomon's work is the most intensive and merits strong consideration in any discussion of developing model programs. Together with Layden, Solomon has worked continuously with the Opportunity Program for over twenty years. Solomon's research in social psychology and commitment to both interdisciplinary learning and social justice makes him a crucial advocate for the program and its students, and one of the key architects in the development of the program supports.

Under the leadership of Solomon and Layden, the summer program has evolved into one in which students are completely immersed in a highly structured and enriching environment. During the course of six weeks, faculty and staff meticulously assess each student's academic, personal, and interpersonal skills as well as their needs in efforts to assist students in choosing courses for the fall and to better tailor student-specific support services. Much is also expected of students, who, for example, need to read to prepare for lecture; are required to attend highly organized lectures (generally presented with ancillary materials such as supplemental handouts and/or quotes and diagrams); and are taught how to take notes. Students are subsequently asked to re-read the materials and their lecture notes and to meet with their faculty/tutors during the mandatory study hours and in the formal study skills acquisition class. This strategy enables students to discuss the readings and lectures in their seminar meeting, and encourages and expects them to model appropriate skills and dispositions in a seminar class: careful and active listening, sharing and developing informed opinions, and the critical examination of ideas (i.e., what do you do when you disagree with an author's premise or thesis?). Students are also given frequent and critical feedback on their work. Many students observe that this is the first time they have received feedback of this nature. While the volume and quality of the feedback is a shock, and often disruptive to how they think about themselves as students (the reader may recall that many OP students are the strongest students from very weak schools), the training provided to faculty and staff working in the program enable students to view this feedback as critical to their academic and social development and, importantly, is tied to very high expectations for their academic success. The following comments by OP students indicate their perceptions of the nature of this feedback:

> For my first couple of assignments, whenever I read the comments on my papers I would never look at them as a way to help me improve my writing, but I would instead take the comments as personal attacks on my efforts to

produce an A paper. As time progressed however, I learned to stop taking the comments I received so personally and understood that the more comments that a professor has on a paper usually signifies how much they care about a student and would like to see that student improve as a writer. The comments I received on my papers during the summer and the fall benefited my writing significantly. It taught me to expand on my ideas and vocabulary, create conclusions that went beyond a summarization of the ideas in my paper and organize my ideas so that my paper is cohesive and flows well from one paragraph to the next. (Female OP Student, Class of 2014)

In high school, I could write an analytical essay in one night, which now I realize how far from analytical it was, while now I can't even imagine doing that. During the OP program, we learned how to be clear and concise but still target the main points of our arguments. (Female OP Student, Class of 2013)

The consistent work with an OP tutor, helps us discover where our grammar/ sentence structure/punctuation needs the most help. With the consistent help/ feedback, we come to know ourselves as writers and we start to prevent the usual mistakes we would usually make. (Male OP Student, Class of 2014)

I'd like to start by saying that the OP summer program was the first time I really started to question, challenge, and learn from readings and class discussions. In all honesty, I felt terrible because it wasn't the feedback I was used to getting in high school, but after I looked over the comments I knew that your feed back was going to help me. It wasn't that your feedback was giving me answers, instead it was constantly challenging me to actually think about what the author is saying in relation to the world around me. It forced me to analyze and question my own writing because I knew that if I didn't, it meant I didn't fully learn the concepts, and I became so engaged with the readings and discussions that I really wanted to learn. With that same paper I saw my writing improve in each draft because I became more critical about what I wanted to say. This was great skill that helped me tremendously in my English and Human Dilemmas classes last fall. (Female OP Student, Class of 2014)

Another significant pedagogy embedded in the summer bridge program is the understanding of cultural difference and how to create supportive learning environments for students from diverse racial, ethnic and economic backgrounds. Faculty and staff teaching and tutoring in the program must work across racial, ethnic and class boundaries on a daily basis, and they must function as "critical mentors" (Steele, 1999; Cohen, Steele & Ross, 1999) in these students' lives. To do so, faculty and staff must continuously confront their own privilege, implicit racism and classism to create classroom environments that avoid the common stereotypes that disadvantage students of color and lower-income students. The result is a learning community that supports students as they become acclimated to the rigor and demands of college life and work. Thus, an important social-psychological dimension to the summer bridge program ensures that students are mentored in ways that bolster their academic confidence and self-esteem while experiencing success in meeting the most rigorous and challenging academic experience of their lives.

Important to this—and to all of the goals of the summer bridge program—is the training that faculty receive in preparation for teaching the pre-Human Dilemmas course during the summer program. Solomon has developed a program of shadowing, wherein a faculty member interested in teaching the pre-Human Dilemmas course during the summer spends one full summer shadowing one of the current instructors. In this way they learn the teaching techniques, the methods for providing substantive feedback, the course materials, and the program philosophy (high expectations and culturally sensitive, student specific support) before they actually teach a section of the course. Faculty members currently teaching in the program describe this shadowing as necessary for effectively understanding curriculum materials and pedagogical goals and strategies for assessing student work and providing critical feedback. They also consider it crucial for understanding the importance of creating a supportive academic and psychosocial environment.

In tandem with the implementation of this iterative design of the pre–Human Dilemmas course for OP students, OP staff and faculty assess students' writing and mathematics skills for placement when they arrive for the summer bridge program. For example, the program staff consider samples of students' high school papers, their overall high school preparation, and their mathematics and verbal SAT or ACT scores when determining the courses in which students are placed, e.g., in either basic math (*HPB: Basic Mathematics*) or quantitative reasoning (*MA 100 Quantitative Reasoning*); and either basic (*HPC: Language Skills*) or academic writing (*HE 100: Academic Writing*). The basic mathematics course (*HPB: Basic Mathematics*) emphasizes basic quantitative skills and the quantitative reasoning course (*MA 100 Quantitative Reasoning*) fulfills the first half of the Quantitative Reasoning Requirement. The *HPB: Basic Mathematics* course carries three credit equivalents and the *MA 100: Quantitative Reasoning* course carries three credits. The OP staff works with the Office of Special Programs to allow those OP students with higher math SAT scores—primarily ESL students with very weak reading and writing skills - to audit a section of MA108: Calculus with Algebra I. The *HPC: Language Skills* course, which carries three credit equivalents, emphasizes basic grammar skills and the writing of one-to-two page essays based largely on readings with an emphasis on interculturalism and identity. The *HE:100 Academic Writing* course, which carries three credits, teaches students how to write short essays and to strengthen their writing through the use of sources and documentation. As previously noted, the historic involvement of key members of the Expository Writing faculty, and the close relationship the Opportunity Program enjoys with the English Department and Writing Center, helps substantially in the delivery of the writing component of the Summer Academic Institute. All students are also required to take *HPG: Pre-First Year Seminar/Study Skills Workshop*, a personal skills and transition course, which carries three credit equivalents. Collectively, these courses represent important areas of preparation for success with the Skidmore curriculum in general, which emphasizes critical and creative writing and thinking.

The grades students eventually receive at the end of the summer academic program appear on their Skidmore transcript. However, only the credit-bearing courses are averaged into students' cumulative grade point averages (Layden, Knickerbocker and Minor 2004). This strategy not only reinforces the significance of the summer program's courses but also reflects OP's commitment to accurately replicate the fall semester. Layden and Solomon emphasize that the implementation of this model has resulted in considerable increases in the mean GPA earned for OP students during their first semester in college (2.8 for Fall 1998 as compared to 3.20 for Fall 2010) (Skidmore College, Office of Institutional Research, Fall 2010). They also suggest that the commonality of the summer bridge experience for all students has positive effects on their achievement.

During the course of the summer, OP students also register for their fall courses. These include the First Year Seminar, which is offered by the Skidmore faculty, and a writing course. Students who were enrolled in HPC: Language Skills in the summer are enrolled in the next course in the sequence, HE 100: Academic Writing. The reader may recall that some OP students took the HE 100: Academic Writing course in the summer program. These students are registered in the next course in the sequence, EN 103, which is a college-wide course offered by faculty in the English Department. Additionally, all first-year OP students are enrolled in HPF: Study Skills Workshop, a course offered by the OP as a continuation of HPG (pre-freshman seminar) offered in the summer. All other course credits can and do lead toward a potential major or toward fulfilling the All-College requirements. Aside from these OP related courses and supports, OP students are registered and engaged in the same courses as their non-Opportunity Program peers.

As noted earlier, the summer academic curriculum is rigorous and intense. This intensity is also reflected in the schedule students follow during the nearly five week program. For example, during the week (Monday through Friday), the students' first course begins at 8:15 am and their last course ends at 4:30 pm. After a few hours' break, students resume their work in compulsory study hours from 7 - 10 pm, Sunday through Thursday. It is important to recognize that the OP staff and professional tutors, not students, actually provide the tutoring students receive during the day and in the evening from 7 - 10 pm. This considerable amount of time spent with students by professionals with diverse academic backgrounds, knowledge bases, and credentials, is uncommon in a higher education context.

The program staff log approximately 7 - 10 contact hours per student each week during the bloc of time allocated for study hours (7-10 pm, Sunday through Thursday) and an average of 25-30 total contact hours per student per week. OP staff and faculty demonstrate their professionalism, dedication and concern not only for students' achievement but also students' general well-being. These multifaceted roles (including those related to advising, faculty, tutoring and counseling), form the basis of strong advising and mentoring relationships with students that begin during the summer program and evolve as students progress in their undergraduate trajectories. Importantly, this academic intensity is balanced with social activities and events (including bowling, roller skating, hikes, movies, mini-golf, a boat cruise on Lake George and barbeques at the program directors' home). Students also participate in community service, including work unloading and packaging food for distribution at the Regional Food Bank. These activities and events are planned and attended by the program staff and are designed to integrate students into campus life. Students' view of the program staff as pivotal to their academic and social integration at Skidmore are thus formed during these important five weeks in the summer program.

Thus, the summer bridge program, with its highly structured pedagogy and support—particularly its emphasis on one-on-one and small group work with students in addition to group study sessions facilitated by faculty/highly capable academic staff and/or tutors—contribute to students' perception that working closely with faculty, tutors and peers is an integral part of being a highly successful student. The integration of help seeking structures within the summer program enables students' awareness that students who excel academically tend to seek help early and often. In this vein, the content of the Pre-Human Dilemmas course assists in this goal as students study progressively sophisticated material that encourages them to consider (1) the contingency of knowledge; (2) the importance of interactions between students and faculty and between and among peers for knowledge acquisition; (3) the centrality of effort in mastering concepts and excelling; (4) the significance of both imagination and knowledge for creative problem solving; and (5) the awareness that their notions of themselves and their identity is continuously shaped and re-shaped in response to interactions with others and the dialectical relationship between self and society. Students come to understand that it is only through meaningful engagement with any content—either academic or experimental—that one can reach an informed opinion. An important byproduct of the strong relationships that students build with OP staff and faculty from the recruitment process through enrollment and attendance at the college is the idea that the OP office (within the purview of the Office of Student Academic Services)—and the Opportunity Program itself—comes to be viewed as what Guitiérrez (2008, 148) refers to as a "collective third space"—a space wherein "students begin to reconceive what they might be able to accomplish academically and beyond."

The Summer Academic Institute is thus rooted in growing empirical evidence that high expectations and academic standards, coupled with relevant and appropriate supports, can influence students' academic and personal success (Bangert-Drowns et al. 1991; Cohen, Steele and Ross 1999; Hogan and Pressley 1997; Kuh et al. 1991; Levine and Nidiffer 1996; Welch and Hodges 1997). These practical and theoretical assumptions undergird the continuous collaborations between the OP staff, Skidmore faculty, and the registrar's office. Layden, Knickerbocker, and Minor (2004, 4) indicate that given the level of preparation the program staff expect and want from students at the conclusion of the summer bridge program, this collaboration between program staff and faculty has resulted in the following integrated goals for the summer program (see table 6).

Supports During the Academic Year

The supports provided by the program staff do not end once the summer program is over. Given their personal and professional commitment to students and the research base on the importance of the first year of college in determining student achievement and retention (Graham 1997; Seymour and

Table 4.6.   Summer Academic Institute Goals

Assess gaps in students knowledge and skills for appropriate placement in summer courses and the selection and registration of freshman (first-year) fall courses;

Expose students to Skidmore's academic expectations and procedures in efforts to provide accurate and relevant information and to nurture self confidence;

Prepare students for academic experiences that privilege different perspectives and ways of knowing;

Expose students to the importance of metacognition, i.e., understanding and taking responsibility for problem solving, reasoning, and decision making relative to their "choosing a major, enrolling in courses, and reviewing career options;"

Encourage students to cultivate valuable time-management skills;

Encourage students to effectively use the computer in their course work;

Expose students to Skidmore's many cultural and social events which they can benefit from and contribute to;

Focus on reducing students' personal and academic difficulties vis-à-vis monitoring, counseling, mentoring and the nurturance of relationships with their peers, administrators and faculty; and

Encourage students to believe in their own capacity to excel as college students.

Hewitt 1997; Ting and Robinson 1998; Tinto 1993), the monitoring, support, advisement and mentoring of first year OP students remain the priority for program staff. This is reflected in the number of academic contact hours between program staff and students, which averaged over 25 hours per staff member per week on a one to one basis with students in 2009-2010. While these resources are emphasized in the first year, as students progress in their sophomore, junior and senior year; the supports provided to them evolve depending on students' academic strengths and weaknesses.

In addition to these supports from the program staff, faculty also assist in monitoring students' academic progress. For example, Skidmore faculty are asked to provide academic evaluations of first year OP students (to the OP staff) in the fourth and eighth week of their fall and spring semester. Faculty are also asked to provide academic evaluations of juniors and seniors in the eighth week of their fall and spring semesters as well. The program staff utilize these faculty evaluations to tailor their support to students, whether it is (1) helping students to understand the material in a different way; (2) reinforcing and/or redirecting students' efforts; or (3) having conversations with students about their study habits, the requirements of subsequent courses, or how a particular course fits into a certain sequence.

This strategy nurtures and strengthens students' trust in the program staff and gives them confidence to pursue mentoring relationships with faculty in other academic departments as they progress in their sophomore, junior and senior years. Additionally, as students progress, the program staff assist them with finding internships, applying for study abroad, fellowship, and research opportunities with faculty, accessing scholarship funds, and applying to graduate school if this is part of their post-undergraduate goals. OP staff spend considerable time with seniors—either with honors thesis, the job search process or graduate school applications. Academic year supports is also balanced with social activities including dinners at program staffs' homes; Office Open Houses with cookies and hot chocolate; dinners at downtown Saratoga restaurants; an OP Family Dinner during Celebration Weekend; holiday get-togethers; an end-of-the-year barbeque at the Saratoga State Park; and a celebration/graduation dinner for seniors. These evolving developments in pedagogy , staffing, and support has resulted in unprecedented changes in academic achievement, graduation and retention rates for OP students at Skidmore (see table 7).

ASSESSMENT: ACADEMIC AND OTHER OUTCOMES

In efforts to improve four-year graduation rates, course completion rates, and cumulative GPAs, Layden, Solomon and their colleagues developed clear programmatic goals, including reducing the number of withdrawals from

Table 4.7.   Comparative OP Achievement, Graduation and Retention Rates

Entering Summer Year	Mean Cumulative GPA	4-Year Graduation Rate	6-Year Graduation Rate
1988	2.29	41.2%	70.6%
2004	3.21	82%	97%

gateway courses (particularly in the sciences); increasing the campus community's understanding of OP and its goals; and developing staff expertise on the experiences of first-generation and underrepresented students in predominantly white and elite contexts. This entailed creating internal assessment structures and mechanisms for collecting data on OP students' achievement outcomes and program support structures, and close work with the College's Office of Institutional Research made this possible. Solomon, Layden and the OP staff, other faculty and Skidmore's leadership, consistently analyze student achievement data each semester to refine program support structures and initiatives. This approach also increased empirical support for the program's outcomes: targeted recruitment, knowledge and skill development, support and motivation, monitoring and advisement, and academic and social integration.

Results indicate that students' grade point averages in their freshman year have increased considerably given the particular focus on implementing and evaluating particular social processes and the provision and arrangement of relevant and appropriate resources. Additionally, recent graduation rates indicate that the majority of OP students are graduating from Skidmore College in less than six years. Indeed, the average four and six year graduation rate for OP students graduating between 2004 and 2008, was 90 percent and 94 percent, respectively. Skidmore's Office of Institutional Research (January 2009) reports the current four and six year graduation rate for non-OP students to be 78.1 percent and 80.9 percent respectively. This important accomplishment has implications for both OP and the College. The program for example, can provide offers of acceptance to more students and the College can channel the funds saved to other students admitted into the program.

The data also indicate that although OP students enroll with SAT scores that are at least 200 points less than their non-OP peers, they are able to perform at similar or higher levels academically. SAT scores notwithstanding, when compared with their non-OP peers, 33 percent of the entering class of 2014 earned term GPAs of 3.5 or above, and 68 percent earned GPAs above 3.0. Indeed, the mean GPA for the entire non-OP entering first year class at Skidmore (N = 768) was 3.315 (mean GPA for all male first year students was 3.154). The mean GPA for the 41 OP students in the class of 2014 was 3.22. Thus, the forty-one "disadvantaged" and "inadmissible" first-year OP students compete with and often outperform their non-OP peers. Indeed, only 30 percent of the entire non-OP entering class (of 2014) at Skidmore had term GPAs of 3.6 or above. OP students' SAT scores, in essence, under-predict their ability to attain comparable GPAs with their non-OP peers. This substantive achievement (on the part of the program staff, faculty and students) is also reflected in the awards and recognition obtained by OP students. For example, OP students have garnered awards on many levels, including international awards (Fulbright, Omicron Delta Epsilon, and Phi Alpha Theta), national awards (National Hispanic Scholarship, National Institute of Health Scholarship, Phi Beta Kappa, Pi Mu Epsilon, Sigma Delta Pi, Psi Chi), and campus levels awards (Periclean Honors Society, the Thoroughbred Academic Society, and other Academic and Leadership prizes). Additionally, more than half of all OP students engage in service to the college community as residential assistants, athletic programs, and student clubs and organizations (Layden, Knickerbocker, and Minor, 2004).

These successes are significant on another level; namely, they serve to temper student perceptions that somehow their race/ethnic status indicates that they are intellectually inferior to other students (Massey et al. 2003; Steele 1997). As indicated earlier, pervasive staff support and ingrained expectations that students will do well, both individually and as part of a learning community, appear to concretize students' sense of belonging in the program. In the aggregate, students are thus able to compete for awards, participate in campus activities and maintain good academic standing. The data however, shows slight continuing differentials in performance between African American and Hispanic males and their Asian American and White male peers in OP (see table 8).Layden and her staff, in collaboration with Skidmore's president and faculty, have begun to assess the reasons behind this phenomenon. To that end, a staff member who is responsible for advising all of the African American males and for coordinating services provided to them was named in the mid-2000s. This change was made in 2004 (Miller et al. 2005).

Several other initiatives have also emerged out of Skidmore's concern with academically and socially integrating males of color. For example, Skidmore's Associate Dean of the Faculty (Office of Academic Advising) and Layden, the Associate Dean of Student Affairs serve as institutional representatives in the Consortium for High Achievement and Success (CHAS) since Fall 2007. In this capacity, students, faculty and administrators attended a CHAS-sponsored conference that Fall at Swarthmore College entitled "The new danger: Black and Latino men facing evolving challenges to their scholarship and community." The team from Skidmore were given an opportunity to craft viable solutions for responding to the needs of males of color on their campus. This experience made a unique impression on the students, who, upon returning to campus, were eager to debrief and discuss

Table 4.8. Graduating Grade Point Averages of OP and Non-OP Skidmore Students by Race/Ethnicity, 2006–2008

Race/Ethnicity	OP Students 2006-2008	# of OP Students 2006-2008	Non-OP Students 2006-2008	# of Non-OP Students 2006-2008
African American	2.917	21	3.216	14
Asian	3.367	17	3.200	79
Hispanic	3.097	20	3.192	44
Native American			3.419	7
Non-resident alien			3.348	13
White	3.121	6	3.352	1256
Race & Ethnicity Unknown	2.969	7	3.372	285
	OP Cum GPA 3.102	Total OP Student count 71	Non-OP Cum GPA 3.343	Total Non-OP student count 1698

Source: Skidmore College Institutional Research Department, January, 2009.

their social and academic experiences on campus with peers, faculty and staff.

Toward this end, the Skidmore team decided to convene a meeting of all Black and Latino men at Skidmore College, including staff, students and faculty (a total of seventy-two Black or Latino males on Skidmore's campus, including fifty-six Black or Latino students, six Latino male faculty/staff members, and ten Black male faculty/staff members). An Assistant Professor of American Studies, Joshua C. Woodfork and Layden spearheaded the planning of this gathering and secured resources from Student Academic Services and the Opportunity Program to sponsor a dinner meeting in the Faculty and Staff Club. This meeting was held in December of 2007. The purpose of the meeting was to share the results of the CHAS meeting and to gather data concerning the attendees' social and academic experiences on campus. Although the Skidmore team anticipated a 50 percent attendance rate, 70 percent of the Black and Latino men on campus attended.

Input from this meeting resulted in a half-day workshop entitled *I, Too, Am Education: Black and Latino Males Achieving Excellence.* This workshop, held in late March 2008, focused on student success and achievement and was geared primarily to Black and Latino males on campus. At least 60 percent of the Black and Latino male students (over forty students) attended this workshop, which featured a keynote speaker, Mr. Lamont Toliver, Director of the Meyerhoff Scholarship Program at University of Maryland,

Baltimore County. The workshop included a session entitled "*Seeing Our-selves in the Curriculum,*" was conducted by the former Director of Intercul-tural Studies and Associate Professor of American Studies at Skidmore Col-lege, Dr. Winston Grady-Willis, and Professor Woodfork. Other staff and faculty, including Skidmore's Registrar and Director of Institutional Re-search, and the Associate Professor of English and Chair of the College Curriculum Committee, assisted in guiding this session. Participants in this session discussed the existence (and the lack thereof) of certain majors and minors at Skidmore, explored pathways to having a passion become a course of study, and examined, in detail, the reflection of their experiences as Black and Latino males in the Skidmore curriculum. Additionally, all students in attendance participated in a *Strategizing for Success* session facilitated by a team of over twenty Skidmore faculty and key campus administrators. Dur-ing this session, eight to ten students were grouped into teams. In their respective groups, students discussed their conceptions of excellence, partic-ularly academic excellence, in addition to institutional supports to which they have access and perceived barriers to excelling at Skidmore.

Data from these sessions were employed in the conceptualizing of follow-up initiatives for the 2008-09 academic year. These include the attendance of a team of Skidmore faculty and staff at a CHAS-sponsored conference, the *Humanities Faculty Forum*. The Skidmore team attended presentations on pedagogy in the humanities, wise mentoring, peer-led learning, writing in the humanities, and best practices. Feedback from the faculty indicated that they would like to integrate their insights from the conference, particularly around stereotype threat, in their coursework. Additionally, Layden has made pres-entations on Skidmore's Opportunity Program and Student Academic Ser-vices at two of the CHAS conferences in 2008. She has also worked with humanities faculty in efforts to increase students' writing skills at the *Human-ities Faculty Forum* in May, 2008 and is also a part of the CHAS Assessment Group. In November 2009, Skidmore hosted the CHAS Annual Black and Latino Males Workshop, attended by students, faculty, and staff from over twenty CHAS institutions. These efforts contribute to a consistent reduction in achievement gaps for males who self-identify as Black, African-American, or Latino. Recent OP GPA data indicate that the mean GPA for these stu-dents (N=24) during Fall 2010 was 2.996. When we further disaggregate the data, 67 percent of these men have mean GPAs above 3.0, and 21 percent have mean GPAs above 3.4. Although these outcomes reflect steady im-provement, it also indicates the importance of continuing work.

CONCLUSION

The combination of factors that seem to influence OP students' persistence, retention and graduation, including a supportive university leadership, congruency between students' academic needs and program staff and faculty support and expectations, a highly structured pre-college and freshman year academic experience, and the integral nature of help-seeking, suggest that the current structure of Skidmore's OP is not random but rather the result of consistent leadership and pervasive expectations that students will excel academically as defined by traditional measures (i.e., high GPAs). This multilevel strategy is reflected in the potency of Skidmore's pre-freshman transitional program which is integrated within a holistic system of supports that not only privilege monitoring, academic support, advising, and mentoring relationships with faculty and staff, but also demand that OP students excel on both academic and personal levels. As a result, the program staff and faculty are able to proactively assist students on both academic and personal levels.

Implicit in the discussion of the Opportunity Program at Skidmore is the idea that both non-cognitive and cognitive factors contribute to student persistence, achievement and completion. That is, in addition to students' growth academically, non-cognitive factors such as a positive self-concept, the ability to work toward long-term goals without being derailed by obstacles, access to strong support person(s) and being able to make and maintain meaningful connections with peers, staff and faculty, and exposure to leadership opportunities and community service, are also essential to their development (Bandura 2001; Schunk 2001; Sedlacek 2004, 37). Some of these non-cognitive factors appear to hinge on students' own personal attributes, including motivation, self-regulation and will (Bandura 2001; Schunk 1995; Schunk & Zimmerman 1994; Sedlacek 2004). These institutional and program supports suggest that Skidmore College has moved beyond a focus on admissions, retention and completion to a more integrated emphasis on providing structural supports to reduce disparities between their majority and minority students.

Introducing The Pre-Medical Program

A Brief Historical Overview of Medical Education

Concerns with increasing access to, participation in, and completion of medical school, is not new. Blackwell (1987, 97) noted, for example, that although black students' access to medical school were initially met with optimism and success during the 1970s, this initial enthusiasm quickly declined; eventually plateauing. Available data indicates that of the 266 black, first-year medical students enrolled in U.S. medical schools in the 1968–1969 academic year, approximately 60 percent were enrolled at Meharry and Howard Medical Colleges (historically black institutions) while fifty-four of the remaining ninety-seven medical institutions enrolled at least two black students each in their first-year classes (Blackwell 1987, 97). Indeed, in the early 1970s, 440 black students, representing 4.2 percent of all first-year classes combined, were still largely clustered at Meharry and Howard Medical Colleges (Blackwell, 1987, 97). The proportion of black students reached a peak of 7.5 percent in 1973 and 1974, and declined noticeably in subsequent years. However, the phenomenon of black medical students who repeated their first year was a confounding factor because they are reported in figures that include enrolled black first-year medical students. In 1978–1979, black students had a repeat rate of 14.4 percent while students who were Mexican American, Puerto Rican, and Asian/Pacific Islander had repeat rates of 9.2 percent, 4.6 percent, and 2.7 percent, respectively (Blackwell 1987, 101).

Nonetheless, the proportional increase in total enrollment in medical school for black students from 1969–1979 more than doubled. This emergent trend was partially the result of rising levels of institutional commitment; increasing availability of financial aid to reduce students' concerns about finances; and "aggressive recruitment, special admissions, and federal mandates to desegregate all components of post-secondary education" (Blackwell 1987, 102). This shift, on a personal level, can be attributed to black students' views that pursuing medicine as a career was not only for the economically and socially advantaged, but also a feasible career regardless of their socioeconomic backgrounds (Blackwell 1987). Given this context, black applicants applying to medical school for the first time grew to approximately 1,600 during the 1980s and by another 50 percent in the mid-1990s (Cooper 2003, 78). Cooper's (2003) analysis also indicated that first-time Hispanic applicants to medical school grew to 900 during the 1980s (from less than 400 in 1973) and by another 65 percent in the mid-1990s. The number of black and Hispanic applicants to medical school decreased however, after the March 1996 decision of the United States Court of Appeals for the Fifth Circuit, which held, in *Hopwood v. Texas*, that the University of Texas Law School, in effect, could consider an applicant's race only if doing so was in the interest of redressing past discrimination by the school itself (Cooper 2003). The ruling in *Hopwood* is striking in that a majority of the judges asserted that the decision in *Bakke* no longer characterized the Supreme Court's perspective; moreover, the use of race to achieve a diverse student body was not a compelling enough state interest to satisfy the standard of strict scrutiny (Killenbeck 2004). It became illegal to take race into account in Texas public colleges and universities (colleges and universities in Louisiana and Mississippi adhere to *Hopwood* because these states are in the Fifth Circuit). During this period as well, the Regents of the University of California declared that the nine universities in the state system were no longer allowed to consider race in admissions decisions. After a heated debate, California voters ended state affirmative action programs when they passed Proposition 209 (Stall and Morain 2006).

In addition to the effects of affirmative action decisions on declines in medical school applications for students of color, Cooper (2003) reminds us that the high dropout rates from high school for black and Hispanic students; low rates of entry into college; entrance into two-year rather than four-year institutions; and low graduation rates from both two- and four- year institutions also play a role in the low numbers of these applicants to medical school. However, when black and Hispanic students do obtain their undergraduate degrees, they tend to apply to medical school at the same rate as their white male peers (Cooper 2003).

Students' undergraduate major also appear to play a role in whether they apply to medical school. A recent analysis by the American Association of Medical Colleges (November 16, 2006) suggests that although more minority students obtain undergraduate degrees in biology (the most common undergraduate major for medical school), minority applicants with undergraduate biology majors declined between 1993 and 2004. Specifically, the number of black applicants to medical school with biology majors declined from 83 percent to 44 percent; the decline for Hispanic and Native American applicants fell from 75 percent to 39 percent and 73 percent to 45 percent respectively.

There are indications however, that declines in minority student's application to medical school may be slowing. American Association of Medical Colleges (October 16, 2007) data indicate that in the aggregate, 42,315 students applied to medical school in 2007, the largest in the nation's history (marking an increase of 8.2 percent from 2006). Of this number, first time applicants numbered approximately 31,946, the highest figure the AAMC has ever documented. Women comprised 49 percent of total applicants (AAMC, October 21, 2008). Of note as well is the strength of the applicant pool. Indeed, applicants had the "highest MCAT [Medical College Admission Test] scores and cumulative grade point averages on record" and demonstrated increases in average amounts of "experience in premedical activities, including time spent in medical research and community service in clinical and nonclinical settings" (AAMC, October 21, 2008).

Applicants to medical school in 2007 also included more underrepresented students. Indeed, the increase in black and Hispanic male applicants by 9.2 percent marks a growth rate larger than that of the entire applicant pool (AAMC, October 16, 2007). Black and Hispanic males however, were not accepted and did not enroll at the same rates. That is, the acceptance and enrollment rates for black males increased by 5.3 percent whereas the acceptance and enrollment rate for Hispanic males was similar to 2006 rates. In 2008 however, Hispanic applicants to medical school increased by 3 percent while applications from black and Native American students declined by 4 percent and 3 percent respectively. Applications from women also decreased to 48 percent (from 49 percent in 2007). Hispanic students accepted to medical school increased their enrollment rates by more than 10 percent in 2008 and comprise 7.9 percent of students in the 2008–2009 entering medical school (AAMC 2008). Although the number of Native American applicants declined (as noted above), Native American students who were accepted increased their enrollment rates by more than 5 percent and comprised 1.0 percent of the entering 2008–2009 class. African American students' acceptance and enrollment rates remained at 2007 levels and comprised 7.2 percent of the 2008–2009 entering class. African American females however, represented approximately two-thirds of the Black/African American students who were accepted and enrolled into medical school in 2007 (Association of American Medical Colleges: Diversity in Medical Education: Facts & Figures 2008).

Despite these trends, Cooper (2003, 81) suggests that the possibility of the high cost of medical school, increasing regulation of health care, insufficient or decreasing reimbursement rates, and the ubiquitous threat of litigation may dissuade some students from a career in medicine. Even so, Cooper surmises that other trends, including the low proportion of minority students (compared with their white and Asian peers) who are enrolled in college; high school graduates who do not have the financial capital to attend college; and the large attrition rates of high school students, may be more impactful on whether minority students eventually apply to medical school.

Given these issues and challenges, understanding how the university leadership, and faculty and staff conceptualize and implement the premedical program at Xavier University, will enable us to rethink how and what we teach in continuing efforts to prepare students for entrance into and success in medical school.

Chapter Five

A Model for Preparing Students for Medical School

Xavier University in New Orleans

INTRODUCTION

Recent literature has documented the many benefits from diversity in medical school, the physician workforce and the nations' physician-scientists (Antonio et al. 2004; Gurin 1999). For example, a larger number of minority physicians are serving generally underserved populations, and research on diseases that disproportionately affect racial and ethnic minority groups are also on the rise (Cohen, Gabriel and Terrell 2002; Marin and Diaz 2002; Smedley, Stith and Nelson 2003). It is thus essential to support (through mentoring and strong, positive role models, for instance), a diverse pool of medical school applicants, physicians and physician-scientists in efforts to both ensure this pool's personal and professional success, and reduce chronic health disparities among diverse racial/ethnic groups (Association of American Medical Colleges [AAMC]: Diversity in Medical Education: Facts & Figures 2008; Institute of Medicine: In the Nation's Compelling Interest: Ensuring Diversity in the Health Care Workforce 2004). These efforts are especially important given increasing numbers of underrepresented students and women who apply to, are accepted, and enroll into medical school (Sullivan Commission on Diversity in the Health Workforce 2004). Indeed, recent AAMC (2010) analysis indicates that in the aggregate, Hispanic enrollment in medical school increased nine percent. When disaggregated by gender, Hispanic male enrollees increased by 17.1 percent from 2009, while Hispanic female enrollees increased by 1.6 percent from 2009. African-American stu-

111

dents increased their enrollment by 2.9 percent in 2010 (compared to 2009). Although the number of American Indian students attending medical school tends to be small, American Indian enrollees in 2010 grew by 24.8 percent. AAMC's (2010) analysis indicates that gains in underrepresented student enrollment across the United States notwithstanding, the West evinced the largest growth; from 14.4 percent in 2009 to 16.1 percent in 2010.

Increases in medical school enrollment for Black or African American and Hispanic/Latino students however, do not accurately reflect their respective population growth. That is, although African Americans, Hispanics/Latinos, and Native Americans comprise 28.8 percent of the U.S. population, in the aggregate, they only comprised 12.3 percent of the physician workforce (AAMC: Diversity in Physician workforce 2010, 17). Additionally, Asian American and Black or African American physicians comprised the largest groups of racial and ethnic minority physicians (12.8 and 6.3 percent, respectively). It is projected that these groups will account for about half of the U.S. population by 2050 (www.census.gov/population/www/pop-profile/nat-proj.html: downloaded May 4, 2012). These dynamics and other economic and lifestyle changes, including a national physician shortage; an increase of 25 million people in the United States in each decade; a doubling of persons over age sixty-five between 2000 and 2030; increasing demands for health care services, particularly by baby boomers; the retirement of one in three doctors over age fifty-five by 2020; and new physicians who place more priority on balancing work and family/personal life; thus working somewhat less than their predecessors (AAMC, June 19, 2006); contributed to the AAMC's recommendation of a 30 percent increase in medical school enrollment by 2015.

Given the importance of preparing more students, including underrepresented students for entrance into medical school (and increasing the diversity of these schools) (Antonio et al. 2004; Gurin 1999), this chapter highlights a premedical program at Xavier University in New Orleans, which consistently ranks first in the nation (since 1993) in preparing and placing African American students into medical schools across the country (including Harvard, Northwestern, Baylor, Emory, Meharry and Tulane). Approximately 92 percent of Xavier University (XU) graduates, who enroll in medical and dental school, graduate and become practicing physicians and dentists (www.xula.edu/admissions/generalinformation.php: downloaded May 4, 2012). When asked what accounts for his program's singular success, Dr. J.W. Carmichael, professor of chemistry at XU, and one of the founders of the pre-medical program, responded as follows:

> When I came to Xavier, I was ready to spend time trying to find ways to improve teaching and I was very skeptical of "conventional wisdom..." As a result, there wasn't any "eureka" moment when we suddenly devised the pro-

gram as it stands. Instead, what you see today is the result of our keeping good data, trying to analyze the data to identify problems, and then developing mechanisms for addressing those problems. (J.W. Carmichael, Interview at Xavier University in New Orleans: July 2005).

Carmichael's implicit premise that teaching, learning and achievement are not mutually exclusive brings into high relief the importance of (1) reconceptualizing teaching, learning and assessment in the service of providing necessary and sufficient supports for undergraduate students in the sciences and mathematics; and (2) utilizing data to continually design and reassess activities, trends and progress. These processes, embedded within several principles of learning, can be understood within the historical context of Xavier University and its nearly two decade success in preparing and placing the largest number of students annually into medical school; a success all the more remarkable given the damage XU sustained after Hurricane Katrina in 2005.

THE HISTORICAL CONTEXT OF XAVIER UNIVERSITY'S PREMEDICAL PROGRAM

Xavier University is a liberal arts college founded in 1925 in New Orleans by Saint Katharine Drexel and the *Sisters of the Blessed Sacrament* order she created to serve African American and Native American students. Considered the only historically Black, Catholic institution of higher education in the United States, control of Xavier University was transferred to a combined lay/religious Board of Trustees in 1970 (www.xula.edu/about-xavier/index.php: downloaded May 4, 2012). Dr. Norman C. Francis, president of XU since 1968, has been associated with Xavier since 1948, when he arrived as a student. Considered the longest-sitting university president in the United States, he is recognized for physically expanding XU'S campus, including the addition of an academic/science complex, the Library/Resource Center, and expansion of the College of Pharmacy's facilities. He has also grown the university endowment to more than $133 million (www.xula.edu/mediarelations/quickfacts.php: downloaded May 4, 2012). In the midst of this work however, academic rigor was not neglected; indeed, a core curriculum and mandatory comprehensives was instituted and XU gained a national reputation for academic excellence. This success is reflected in the near doubling in enrollment over the past fifteen years to 3,401 current students (XU's enrollment before Hurricane Katrina in 2005 was 4,100) (www.xula.edu/mediarelations/quickfacts.php: May 4, 2012). Current demographic information indicates that more than one-half (57.1 percent) of Xavier students are from the New Orleans area (www.xula.edu/about-xavier/index.php). There are also students from thirty-nine states (with heavy representation from Texas and

Georgia) and seven foreign countries on XU's campus. African American students comprise approximately 90 percent of the University's enrollment and nearly 40 percent of these students are Catholic; further reflecting XU's historical mission of educational service to the African American Community (www.xula.edu/admissions/generalinformation.php: downloaded May 4, 2012).

XU's admissions office indicate that in the past few years, 74 percent of new freshman students have declared majors in the natural sciences; 11 percent in the social sciences and education; 7 percent in business; 5 percent in the arts and humanities; and 3 percent in other areas (www.xula.edu/admissions/generalinformation.php: May 4, 2012). All Xavier students, irrespective of major, are required to enroll in the following courses: African American studies, art, foreign language, history, literature, mathematics, music, philosophy, science, social science, speech, and theology www.xula.edu/mediarelations/quickfacts.php: downloaded May 4, 2012). XU's major academic units include the College of Arts and Sciences, which awards baccalaureate degrees; the College of Pharmacy, which awards the Doctor of Pharmacy degree; and the Graduate School, which awards masters degrees in Education and Theology. XU's Drexel Center serves the surrounding community via community outreach and continuing education programs. Taken together, XU offers preparation in 44 major areas at the undergraduate, graduate, and professional levels. Tuition at XU's college of Arts and Sciences and Pre-Pharmacy for a full-time student (12-18 hours) is currently $8,850.00 per semester. Tuition for the College of Pharmacy (Pharm. D.) for a full-time student (12-18 hours) is $13,400.00 per semester (www.xula.edu/fiscal/tuition.php: downloaded May 4, 2012).

XU is recognized by the National Science Foundation as a Model Institution for Excellence (MIE). This recognition rests on the large number of Black undergraduates who receive degrees in the physical, life and health sciences. XU is also considered a "top producer" in placing African American students into pharmacy school. Indeed, Xavier has educated nearly 25 percent of the more than 6,000 black pharmacists currently practicing in the United States (http://www.xula.edu/admissions/generalinformation.php: downloaded May 4, 2012). And as noted in the introduction, XU's premedical program sends the largest number of African American students to medical school since 1993.

One of the faculty members at the heart of this achievement is Dr. J.W. Carmichael, Professor of Chemistry, who was selected as the National Professor of the Year by the Council for the Advancement and Support of Education in 2008. Carmichael was chosen from a pool of 537 nominations submitted by colleges and universities across the nation. He has also been honored with the Charles A. Dana Foundation Award for his innovations in teaching science and has won the McGraw Hill Prize in Education in 1997.

He has also received an honorary degree from Meharry Medical College in 2008 for "his success in making Xavier the undisputed leader in African American medical school acceptances" (www.xula.edu/mediarelations/quickfacts.php: downloaded May 4, 2012).

XAVIER UNIVERSITY'S PREMEDICAL PROGRAM

Until the mid-1970's, students entering Xavier with an interest in medicine were automatically placed in the Chemistry Department. With a view to growing the number of XU students enrolling in medical school, XU decided to allow students to major in other areas (particularly Biology and psychology), and a separate Premedical Office was created to ensure that students—in any department—with an interest in medicine will receive assistance in obtaining their career goal (J.W. Carmichael, personal communication, Xavier University, July 2005). Thus, the purpose of Xavier's Premedical Office is to prepare students to enroll and succeed in schools of Medicine, Osteopathic Medicine, Dentistry, Veterinary Medicine, Optometry, Podiatry, and Public Health (MODVOP+PH—to use Carmichael's term). The Premedical Office provides information about and assistance in applying to Public Health/ Health Administration (PH) schools given students' interest in preparing for eventual administrative posts in their fields (J.W. Carmichael, personal communication, July, 2005; XU Profile: Office of Planning and Institutional Research, 2005). The premedical office also provides special Pre-Pharmacy Advisers who work closely with XU's College of Pharmacy to advise students interested in Pharmacological studies (J.W. Carmichael, personal communication, Xavier University, July 2005).

XU's premedical program is structured to assist all students interested in MODVOP, to meet certain criteria before applying to medical school in these areas. Accordingly, since all MODVOP schools/programs expect undergraduates to have completed at least forty hours of coursework in mathematics and science, XU's premedical program is strategically located in the College of Arts and Sciences as an actively cooperative effort between the Biology, Chemistry, and Psychology departments. Several faculty members from each of these departments serve in the program as premedical advisors. The premedical director and advisor(s) report to the Dean of Arts and Sciences and receive partial release time from their respective departments in order to staff the premedical program. This arrangement does not mean that only premedical advisors from Biology can advise only Biology majors, however. Rather, the premedical advisors are responsible for supporting all students enrolled as premedical majors in biology, chemistry or psychology. They collectively decide their roles and related tasks and perform them in collaborative ways.

Carmichael (personal communication, Xavier University, July 2005) suggests that this structured approach has enabled the program to effectively evolve and operate with minimal conflict between and among departments. For example, the premedical advisors, who are fulltime, tenured faculty members, work closely with faculty from the Biology, Chemistry and Psychology departments not only in monitoring student progress, but also in assessing the effectiveness of current teaching methods if students are not learning major concepts taught across the three departments. Additionally, the premedical advisors regularly consult Officers of Alpha Epsilon Delta (Premedical Honor Society), Beta Beta Beta (Biology Honor Society), and Phi Lambda Upsilon (Chemistry Honor Society) in efforts to remain at the forefront of the knowledge, skills and abilities students are expected to know and have when applying to medical school. At the heart of the three departments' synergy, Carmichael (personal communication, Xavier University, July 2005) emphasized, is an overarching charge each take seriously: that of systematically preparing students for eventual acceptance and enrollment in the health professions and graduate schools. When operationalized, this charge takes the form of careful analysis of the teaching and learning functions and processes in the biology, chemistry and psychology departments. This approach, created and refined over a 40 year life span by a group of committed faculty members with expertise in the sciences and mathematics, is widely perceived as an effective strategy for nurturing underrepresented students to eventually gain admittance to health professional schools (Council of Graduate Schools 2009; National Center for Education Statistics 2008).

Remarkably, the costs of Xavier's premedical program are relatively minimal. In the main, funding is provided by the Howard Hughes Medical Institute for the freshman summer program offered by the premedical program (although students are expected to contribute a small fee). The costs of supports offered to premedical students during the academic year is integrated and absorbed into XU's core budget; thus the program is not dependent on external funding — hence its longevity. The cost of faculty release time to staff the premedical program was the only expense identified by the premedical director (J.W Carmichael, personal communication, Xavier University, July, 2005). Interestingly, XU's per student expenditures are actually lower compared to the average for other historically Black colleges and universities (Gandara and Maxwell-Jolly 1999; U.S. Commission on Civil Rights 2010).

Program Outcomes/Studies Attesting to XU's Premedical Program Effectiveness

The most recent figures indicate that 248 premedical students at XU were accepted into medical school for the 2010–2011 academic year (www.xula.edu/premed/ downloaded September 7, 2011) and an additional

111 students were accepted in the following health professions schools: osteopathic medical school (8 students); dental school (42 students); veterinary medical school (3 students); podiatry school (12 students); optometry school (5 students); chiropractic school (7 students); and public health or health administration school (34 students).

XU's premedical program's success raises several questions; namely what factors predict or are strongly associated with how well students do in XU's premedical program and in medical school once they arrive. With regard to students' entering characteristics, a prior study (Carmichael et al. 1988) found strong correlations between students' ACT scores and high school grade point average (GPA) and the probability of their gaining entry into medical school. That is, students who enrolled at XU with a composite ACT ≥ 22 (combined SAT score of 953) and high school GPAs ≥ 3.0 had a good chance (50 percent or higher generally) of completing coursework in XU's premedical program and gaining entry into medical school; whereas, students with a composite ACT <19 (combined SAT <953) and high school GPA < 2.75, had relatively little chance of persisting and gaining entry into medical school (J.W. Carmichael, Personal communication, Xavier University, July, 2005). Carmichael and colleagues (1988) also discovered that some students with lower ACT's and high school GPA's actually have some chance of gaining entry into podiatry or dentistry and a better chance of gaining entry into XU's College of Pharmacy and succeeding there than they do in getting into medical or dental schools.

With regard to medical school, Carmichael and colleagues (1987) indicate that students' grades at XU, particularly in biology and chemistry, are better predictors of their success in medical school than are MCAT scores. (Even so, the premedical faculty has focused continuing efforts on enabling students to improve their MCAT scores, particularly since scoring in a certain range (e.g., 5–15) increases the likelihood of gaining admittance into medical school.) More recent internal analysis by the premedical office reinforces the integral relationship between students' grades and their probability of getting into medical school (www.xula.edu/premed/PMInfo/a.HPInfo/Info02Advice: downloaded May 4, 2012). That is, a premedical students' overall GPA and aggregate GPA in Biology, Chemistry, Physics, and Mathematics at the end of their junior year, can give them a sense of the probability of acceptance into their school of choice. This current analysis of students' cumulative and discipline specific GPAs and their MCAT scores are employed in advising students not only about the probability of their gaining entry into health professions schools, but also whether they should retake the MCAT (J.W. Carmichael, personal communication, Xavier University, July 2005 & January 2010). Advisement thus includes the emphasis that many factors are considered in the admissions calculus, including cumulative and science grades, students' summer research experiences, MCAT scores, faculty recommendations, community service, etc.

The above analyses comports with Carmichael and colleagues' internal analyses, which show that in general, premedical students with GPA's of 3.3 or above can succeed in any medical school; students with GPA's between 3.0 and 3.3 can generally succeed in most medical schools; and those students with GPA's between 2.75 and 3.0 need to consider medical schools with strong support systems. The premedical director notes that these guidelines are adjusted to account for "late bloomers" — including students who have especially heavy work-loads (J.W. Carmichael, Personal communication, Xavier University, July 2005).

Carmichael notes that he and his colleagues' past studies and current internal analysis demonstrate that XU is not preselecting students who would have succeeded irrespective of the program; that is, XU "does not accept only the cream of the African American high school crop" (J.W. Carmichael, Personal communication, Xavier University July 2005 and January 2010). This is evidenced by Fall 2011 data indicating that freshman students enter XU with ACT composite scores ranging from 19 to 25, and SAT scores ranging from combined math and verbal scores of 860 to 1080 (nces.ed.gov/collegenavigator/?q=xavier+university&s=all&id=160904#admsns: downloaded May 4, 2012).

Recruitment

The recruitment process for XU's premedical program has evolved over time. In its early stages, the premedical program offered entering ninth, tenth, eleventh and twelfth graders a coordinated sequence of four summer enrichment programs created to prepare them for the algebra (MathStar), biology (BioStar), and chemistry (ChemStar) courses they will take during their upcoming academic year. Students entering their senior year in high school can enroll in a program called SOAR (Stress on Analytic Reasoning), the last in this series of four summer enrichment programs. SOAR emphasizes skill development in problem-solving and vocabulary (Whimbey et al. 1980; Whimbey 1985). Taken together, the summer enrichment programs were not remedial in nature but rather rigorous in their course content and expectations that students will work hard and succeed in highly competitive fields, including medicine, dentistry and science graduate school. These programs are now integrated within the overall range of summer programs offered by XU's Drexel Center, and are taught by XU faculty members in collaboration and cooperation with high school teachers, and if available, upper level XU premedical students and graduates currently in medical and dental school.

It is important to note here that XU faculty in biology, chemistry and psychology designed these enrichment programs in close and active collaboration with a range of teachers from the local public and parochial schools. Despite the different content area of each, all of the courses share common features, including the integration of problem solving exercises within the curriculum; several hours of homework daily; frequent quizzes that test conceptual mastery; feedback provided early and often; knowledge and skill development in vocabulary and reading; and the assistance of successful Xavier students who function as group and role models. The referenced partnership and collaboration between faculty members and high school teachers is part of a long tradition at XU. Indeed, high school teachers are viewed as equal partners in XU's endeavors to prepare students for the rigor of their high school mathematics and sciences courses, and possibly XU's premedical program if that is their goal. This partnership has resulted in extensive assistance to teachers, including audio visual materials, textbooks, guest lecturers from the University, and professional development workshops in teachers' content areas. Additionally, teachers' contributions to XU's success are often publicly recognized by faculty. This model of university/school/community partnership is integral to XU's recruitment approach and appears to be gaining momentum in other parts of the country (www.tc. edu).

Reconceptualizing Teaching, Learning and Assessment

The focus group and individual interviews with faculty, staff and students revealed the deeply integral nature and active implementation of several principles of learning in XU's premedical program. That is, this program (1) structures knowledge around the major concepts and organizing principles of several disciplines, including biology, chemistry, mathematics and physics (a knowledge-centered environment); (2) structures and shapes student learning around particular tasks and activities (a learner-centered environment); and (3) academically and socially supports students' capacity to learn with understanding vis-à-vis learning communities at many levels (a community-centered environment) (Bransford, Brown and Cocking 2000; Brown and Campione 1994; Vye et al. 1998).

A Knowledge-Centered Environment

As noted in other chapters in this volume, the practice of "weeding" out large numbers of students of color from engineering, mathematics, and the biological and physical sciences, is the norm at many colleges and universities (Hurtado et al. 2009; Maton et al. 2008). Carmichael (personal communication, Xavier University, July 2005) noted that "other practices that emphasize the lowering of standards for underprepared students, is not conducive either to nurturing their persistence and achievement in these disciplines." One key aspect that distinguishes the premedical program at XU is the enduring belief (on the part of the premedical director, the university leadership, and affiliated faculty and staff members), is that given high expectations and supports that are appropriate and consistent, underrepresented students can and do excel in mathematics and the biological and physical sciences. These beliefs are manifested in the premedical faculty's relinquished independence in their classrooms and their exceptional cooperation and collaboration across departments and with their peers. Their beliefs and actions appear to be motivated by a steadfast commitment to not only rigorously prepare students for medical school, but also prepare them to persist and graduate once there. "Our focus is on exit criteria rather than entrance requirements" (J.W. Carmichael, personal communication, Xavier University, July 2005).

This focus informs the premedical faculty and staffs' perspective that "course content, teaching methodology, and the rate of presentation should be determined by the relevant department as a whole, not by individual lecturers or textbooks." Toward this end, faculty members in the biology, chemistry, mathematics, and physics department moved to adapt and standardize several foundational courses, including general biology, general chemistry, organic chemistry, general physics, and pre-calculus/calculus I. Faculty emphasized that as a department, they "decide the material covered, the rate at which it is presented, and even the algorithms students will use in solving problems. This material is integrated in the workbooks students receive, which have learning goals and sample problems, for example." As a result, "all faculty are aware of the content in basic courses and where to begin upper level courses." This ensures that "the responsibility for providing support is shared by all faculty; including new and adjunct faculty."

This integrated curriculum not only removes redundancies, but it also reinforces difficult concepts and promotes conceptual mastery vis-à-vis interdisciplinary course work (Gandara and Maxwell-Jolly 1999). As an indication of faculty commitment and dedication, this effort, which began in the early 1970s, continues today, forty years later. What were some of the factors that led XU's faculty to considerably modify the curriculum? They found, for example, that "students often struggled to conceptually link their mathematical knowledge with scientific concepts in general chemistry." They also found that "students tend to view additional tutoring in this area as embarrassing" and as a consequence, did not actively avail themselves of tutoring and other supports. They moved thus to deliberately integrate academic supports as part of the course. This strategy ensured that "students are neither pre-judged because of their background nor punished for poor performance." Thus, the standardization of biology and chemistry courses "helps to provide structure. It helps tremendously because we have students with a wide variety of backgrounds and it helps to get everyone up to speed in one year. We believe we need to be very explicit about what students have to do. We are correcting for years and years of poor education. Everyone goes to tutoring.

There is no stigma attached to tutoring. Standardized courses really make a difference" (personal communication, J.W. Carmichael, July 2005 and January 2010).

The premedical faculty also discovered that "students need to increase their problem solving skills." They thus redesigned the general chemistry laboratory as a space in which students can investigate and analyze a phenomenon as opposed to simply confirming something already known. To that end, "students directly experience collecting and analyzing data, and testing and forming ideas." This iterative process can result in students achieving an A for a laboratory report that demonstrates an exhaustive analysis but scientifically incorrect inferences. Recent internal and other analysis (Carmichael et al. 1986), indicate that this strategy enables students to acquire critical reasoning skills for real-world scientific work. The faculty have also integrated this approach in their lectures. That is, they employ error-free data, rigorous analyses and relevant equations/formulas to introduce subject matter content. This approach enables students to correct misconceptions that may have emerged from variations in their experiments. The laboratory manual serves as the foundations for the general chemistry program (Carmichael 1976; Carmichael et al. 1986; Ryan et al. 1980).

The premedical faculty have also instituted the Whimbey and Lochhead 1979; Lochhead and Whimbey 1987) approach to problem solving in entry level courses in mathematics, chemistry and physics. This approach entails deconstructing problems into basic steps that students are able to solve consecutively (Greeno 1991; Goldman 1994; Schoenfeld 2010). One of the goals underpinning this approach is to reduce both student and faculty perception that complex problems can be solved quickly or in one's head (Asera 2001; Treisman 1992; Treisman and Asera 1995). This strategy reinforces the idea that sustained effort is necessary to achieve conceptual mastery rather than reliance on one's ability (Hrabowski and Maton 1995; Maton, Hrabowski and Schmitt 2000; Resnick 2000). Thus, according to faculty, students in XU's premedical program are expected to "work thoroughly, with all steps clearly articulated and verified for accuracy. Students often work in pairs, which enables them to defend and confirm their work" (personal communication, J.W. Carmichael, July 2005 and January 2010).

The algorithms for solving certain problem are also the result of faculty consensus. All of the procedural steps to solve a particular problem are discussed in the classroom, where students are given opportunities to immediately put into practice what they have learned. Students are also encouraged to demonstrate these steps in weekly quizzes, exams and projects done outside of class. Additionally, given the importance of conceptual mastery in general and organic chemistry, mathematics and the sciences, and the ability to visualize in three dimensions, students are taught how to use relevant models in the course of their studies to increase their ability in this process.

Faculty iteratively assess their modifications of entry level courses in the context of whether students are able to pass these courses. For example, prior studies and internal analysis from the premedical program demonstrate that before modification of the freshman biology and chemistry courses, approximately 40 percent of students passed these courses with a grade of "C" or better. Given the iterative modifications in place, more than 60 percent of students now pass these courses with a "c" or better (Carmichael et al. 1988; J.W. Carmichael, personal communication, Xavier University, July 2005). Additionally, program data indicate that, on average, current students are achieving stronger scores on their exams in foundational courses, which is reflected ultimately on standardized tests. Faculty note that "these modified foundational courses enable students to gain strong conceptual mastery in the course of their freshman and sophomore years, which is foundational for more advanced coursework in the sciences and mathematics." This strategy is especially important since "students take more traditional science and mathematics courses after their sophomore year." Thus, students enrolled in the traditional courses are able to "perform at a competitive level — without crutches" (Personal Communication, J.W. Carmichael, July 2005 and January 2010; Carmichael et al. 1993; Carmichael et al. 1988; Dawson 2005).

A Learner-Centered Environment

Matriculating students with strong high school GPAs and ACT/SAT scores, and with the intent to major in Biology-premedical, Chemistry-Premedical, or Psychology-Premedical, are invited to participate in the only pre-freshman summer program offered by the premedical staff — the Howard Hughes Biomedical Scholar Summer Program (HHBSSP). (There is no separate application for this program. Participants are selected from students who apply to attend Xavier.) This program gives students the opportunity to complete the first half of General Chemistry (Chem 1010) lecture the summer before their first semester of college. Students earn three hours of academic credit for this course and are permitted to take the second half of this course (Chem 1020) in the fall semester of their freshman year. During this five week program (which begins the last week in June and ends the first week in August), students are expected to attend all classes from 7:30 am to 5 pm, Monday to Friday and are required to participate in daily lectures by XU's Chemistry faculty; daily two-hour tutorial sessions conducted by their "mentor," who faculty describe as a high achieving XU sophomore who previously completed the program and is able to interact effectively with incoming students. Students are also required to attend a daily two-hour drill (recitation) class conducted by an upper-level science major, again a high achieving student with conceptual mastery in General Chemistry and able to conduct the drill classes. During drills, students are expected to have completed their chemistry homework; take quizzes on concepts covered in previous lectures and general vocabulary words; participate in skill building modules which emphasize review of mathematical concepts that are foundational to chemistry; and construct ball-and-stick models of common molecules designed to improve their ability to visualize in three dimensions. It is also mandatory for students to attend a two-hour study hall supervised by a faculty member (Carmichael and Sevenair 1991).

The premedical director suggests that the HHBSSP is especially "beneficial to students who hope to enter medical school after their junior year at Xavier through one of the Accelerated Premedical Programs." Additionally, it enables students to enroll in advanced courses or to reduce their course load during demanding semesters (such as those in which they have to prepare for the MCATs), when they have completed this course during their pre-freshman summer.

The integration of vocabulary quizzes in students' course work is a unique feature of XU's premedical program. Faculty are clear that the level of reading demanded of students in freshman biology and chemistry necessitate that premedical students know and understand approximately forty to eighty general vocabulary words on a weekly basis throughout the academic year. Students are tested weekly on these words. These vocabulary grades are considered just as important as those students receive from their subject matter exams. Additionally, the premedical faculty consistently integrate questions from the MCAT into students' subject matter exams. This strategy serves several purposes for faculty and students in that it: (1) keeps faculty abreast of content changes in the MCAT; (2) helps faculty to expose students early and often to how questions are phrased in the MCAT; and (3) frequently reminds students of the importance of developing strong vocabulary and verbal reasoning skills. Carmichael suggests that his students do well on the verbal section because he expects and encourages them to read books and magazines weekly and to maintain an active reading schedule in the summer.

A Community-Centered Environment

With regard to the community of learners within the premedical program itself, students are exposed to more than just better designed foundational courses. They are expected and encouraged to work closely with core faculty members. The premedical director asserts that "this is not difficult for students to do since most have declared a major upon admittance to XU and are assigned an academic advisor in their department. Students enrolled in freshman biology and chemistry are expected to maintain current records of their grades, which are signed weekly by their academic advisor. Students also receive points for keeping an up-to-date record of their grades."

Students enrolled in foundational science and mathematics courses have access to a tutoring center, located in the premedical offices. Upper level students who have previously taken the same courses and performed well, provide tutoring services for freshman and sophomore students. The premedical director indicates that given the standardization of content across foundational courses, "training tutors to assist students is a straightforward task." This standardization thus enables tutors to more effectively provide assistance, which students seek early and often (personal communication, J.W. Carmichael, July 2005 and January, 2010).

Additional support is available via the Biomedical Honor Corp (BHC) program for freshman students who are interested specifically in careers (i.e., as dentists, optometrists, physicians, podiatrists, and veterinarians) in the biomedical sciences. (The BHC is not a summer program but one that operates from August–April of students' freshman year. It is also a program is for freshman students—those students in other phases of their trajectories do not qualify.) There is not a separate application process for this program; rather all students are considered for admission when they apply to the university. In order to be invited to participate in this program, students need to have ACT composite scores of 20 or higher (combined SAT scores of 930 or higher), and high school GPAs of 3.0 or higher in core content courses (mathematics, the sciences, English and the social sciences). The premedical offices' current internal analysis reinforces a past study which suggests that over half of the freshman students majoring in biology, chemistry or psychology premedical, are selected to participate in the BHC (Carmichael et al., 1988). Second semester freshman students already in the premedical program must have a cumulative GPA of 2.75 or higher and meet the criteria for interest in the biomedical sciences in order to be considered for the program. Incoming freshman students with potential and interest in the biomedical sciences but who do not meet the grade/ACT criteria, are supported through a parallel program (personal communication, J.W. Carmichael, July 2005).

The BHC, funded by the Howard Hughes Biomedical Institute, focuses on preparing students for graduate and professional study in the biomedical sciences. In this program, students (1) participate in seminars by professionals with terminal degrees, including PhD, MD, DDS; (2) are exposed early and often to the range of available health professions and graduate programs; (3) receive detailed assistance in preparing applications for health professions schools and graduate programs; (4) receive assistance in preparing for the Graduate Record Exam (GRE), Medical College Admissions Test (MCAT), and Dental Admissions Test (DAT); (5) receive assistance in finding summer jobs and/or positions in programs that exposes them to the demands and opportunities of a career in the biomedical sciences; and (6) receive assistance in improving test-taking and note-taking skills. Activities related to improving students' test-taking and note-taking skills are integrated into their biology and chemistry courses. For example, time is allocated during certain lectures to expose students to MCAT and GRE questions, and for instruction in writing career essays and curriculum vitaes. Additionally, students are exposed to high performing upper level premedical students in biology and chemistry through social events and other opportunities. Faculty assert that given the critical nature of the freshman year for many underrepresented students, their "academic progression is thoroughly monitored to ensure that they are not derailed by personal or academic difficulties." Interviews with the premedical director and his colleagues indicate that many BHC participants are admitted into professional and medical schools. That is, "more than three times as many of a wider range of students (those from the top 20 percent of African Americans nationally) who enter Xavier University as biology or chemistry majors persevere and gain entry into biological science graduate or professional schools" (Carmichael et al.1988).

Additionally, students majoring in biology and chemistry are provided information about the health professions the moment they begin their freshman year. Students indicate that they "are given lots of opportunities to meet with people who make presentations and recruit on campus." Students note that this strategy sensitizes them, early and often, "to entrance requirements for graduate or health professional school, the application process," and potential careers.

Thus, students at all phases of study in XU's premedical program are given detailed, step-by-step information on what to expect, prepare for, and how to conduct themselves as they progress toward further study in the health professions. Freshman students in particular are expected to attend a series of approximately twenty group workshops/advising sessions over the academic year that are geared specifically for them. In these forums (which are conducted by the assistant premedical advisor), for example, students are given information regarding careers in the health professions, summer premedical and research opportunity programs, instructions for writing a curriculum vitae, and instructions for writing a career essay. This structure demonstrates that the academic and practical work in which students are expected to engage, are reinforced not only in and out of the classroom, but also throughout students' trajectory in the premedical program.

Sophomore students, for example, are expected to attend three workshops in the course of the academic year. These workshops/advising sessions focus on (1) student' self-assessment of their progress, grade-wise, toward entry into their desired field; (2) summer premedical and research opportunity programs; and (3) the procedures for early admissions at Tulane and the University of Rochester. Students interested in the early admission program are assisted throughout the application process by the premedical director, faculty and staff. For example, students indicate that their "applications are proof-read; interviews with the faculty selection committee are arranged; and applications are submitted to both the University of Rochester and Tulane in a timely manner." Additionally, if applications for summer premedical and research opportunities are available, they are scanned so students are able to print copies in the Premedical Office. This assistance has enabled approximately 13–15 percent of Biology, Chemistry, or Psychology-Premedical students to participate in such programs on a consistent basis. The premedical staff assist students interested in summer programs by proof-reading their applications and providing relevant feedback. Additionally, students are made aware of peers who have previously worked on particular research projects. They are encouraged to contact these students, who can and do serve as mentors.

Students who are juniors are given an overview (in early September) of tasks they need to do throughout the year in preparation for applying to schools in the health professions. They are also provided with templates to craft and update their career essays and curriculum vitas. Students indicate that "the premedical staff helps us with editing and finalizing our essays and CVs. We also meet on a one to one basis with the staff to discuss if we have prepared and submitted all of our materials. We also talk about which faculty will provide recommendations and which schools we will apply to." Students also indicate that they "make plans to take preparation courses for the MCAT." Both Princeton Review and Kaplan have arrangements with the premedical staff to provide MCAT preparation courses. Additionally, students are often reminded, via email and verbally, to remain focused and on task. Students also note that their "parents know if [they are] making progress or not." By the time students become seniors, they would have already applied (the summer before their senior year) to health professions schools. Seniors are thus individually assisted as needed.

Community of Faculty Learners—Science Education Research Group (SERG)

In addition to the pervasive supports and iterative curriculum modifications in which the premedical faculty are engaged, they have also organized themselves into a group called the Science Education Research Group (SERG). The premedical director indicated that in the early stages of developing the premedical program, SERG, comprised of faculty members in biology, chemistry, mathematics, and physics, "met on a weekly basis to assess whether students are indeed learning course content and if not, to evaluate their teaching methodology and effectiveness and/or pedagogical approach. [They] strategize and self-correct constantly in efforts to refine freshman and sophomore courses. The summer enrichment programs, originally within our scope is now integrated within the university. SERG is able to strategize because [they] know [their] students' cumulative GPA at XU, whether students have changed their major, graduated, entered a health professions school, etc. These monitoring strategies enable [them] to assess student persistence, retention and attrition rates and to address quickly any emerging issues or challenges." The premedical director also noted that the premedical's faculty respect for each other, and the resulting support and camaraderie inherent in SERG has enabled it to maintain its focus and commitment to student achievement. He acknowledges however, that one potential challenge to the premedical program is recruiting and maintaining a core group of faculty members with a similar sense of commitment and level of dedication. This is a particularly weighty concern "since XU faculty are not highly compensated for their heavy course loads — the premedical faculty can teach up to five courses per semester — when compared with other colleges/universities" (J.W. Carmichael, personal communication, Xavier University, July 2005).

CONCLUSION

The significance of preparing students, including underrepresented students, for enrollment in and graduation from medical school can be established on many levels. On a macro level, for example, the United States is in the midst of debates concerning the affordability of, and access to, quality health care as evidenced by current Supreme Court deliberations regarding the constitutionality of one of the Patient Protection and Affordable Care Act (ACA) requirements, which stipulates that individuals purchase health insurance. (The ACA was signed into law by President Obama in 2010.) These debates bring other issues and challenges to the fore; including an anticipated shortage of 124,000 physicians by 2025; and both an increasing and aging population who will not only live longer but also require more medical care (AAMC, 2008; Census Bureau 2010).

The findings from this study and current work in increasing access for underrepresented students in the health professions, suggest several levels of ideas for policymakers and educators to consider in preventing anticipated physician shortages (Cohen, Gabriel and Terrell 2002). At the higher education level, the focus of the premedical program at Xavier University on exit rather than entrance criteria suggests the importance of reconceptualizing the curriculum, teaching, assessment and learning in foundational courses. This strategy is challenging however, when we consider existing incentive structures in most American higher education institutions. That is, successful teaching is not consistently rewarded, often resulting in large numbers of students in entry-level courses being taught by less experienced and/or effective faculty and teaching assistants (Bridglall, Hrabowski and Maton this volume; Carmichael et al. 1993; personal communication, J.W. Carmichael, July 2005 and January 2010; Hurtado et al. 2009).

Other considerations for policymakers include (1) providing supports for conceptualizing and designing interventions that cultivate a pipeline of students (starting at the elementary and/or middle school level) interested in the health professions; (2) reducing the drop out/attrition rates of high school students; (3) increasing the proportion of underrepresented students who are prepared for and enroll in college; and (4) providing access to financial capital for high school and college graduates to attend college and medical school, respectively (Cooper 2003). Implicit in these ideas is the centrality of accurate and relevant information, creative strategies, and committed leadership which become particularly salient for students who access higher education institutions vis-a-vis multiple pathways, including public and private colleges and universities.

III

Research and Policy Implications

Chapter Six

Recommendations and Policy Implications

INTRODUCTION

The overarching emphasis of this study hinged on exploring and understanding how institutional contexts, particularly those that are selective, promote student persistence, learning and completion on their campus. Toward this end, three discrete programs were examined; namely the Meyerhoff Scholars Program at the University of Maryland, Baltimore County; the Premedical Program at Xavier University in New Orleans; and the Opportunity Programs at Skidmore College in Saratoga Springs, New York. One of the themes resonating across the three programs is the collective responsibility for student learning and development. This institutional ethos undergirds the targeted and sustained allocation of resources that ultimately enables students to perform academically at high levels.

We are reminded at this juncture however, of the pivotal roles played by the founders of UMBCs Meyerhoff Scholars Program, XU's Premedical Program, and Skidmore's Opportunity Programs. Indeed, the vision and focused work of Drs. Hrabowski, Carmichael, Layden and Solomon and their colleagues and staff at their respective institutions, is considered integral to their program and institution success. Even so, these individuals and their colleagues have taken steps to institutionalize their programs independent of their continued involvement. With the recognition that individual leadership, vision and commitment play salient roles in these programs' success, this chapter concludes with a set of general recommendations, culled from the analysis of these three programs (and substantiated in the literature), which have implications for higher education. Importantly, the implementation/adaptation of these recommendations will necessarily vary, depending on the particular institutional context and culture. However, a particular recommendation by itself may not produce substantial differences with regard to student learning and development (Kuh et al. 2010). Rather, it is important to consider implementing (and consistently evaluating for effectiveness), a constellation of integrated activities given differing institutional contexts and student needs (Collins 2001; Fleming 2012; Pascarella and Terenzini 2005; Rhatigan and Schuh 2003). In this vein, the recommendations are categorized under institutional commitment to students; supports for their education; and the social and intellectual learning communities that promote their achievement, retention and completion in higher education.

INSTITUTIONAL COMMITMENT TO STUDENTS

It is increasingly apparent that an institution's focus on student learning and development must be reflected in its mission, vision, values and culture (Arum and Roksa 2011; Bowen, Chingos and McPherson 2009; Kuh et al. 2010). Solomon and Layden (Opportunity Program Summer Academic Institute Lecture and Discussion, Skidmore College, July 2011) articulate these values within the context of discussions regarding the purpose of education. That is, these teacher-scholars and architects of the current Opportunity Program at Skidmore College, suggest that education comprise five components (including socialization, acquisition of facts and skills, critical thinking and aesthetic awareness, moral courage, and the reconstruction of personal experience in the service of maximizing unique individual potential), which are all necessary but not sufficient. These concepts however, are not simply articulated but actually integrated and manifested in all work done for and with students, often beginning with students' first contact with Skidmore College. The significance of these five elements of education, are explicitly articulated in the first lecture to which students are exposed and in subsequent discussion sections led by faculty and staff. Solomon and colleagues emphasize that despite the "shift in the onus of responsibility at college," OP faculty and staff "view themselves as teachers and will not leave students out there" (Solomon and Layden, Opportunity Program Summer Academic Institute Lecture and Discussion, Skidmore College, July 2011).

This explicit institutional commitment to students is also apparent in the Meyerhoff Scholars Program at UMBC and the premedical program at Xavier University. At UMBC, Hrabowski and his faculty and staff speak of student achievement as an institutional priority, not a minority issue; and at XU, Carmichael and his colleagues and staff, speak of a focus on preparing students to meet exit criteria rather than entrance requirements/criteria. That is, if students want to become doctors, it is their job to prepare them to meet the requirements and preparation expected of applicants to medical school.

This institutional commitment to students result in the admission of a critical mass of academically motivated students, including underrepresented students and women, who are provided with comprehensive financial aid that reduces students' financial concerns and increases their ability to focus on attaining conceptual mastery in their course work.

Creating a Critical Mass of Academically Motivated Students, Including Women and Underrepresented Students

The literature suggests that being one of few underrepresented students can be psychologically, academically and socially isolating (Gandara 1999; Miller 1995; Thayer 2000). Indeed, the absence of academically and socially supportive peers with whom a student can share his or her self-doubts, and/or seek academic help without fear of reinforcing extant stereotypes about ethnic inferiority, places students at risk of marginalization (Steele, Spencer and Aronson 2002). Extant evidence suggests that these students are much more likely to underachieve academically or leave the university system (Aronson, Fried and Good 2002; Aronson and McGlone 2009). An emphasis on creating a critical mass of academically motivated women and underrepresented students who have access to and substantive contact with faculty outside of the classroom, and mentoring relationships with faculty (including with minority faculty), seem to increase the likelihood of student persistence and academic achievement (Gladieux and Swail 2000; Maton, Hrabowski and Schmitt 2000; Swail 2002).

It is informative at this juncture, to consider the implications of gender, particularly in the STEM disciplines. A recent AAUW report (Hill, Corbett and St. Rose 2010, xiv) entitled *Why so few? Women in Science, Technology, Engineering and Mathematics* suggests that although approximately "as many girls as boys leave high school prepared to pursue science and engineering majors in college…fewer women than men pursue these majors." At the higher education level, women who do take courses in these fields tend to have lower rates of persistence, retention and completion. Hill and colleagues (2010) suggest that this underrepresentation of women in STEM is influenced by social and environmental factors. On the K–12 level, the literature notes that when girls are told by their parents and teachers that increased experience and learning with math will help them to become more competent, girls tend to excel in mathematics and may be more likely to have future plans to persist in the discipline (Dweck 2006, 2008). This finding is particularly important in that it can help to dispel negative stereotypes about whether girls have the capacity for the study of mathematics, and positively encourage girls' interest in the sciences and math (Aronson, Fried and Good 2002; Good, Aronson and Harder 2008).

In addition to the issues related to negative stereotypes, girls' self-assessment of their mathematical abilities tend to be lower than those of boys with similar mathematical achievements (Correll 2001, 2004; Good, Rattan and Dweck 2009). This phenomenon results in fewer girls than boys who aspire to careers in STEM despite excellent academic performance as evidenced by strong grades and test scores (Hill, Corbett and St. Rose 2010). Hill and colleagues (2010, xvi) also emphasize the importance of providing appropriate supports for girls to learn spatial skills, which many consider as pivotal for success in engineering and other scientific fields (Baenninger and Newcombe 1989). Supports of this nature can help girls not only to develop skills in this important area, but also the confidence and envisioning of possible future selves in STEM careers. On the college and university level, the issues and challenges facing women include a dearth of female faculty members (Hill, Corbett and St. Rose 2010). This dynamic may result from female professors who do not find academia to be supportive or satisfying and thus may leave earlier in their careers than male peers (Ginther and Khan 2006; Kulis, Sicotte and Collins 2002; Massachusetts Institute of Technology 1999). This dissatisfaction may also be compounded by the idea that math and the sciences are predominantly "masculine" disciplines; whereas the humanities and the arts are more "feminine." These biases may precipitate negative perceptions of women in "male" disciplines, further impacting whether they are perceived as likable and/or competent (Holmes and O'Connell 2003).

When we consider current work in understanding the phenomenon of the underrepresentation of women and underrepresented students in STEM disciplines, several ideas for policymakers and educators to consider emerge. These include (1) improving the academic preparation of girls and underrepresented students in mathematics and the sciences; (2) helping secondary teachers understand the demands of undergraduate academic work in STEM fields; (3) providing students with a better introduction to academic requirements; (4) strengthening incoming students' ability to conceptually understand calculus and the sciences; and (5) offering more support for women and underrepresented students on campus, including adopting new instructional strategies and providing more role models and mentors. On a practical level, this includes: 1) crafting, implementing and evaluating comprehensive student orientation programs; including pre-freshman/transition interventions; and 2) providing targeted support throughout students' academic trajectories. These ideas are considered in more detail below.

Provide Comprehensive Financial Support

In deliberate attempts to increase student persistence and reduce the negative impact of inadequate finances on underrepresented students' academic achievement and completion (St. John 2000) of rigorous study in the sciences, engineering and the social sciences, students in the three programs are provided with full or partial scholarships. In the Meyerhoff Program, for example, financial aid is contingent on consistently high GPAs. Bowen and colleagues (2009) suggest that students in selective universities are more likely to receive generous financial aid than their peers elsewhere. Additionally, the research, mentoring and work opportunities provided by faculty, particularly in the sciences and engineering, can promote student participation with and engagement in with the academic process; hence moving them toward eventual degree completion (Bowen, Chingos and McPherson 2009).

EDUCATIONAL COMMITMENT TO STUDENTS

Given the importance of actively conceptualizing and structuring supports and learning opportunities for students whose standardized test scores and high school GPAs can under- or over-predict their achievement trajectories, an integrated approach that emphasizes the nurturance of talent and addresses the under- and over-prediction phenomenon is necessary and essential. Toward this end, the inputs, processes, and learning contexts of the MSP, OP and XU's premedical program enable the development of high achieving students who are academically and socially integrated, and have developed knowledge and skills as a result of targeted support, motivation, monitoring and advising. The following strengths-based, theoretically driven practices are foundational to these programs' success.

Require Student Participation in Pre-Freshman Transitional/Bridge Interventions

In each of the three programs, students' attendance in a required pre-freshman summer transitional intervention is one of the venues for socializing them to the explicit and tacit academic and social expectations of the college or university (Maton, Hrabowski and Schmitt 2000). In addition to an emphasis on content mastery in courses taken (including mathematics, the sciences, writing, etc.), the summer bridge component gives special attention to promoting strong work ethic, discipline, teamwork and the cultivation of trust between and among students, staff and faculty. Students also register for the fall and begin working with a team of advisers and mentors with whom they will continue throughout the academic year. The comprehensive support of students within a specific structure has been shown to increase their sense of belonging in the campus community (Flowers 2004; Strayhorn 2011) and enable their academic and social integration (Kuh et al. 2010), outcomes vital to these three institutions.

Iteratively Study and Refine the Curriculum

As noted in their respective chapters, faculty and staff members from differ- ent academic departments collaborate on a consistent basis to discuss student progress and align their curriculum to reinforce conceptual mastery. A focused emphasis on student learning and development is demonstrated by the faculty's commitment to continued study of their curricula in their particular discipline (and across disciplines), including the sciences, mathematics, engineering, technology, the social sciences and humanities. Faculty, for example, make deliberate attempts to: (1) weigh the importance of certain concepts in their discipline; (2) determine whether and how these ideas should be taught and reinforced; and (3) identify aspects of the knowledge base that require more time and concentrated study to internalize. The data also demonstrate the deeply integral nature and active implementation of several principles of learning in how knowledge (curriculum and instruction) is organized and student learning monitored. That is, these programs (1) structure knowledge around the major concepts and organizing principles of particular disciplines, including psychology, biology, chemistry, mathematics and physics (a knowledge-centered environment); (2) structures and shapes student learning around particular tasks and activities (a learner-centered environment); and (3) academically and socially supports students' capacity to learn with understanding vis-à-vis learning communities at many levels (a community-centered environment). Thus, the rigor of the curriculum, and its implementation and iterative evaluation, is not by happenstance.

Integrate Diverse Perspectives within the Curriculum

Additionally, with the understanding that exposure to diverse ways of thinking, through both the curriculum and interactions with peers from various backgrounds, is just as important as structural diversity, faculty and staff in the three programs have also made substantive attempts to integrate diverse perspectives in the curriculum (Hurtado et al. 2003; Umbach and Kuh 2006). This practice; aimed at enabling students to consider the diverse experiences of others in open and positive ways; tends to facilitate more nuanced and complex ways of interacting and responding to others. Kuh and Umbach (2005) indicate that students with more exposure to diverse perspectives appear to enjoy more supportive environments; opportunities for participation and collaboration; and higher levels of academic challenge. These efforts are considered essential in enabling students' steady advancement in their fields vis-à-vis learned habits of mind that, over time, become foundational in pursuing excellence (Kuh et al. 2010).

Increase Student Awareness of the Curriculums' Rigor

Students in the MSP, Skidmore's OP and XU's premedical program are exposed to curriculum that is rigorous and demanding. This approach is balanced with student awareness of the curriculum's specific requirements, which are made clear early and often (Barton 2003). In the MSP, for example, faculty and more advanced students share examples of exemplary work—a test bank of former exams and essays are available to students. Additionally, students who earn a grade of C or below in foundational courses, are required to retake the particular course and earn at least a grade of B. With the understanding that challenging students to achieve at high levels is a complex task, the teaching and learning of the curriculum (in each program), is supplemented with peer study groups and tutoring to ensure that difficult concepts are conceptually mastered and can be practically applied.

Create and Sustain Teaching and Learning Centers

Structural resources provided to faculty in support of students' academic learning, including teaching and learning centers, are directly associated with student' cognitive gains (Kuglemass and Ready 2010). These centers can reinforce the ideas detailed above, namely faculty collaborative efforts in studying and refining the curriculum within and across departments, and informing the integration of diverse perspectives within the curriculum. These centers can also serve as the catalyst for pedagogical innovation by providing seed funding for efforts and ideas to improve teaching and learning, and institution-wide recognition of faculty engaged in this work (Kuh et al. 2010).

Assign the Best Faculty to Teach Freshman Courses

Bowen and colleagues (2009) and others (Arum and Roksa 2011; Kuh et al. 2010) remind us that often, students' contact with their institution happens mainly through their classrooms. This provides faculty members with important opportunities to not only facilitate student learning and success but also recognize those who may be having academic or personal difficulties in meeting expectations. In providing constructive feedback to students, faculty and staff in the MSP, Skidmore's OP and XU's premedical program, often begin by noting the particular strengths in students work before identifying areas in which the work can improve. This strategy assists faculty and staff in maintaining student confidence, persistence and motivation. The higher attrition rates for freshman and sophomore students suggest to the faculty and staff in these programs, that underrepresented students are more sensitive to teaching quality than majority students from more advantaged backgrounds. As a result, freshman students are taught by tenured and tenure track faculty who are considered effective; who interact substantively with students; and who can play vitally important roles in engaging, encouraging and guiding students in seeking and employing appropriate resources at the university and department level. This approach ensures that the crucial freshman and sophomore years are successful experiences for students not only academically, but also developmentally.

Comprehensively Monitor, Mentor, and Advise Students throughout their Undergraduate Career Rather Than Emphasizing Only the Freshman Year

Each of the three programs provides support throughout students' academic trajectories rather than focus exclusively on the freshman year as the most critical point in time. Indeed, continuous monitoring and the provision of services to students throughout their undergraduate career is an institutionalized aspect of these programs. The overarching assumption is that given the referenced support and resources, competitively selected underrepresented students are capable of succeeding in the social sciences, humanities and STEM fields. These strategies, which are deliberate attempts at addressing the under- and over- prediction phenomenon, are predicated on research-based approaches that emphasize motivating *and* expecting academic excellence from students, including those who are underrepresented. In this vein, Hrabowski has observed certain characteristics prevalent among students who succeed, most notably: (1) the ability to read well, take notes, and study; (2) a willingness to go to class regularly; (3) willingness to seek and take advice; (4) "fire in the belly" — a passion for learning and excelling; and (5) the resilience to recover and learn from mistakes and setbacks.

Use Data to Strategically Inform Goals and Efforts

The strategies noted above, namely pre-freshman transitional interventions, curriculum modification that emphasize conceptual mastery and the garnering of diverse perspectives, teaching and learning centers that encourage modifications in curriculum and instruction, and focused efforts on comprehensive mentoring, monitoring and advising students, are anchored in the judicious use of data. That is, the faculty, staff and institutional leadership associated with each of the three programs, actively study student and course data and are thus aware of the effect of policies and practices on teaching and learning. This knowledge serves as the basis for maintaining programmatic activities that are effective, and modifying or eliminating those that are less so. In addition to collecting data on the teaching and learning process, faculty and staff in each of the three programs are also very much aware of who their students are and their particular needs; information that emerges in the course of interaction with students and their active participation in their respective learning communities (Carini, Kuh and Klein 2004).

Institutional Commitment to Students' Intellectual and Social Development

In addition to important aspects of institutional commitment to students and to their education, is an equally salient emphasis on providing leaning communities/environments that support student effort (Smith et al. 2004). On another level (and as noted in their respective chapters), UMBC, Skidmore College and Xavier University actively engage with their surrounding community. This enables collaborations with community organizations and secondary education faculty, for example, that can result in community service opportunities for students and the revising of secondary curricula, for example, that are aligned with the knowledge and skills colleges expect from high school graduates.

Create and Sustain Learning Communities

In the MSP, OP and XU's premedical program, students are offered access to relevant and appropriate resources, combined with high expectations that they will avail themselves of these resources. These practices are associated with increased student engagement and college completion (Fleming 2012; Kuh et al. 2010; Bowen, Chingos and McPherson 2009). Tinto (1993) and others (Just 1999; Nagda et al. 1998; Smith et al. 2004), reminds us that supportive learning communities are especially important for low-income students and those who are underrepresented. That is, underrepresented students in predominantly majority campuses can benefit from structures and supports as they engage in establishing themselves academically and otherwise. These resources can take the form of providing appropriate academic advising and encouraging students to actively engage in help-seeking behaviors (strategies prevalent across each of the three programs). It also means affording opportunities for mentoring, including peer mentoring, which faculty and staff initiate and supervise (Carini, Kuh and Klein 2004). The provision of adequate physical spaces in which these activities are conducted is also an integral part of the resources students receive. Students in each of the three programs are thus integrated in learning communities that are inclusive, and in which they can participate in the co-construction of their academic trajectories. Supports such as these can guard against student perceptions of marginality and their possible attrition, concerns that are increasingly salient in the higher education context (Maton et al. 2008; Swail 2002; Swail, Redd and Perna 2003).

Provide Institutional Support for Cumulative Knowledge and Skill Development

Faculty and staff in each of the three programs operate on the assumption that their students are intellectually competent and motivated. They recognize however, that some students may not have adequate or the requisite preparation for success in certain foundational courses. Correcting for these gaps in knowledge or understanding becomes the focus of faculty, peer and tutorial interventions. The peer effects of peer study groups and tutors, for example, are associated with student perceptions that they are part of learning contexts that are effective and positive educational outcomes, such as timely completion/graduation (Bowen, Chingos and McPherson 2009; Swail, Redd and Perna 2003). Given the importance thus, of exposure to highly capable peers, supports of this nature are integrated in the course of students' undergraduate lives in each of the three programs. This approach appears to work particularly well for student persistence and completion in the STEM disciplines emphasized by the MSP and XU's premedical program.

Encourage Student-Faculty Interactions

Faculty-student interaction is positively associated with student success (Lundberg and Schreiner 2004; Kuh 2003). Faculty and students in the three programs confer, early and often, over grades, assignments and career plans. Students also work closely with faculty as peer mentors and research associates.

Enlist Residential Services in the Support of Students

Resident life staff members, who work closely with program staff and faculty, are considered integral in each of the three programs. In their official capacities as campus staff who are concerned with maintaining student safety and providing students with relevant information regarding counseling, relationships, academic and social activities, for example, resident life staff members can determine how students spend their time and apprise faculty, staff and academic advisors in focused efforts to assist struggling students.

Encourage Service to the Community

In addition to an emphasis on academic and social supports for students, faculty and staff in each of the three programs maintain ties with community organizations that are leveraged to provide students with opportunities for community service, internships and tutoring, for example. These opportunities serve several purposes in that they (1) promote coherence between students' conceptual and practical knowledge, and (2) enable students to think of and apply their knowledge in ways that can benefit others (Fleming 2012; Kuh et al. 2010; Lotkowski, Robbins and Noeth 2004).

CONCLUSION

The set of recommendations detailed above offers a framework for how the University of Maryland, Baltimore County, Xavier University in New Orleans, and Skidmore College in Saratoga Springs, New York, views the issues confronting their institutions and their students. Their commitment to not only students' welfare but also to their students' education; is apparent in their considered allocation of resources and the high expectations to which all faculty, staff and students are held. It is also evident in the targeted and sustained learning communities they have provided for students' intellectual and social development. The study of these three programs and others throughout the country (Battaglini 2004; Fleming 2012; Kuh et al. 2010; Smith 1998; Smith et al. 2004; Swail 2000); are attempts to understand and disseminate lessons learned; further refine practical knowledge; and codify best practices for others to emulate. The unwavering commitment of administrators, faculty, and staff at UMBC, Xavier University and Skidmore College, to student academic excellence and achievement prompts them to consistently consider how they can enable their students, including underrepresented students and women, to develop the ability to compete successfully for admission to graduate school and to prepare for productive careers; and develop and implement strategies to increase the presence of underrepresented students and women at the highest levels of achievement in society, e.g., physicians, research scientists and university professors. This commitment is especially significant and relevant given the moderate success of various programs at increasing the achievement of underrepresented students and women in engineering, and mathematics achievement at the undergraduate level and relatively little success at the graduate level. Hrabowski believes that only by creating and supporting a larger pool of high-achieving minority students can they ultimately increase the number of underrepresented faculty in the nation's colleges and universities and the number who become leading professionals.

Cultivating an institutional ethos that parallels that of the three programs will increasingly become a necessity when we consider the conceptual and talent age in which we find ourselves. Friedman (2006) suggests that this age can be traced to a more than two decades long convergence of technological, social and economic trends that are reverberating around the world. These forces are simultaneously integrating the world and leveling the playing field for millions of people, allowing many to collaborate, compete and innovate in unique ways. The flexible movement of ideas and information enabled by rapidly evolving communication technologies, for instance, has important implications for how knowledge is conceptualized, produced and utilized in a world in which traditional boundaries are called into question (Friedman 2006; Rizvi and Lingard 2009). Equally significant, these emerging shifts in boundaries and expectations are changing the nature of the social contract, making it imperative that nation states cultivate more egalitarian societies by enabling their citizens to not only acquire the tools and experiences that will promote their role as citizens and employability as adapters, synthesizers and collaborators in the flat world, but also take responsibility for their own lives, careers and economic security (Friedman 2006). Friedman (2006) reminds us that the United States has encountered similar challenges in transitioning from an agricultural society 150 years ago to an industrial one; yet, by mandating secondary education in the early twentieth century, the living standards for many Americans increased. Indeed, from 1900 to 1975, the increase in students who attended high school and the evolution of higher education into a universal system resulted in significant educational progress for the United States and higher wage premiums earned by college graduates (Goldin and Katz 2008).

Unfortunately (as noted in earlier chapters), low levels of human capital development in the United States have been the norm since 1975 and appears to be further compounded by the existence of a numbers gap, a knowledge gap (education gaps both *between* high and low performing students and *within* these student populations), an ambition gap, a funding gap and an infrastructure gap (Friedman 2006). Growing debates regarding these gaps reflects several concerns, including the idea that the United States will be increasingly unable to effectively compete in the global marketplace if these gaps are not systematically addressed. The work of administrators, faculty and staff in each of the three programs provides important and usable strategies for addressing these challenges. It also makes clear that these issues and challenges are not intractable (Bowen, Chingos and McPherson 2009; Seidman 2005). Thus, considerations of the above strategies and similar studies can begin to lay the groundwork for the conceptualization, implementation and evaluation of relevant and appropriate policies and interventions to address the underrepresentation of women and underrepresented students in STEM and other disciplines. When done on several fronts, including structural, organizational, cultural and environmental, we can begin to address the pervasive and persistent dilemmas of low completion rates and increases in time to degree for our nation's students.

Appendix A

Overview of the Study

The study of the Meyerhoff Scholars Program at the University of Maryland, Baltimore County; the Premedical Program at Xavier University in New Orleans; and the Opportunity Programs at Skidmore College in Saratoga Springs, New York, contributes to a decades long tradition of ethnographic and mixed-methods studies of institutions, programs and students in higher education (Beyer, Gillmore and Fisher 2007; Hrabowski, Maton and Grief 1998; Hrabowski et al. 2002; Kuh et al. 2010; Lenning and Ebbers 1999; Seymour and Hewitt 1997; Smith et al. 2004). In the main, these salient multi-and single- site studies examined the factors, including institutional and personal, that influence student aspirations, motivation, persistence in their course of study and eventual degree completion. These findings provide important contextual and qualitative analysis that complement macro level studies (Bowen, Chingos and McPherson 2009; Arum and Roksa 2011). Toward this end, the study of the three programs seek to influence not only policy and practice but to also serve as a catalyst for research that is conceptualized, conducted and analyzed from a multi- and inter- disciplinary perspective. Given these aims, the within- and cross- site analysis serves to empirically anchor this work. This appendix details the study's design and analytic procedures of the qualitative data.

SELECTION OF PROGRAMS, DATA SOURCES AND COLLECTION

In the course of my graduate study at Teachers College, Columbia University, Emeritus Professor Edmund W. Gordon initiated and supported the study of the Meyerhoff Scholars Program at the University of Maryland, Baltimore County. While examining the Meyerhoff Program, we added the premedical program at Xavier University in New Orleans, to the list. Subsequent conversations with L. Scott Miller led to his suggestion to consider and integrate study of the Opportunity Programs at Skidmore College in Saratoga Springs, New York. The initial data collection work was conducted jointly with Professor Gordon. In this collaboration and subsequent research with faculty, staff and administrators at each institution, visits were planned and conducted over the course of nearly a decade.

These visits comprised of interviews (with administrators, faculty, and staff in each program and institution); focus groups (separately with students and program staff); shadowing students during the course of their day and week; observations of interactions in the dining hall, tutoring centers, classrooms; faculty meetings; and student-focused meetings; attendance at special events (viewing a film that has implications for a particular theme students are exploring; mentors' reception; graduation ceremonies; team-building exercises; community service work) that occurred during visits; collecting documents relevant to the program structure and focus; and learning about the larger institutional context in which each program was implemented. Depending on the context, all interviews and focus group discussions were either audio-taped or described in field notes. Taped interviews were transcribed verbatim and verified. Unrecorded interviews were detailed in field notes. The interviews and focus group discussions, which comprised the majority of data collected, were supplemented by other data sources, including extensive and focused field notes each researcher prepared concerning his or her observations and impressions, and relevant documents, including internal analyses, assessments and reports made available by staff in each program (Yin 2003).

In the main, we utilized the initial round of data collection to gain an awareness of the context, resources and processes of each program and institution. This enabled a growing understanding of both the implicit and explicit structures and processes inherent in each program. Subsequent conversations and visits resulted in the beginnings of program/institution specific study that considered both commonalities and differences between and across each program. In the course of this work, findings and themes (both common and program-specific) were considered and the focus of the data collection revised given our evolving understanding of each program/institution. It should be noted here that every attempt was made by the researchers to ensure that data-gathering was not conducted in an invasive or disruptive manner for students, faculty, program staff or administrative leadership.

In the course of data collection efforts in each program, we focused on exploring program outcomes vis-à-vis the program's components, which details the individual and institutional factors that influence students' persistence and completion in their course of study, pre-freshman transitional interventions; the provision of financial aid; a supportive campus climate; pervasive expectations that students will engage in help-seeking behaviors; and supports and motivation as students progress in their major of choice.

This resulted in an updated, expanded and refined study, the product of which can be seen in each program's respective chapters. Thus, the methodological framework we utilized; the "collective case study," assisted the refinement of our conceptual approach and afforded particular insight into specific ideas that iteratively informed our evolving data analysis. This strategy reinforces Stake's (1994, 237) idea that a collective case study is "not a study of the collective, but [rather] an instrumental study extended to several cases."

PARTICIPANT-ORIENTED MODEL OF EVALUATION

Given the collaborative nature of the research, we employed a participant-oriented approach to our examination of each program/institution (Cousins and Earl 1995; Fitzpatrick, Sanders and Worthen 2004; Patton 1997; Stake 1967). This strategy comprised of collaborations between researchers, program sponsors and primary stakeholders to craft both practical and constructive information to assist in relevant decision-making. This type of collaboration tends to increase stakeholder buy-in and potential utilization of evaluation results to continuously inform and improve program implementation (Chatterji and Iyengar 2009). Thus, questions of interest, related timelines and responsible personnel were jointly agreed upon.

ANALYTIC APPROACH

The analytic strategy involved an iterative approach – that is, the observational and interview/focus group data were analyzed with a view to determining emerging themes and conclusions. Although coding of the data was begun with a theoretical framework derived from the literature, we did not begin with any predetermined analytic codes or categories. That is, the analysis was "free flowing" and not "structured or rigid" (Strauss and Corbin 1998, 58). The codes themselves were derived from the data (Merriam 1998) and as Maxwell (1998) suggested, were generated inductively through the evolving, iterative coding process. This strategy confirmed that the themes, subthemes and analytic categories that eventually emerged during the analysis were empirically grounded and in alignment with the data (Miles and Huberman 1994). Thus, our first step included reviewing all of the data and recording both possible and latent patterns that might eventually materialize into codes (Goetz and LeCompte 1984; Marshall and Rossman 1999; Merriam 1998).

The second step entailed another round of thoroughly reviewing the data and applying the codes derived from the first step. Notably, a salient aspect of this step entailed recognizing disconfirming evidence in respondents' comments and related documents (Bogdan and Biklen 1997). This data however, was not neglected; rather, it was appropriately coded and analyzed.

Thirdly, the coded text was organized into categories and subcategories based on the codes established in the steps noted above. Guba and Lincoln (1981) indicate that this third step is both divergent and convergent; that is, some categories will be further refined and expanded upon while other categories and/or subcategories that are strongly related to each other will be integrated. Similarly, we anticipated that several categories and/or subcategories will be eliminated due to insufficiency of data. At the same time, new categories and ideas that were not previously identified during the initial coding phases, surfaced. Additionally, the subtle nuances in the data indicated that particular categories needed to be further refined into subcategories for a more fine-grained analysis and understanding.

This iterative process, which entailed constantly analyzing data and emerging codes and categories, can be construed as comparative analysis. In this vein, we contrasted the quotes and themes with one another in efforts to discover inherent differences and similarities (Corbin and Strauss 2008). The aim of this approach, called pattern coding, is to arrive at plausible interpretations vis-à-vis the categorization of codes into themes and constructs (Miles and Huberman 1994). This process was concluded when we arrived at adequate numbers of regularities (Lincoln and Guba 1985). Miles and Huberman (1994, 72) suggest that the grouping of codes and themes resulting from this process "often turn out to be the conceptual hooks [upon] which the analyst hangs the meatiest part of the analysis."

TRUSTWORTHINESS OF THE DATA

As our selection of data sources, data collection procedures and data analysis suggest, we engaged in focused efforts to increase the trustworthiness of the qualitative data. That is, we employed certain strategies, including member checking, triangulation, peer debriefing, and identified disconfirming evidence to ascertain credibility (Creswell and Miller 2000; Lincoln and Guba 1985). During site visits and subsequent conversations, we not only tested our preliminary and evolving hypotheses but also sought to challenge our assumptions and sometimes varying interpretations. Additionally, we continually shared drafts of the analysis and results as they became available. This strategy was extended to the eventual writing of the results for publication. The concluding chapter demonstrates, moreover, an informed awareness of the significance of recognizing commonalities that were salient across the three programs (Lincoln and Guba 1985). This approach is in line with one of the study's goals; that of meaningfully contributing to evolving policy, practice and research.

References

Allen, M. L. Bradford, D. Grimes, E. Cooper, L. Howard, and U. Howard. 1999, November. Racial group orientation and social outcomes: Summarizing relationships using meta-analysis. Paper presented at the annual meeting of the National Communication Association. Chicago IL.

Allen, Walter. 1992. "The color of success: African-American college student outcomes at predominantly White and historically Black public colleges and universities." Harvard Educational Review 62(1):26–44.

Alter, Adam, Joshua Aronson, John Darley, Cordaro Rodriguez et al. 2010. "Rising to the threat: Reducing stereotype threat by reframing the threat as a challenge." Journal of Experimental Social Psychology 46:166–171.

Anderson, Eugene, and Dongbin Kim. 2006. Increasing the success of minority students in science and technology. Washington, DC: American Council on Education.

Aronson, Joshua, Carrie Fried, and Catherine Good. 2002. "Reducing the effects of stereotype threat on African American college students by shaping theories of intelligence." Journal of Experimental Social Psychology 38(2):113–25.

Aronson, Joshua, and Matthew McGlone. 2009. "Stereotype and social identity threat." In Handbook of prejudice, stereotyping and discrimination, edited by T Nelson. New York: Guilford.

Aronson, Joshua, Michael Lustina, Catherine Good, Kellie Keough et al. 1999. "White men can't do math: Necessary and sufficient factors in stereotype threat." Journal of Experimental Social Psychology 35:29–46.

Arum, Richard, and Josipa Roksa. 2008, November. Learning to reason and communicate in college: Lessons from the CLA longitudinal project. Presented at the Social Science Research Council's conference on learning in higher education, Chicago.

Arum, Richard and Josipa Roksa. 2011. Academically adrift: Limited learning on college campuses. Chicago: The University of Chicago Press.

Asera, Rose. 2001. Calculus and Community: A History of the Emerging Scholars Program. A Report of the National Task Force on Minority High Achievement. New York: The College Board.

Association of American Medical Colleges. 2006. Nov 16. AAMC launches campaign to increase diversity in medicine: New analysis reveals growing gap between undergraduates and medical school applicants. AAMC: Washington, D.C.

American Association of Medical Colleges. 2010. Oct. 13. Medical school enrollment shows diversity gains: Number of first-time applicants also up, demonstrating interest in medicine as a career. AAMC: Washington, D.C. https://www.aamc.org/newsroom/newsreleases/2010/152932/101013.html

American Association of Medical Colleges. 2008. Diversity in Medical Education: Facts and Figures 2008. AAMC: Washington, D.C.

American Association of Medical Colleges. 2008. Policy priorities to improve the nation's health from America's medical schools and teaching hospitals. AAMC: Washington, D.C.

American Association of Medical Colleges. 2010. Diversity in the physician worksforce: Facts and Figures 2010. AAMC: Washington, D.C.

Antonio, Anthony, Mitchell Chang, Kenji Hakuta, David Kenny et al. 2004. "Effects of racial diversity on complex thinking in college students." Psychological Science 15:507–10.

Astin, Alexander. 1985. Achieving Educational Excellence. San Francisco: Jossey-Bass.

Astin, Alexander. 1993. What matters in college: Four critical years revisited. San Francisco: Jossey-Bass.

Baenninger, Maryann, and Nora Newcombe. 1989. "The role of experience in spatial test performance: A meta-analysis." Sex Roles 20(5–6):327–44.

Bailit, Howard, Allan Formicola, Kim Herbert, Judith Stavisky et al. 2005. "The origins and design of the dental pipeline program." Journal of Dental Education 69:232–238.

Bandura, Albert. 1997. Self-efficacy: The exercise of control. New York: Freeman.

Bandura, Albert. 2001. "Social cognitive theory: An agentic perspective." Annual Review of Psychology 52:1–26.

Bangert-Drowns, Robert, Chen-Lin Kulik, James Kulik, and Mary Morgan. 1991. "The instructional effect of feedback in test-like events." Review of Educational Research 61:213–238.

Barefoot, Betsy, Carrie Warnock, Michael Dickinson, Sharon Richardson et al. 1998. Exploring the evidence: Reporting outcomes of first-year seminars 2. Columbia SC: University of South Carolina.

Barton, Paul. 2003. Parsing the Achievement Gap: Baselines for Tracking Progress. Princeton: Educational Testing Service.

Battaglini, Janis. 2004. Retention and graduation rates at Maryland public four-year institutions. Annapolis, MD: Maryland Higher Education Commission. ED484153.

Bembenutty, Hefer. 2010. "Homework completion: The role of self-efficacy, delay of gratification, and self-regulatory processes." International Journal of Educational & Psychological Assessment 6(1):1–20.

DeMarrais, Kathleen, and Margaret LeCompte. 1998. The Way Schools Work: Sociological Analysis Education. White Plains NY: Longman.

Berkner, Lutz, Shirley He, and Emily Cataldi. 2002. Descriptive Summary of 1995–96 Beginning Postsecondary Students: Six Years Later (NCES 2003–151). U.S. Department of Education. Washington, DC: National Center for Education Statistics.

Beyer, Catherine, Gerald Gillmore, and Andrew Fisher. 2007. Inside the undergraduate experience: The University of Washington's Study of Undergraduate Learning. Bolton MA: Anker Publishing.

Blackwell, James. 1987. Mainstreaming outsiders: The production of black professionals. Rowman & Littlefield Publishers.

Blake, J. Herman. 1998. "The full circle: TRIO programs, higher education and the American future." The Journal of Negro Education 67(4):329–454.

Bloom, Allan. 1987. The closing of the American mind. New York: Simon & Schuster.

Bogdan, Robert, and Sari Biklen. 1997. Qualitative research for education. Boston: Allyn & Bacon.

Bok, Derek. 2003. "Closing the nagging gap in minority achievement." Chronicle of Higher Education 50: B20.

Bonsangue, Martin, and David Drew. 1995. "Increasing minority students' success in calculus." New Directions for Teaching and Learning: 23–33.

Boud, David, Ruth Cohen, and Jane Sampson. 1999. "Peer learning and assessment." Assessment and Evaluation in Higher Education 24(4):413–426.

Bouffard-Bouchard, Therese. 1990. "Influence of self-efficacy on performance in a cognitive task." Journal of Social Psychology 130(3):353–363.

Bouffard-Bouchard, Therese, Sophie Parent, and Serge Larivee. 1991. "Influence of self-efficacy on self-regulation and performance among junior and senior high-school aged students." International Journal of Behavioral Development 14:153–164.

Bourdieu, Pierre. 1986. The forms of capital. In Handbook of theory and research for the sociology of education, edited by J Richardson, 241–258. Westport: Greenwood Press.

Bowen, William, and Derek Bok. 1998. The Shape of the River: Long-Term Consequences of Considering Race in College and University Admissions. Princeton: Princeton University Press. Bowen, William, and Sarah Levin. 2003. Reclaiming the game: College sports and educational values. Princeton: Princeton University Press.

Bowen, William, Matthew Chingos, and Michael McPherson. 2009. Crossing the Finish Line: Completing College at America's Public Universities. Princeton: Princeton University Press.

Bowlby, John. 1988. A secure base: Parent-child attachment and healthy human development. USA: Basic Books.

Bowman, Barbara, M. Suzanne Donovan, and M. Susan Burns. 2001. Eager to Learn: Educating our preschoolers. Committee on Early Childhood Pedagogy. National Research Council. Commission on Behavioral and Social Sciences and Education. Washington, D.C.: National Academy Press.

Bransford, John, Ann Brown, and Rodney Cocking. 2000. How People Learn: Brain, Mind, Experience, and School. Committee on Developments in the Science of Learning. Commission on Behavioral and Social Sciences and Education. National Research Council: National Academy Press.

Bridglall, Beatrice L. 2004. Structural and individual characteristics that enable high academic achievement in underrepresented students of color. Diss. Columbia University, Teachers College.

Bridglall, Beatrice L. and Gordon, Edmund. 2004a. "The nurturance of African American scientific talent." Journal of African American History 89(4).

Bridglall, Beatrice L. and Gordon, Edmund. 2004b. Nurturing talent in underrepresented students: A study of the Meyerhoff Scholars Program at the University of Maryland, Baltimore County. Pedagogical Inquiry and Praxis, 6. New York: Institute for Urban and Minority Education, Teachers College, Columbia University and The College Board.

Bridglall, Beatrice L. Freeman Hrabowski, and Kenneth Maton. (This Volume). Preparing students for research careers: The Meyerhoff Scholars Program at the University of Maryland, Baltimore County. Lexington Books: Rowman and Littlefield Publishers.

Brophy, Jere. 1981. "Teacher praise: A functional analysis." Review of Educational Research 51: 5–32.

Brophy, Jere. 1985. "Teacher–student interaction." In Teacher expectancies, edited by J. Dusek, 303–328. Hillsdale: Erlbaum.

Brophy, Jere. 1987. "Teacher in fluencies on student achievement." American Psychologist 41: 1069–1077.

Brophy, Jere. 2006. Observational research on genetic aspects of classroom learning. In Handbook of educational psychology, 2nd Edition, edited by P. Alexander and P. Winne, 755–780. Mahwah: Lawrence Erlbaum Associates.

Brown, Ann, D. Ash, M. Rutherford, K. Nakagawa, et al. 1983. Distributed exercise in the classroom. In Distributed Cognitions: Psychological and educational considerations, edited by Gavriel Solomon, 188–228. New York: Cambridge University Press.

Brown, Ann and Joseph Campione. 1994. Guided discovery in a community of learners. In Classroom lessons: Integrating cognitive theory and classroom practices, edited by K. McGilly, 229–270. Cambridge: MIT Press.

Bryk, Anthony, Valerie Lee, and Peter Holland. 1993. Catholic schools and the common good. Cambridge: Harvard University Press.

Bryk, Anthony, and Barbara Schneider. 2002. Trust in schools: A core resource for improvement. New York: Russell Sage Foundation.

Burt, Ronald. 1997. "The contingent value of social capital." Administrative Science 42(2):339–365.

Bush, Vanevar. 1945. As we may think. The Atlantic Monthly. July.

Callan, Patrick. 2006. Measuring up 2006: The national report card on higher education. The National Center for Public Policy and Higher Education Report, 6. measuringup.highereducation.org/commentary/introduction.cfmhttp:/

Carini, Robert, George Kuh, and Stephen Klein. 2004. Student engagement and student learning: Insights from a construct validation study. Paper presented at the annual meeting of the American Educational Research Association, San Diego CA.

Carmichael, J.W., Diedre Labat, Jacqueline Hunter, Ann Privett, et al. 1993. "Minorities in the biological Sciences: The Xavier Success Story and Some Implications." Bioscience 43(8):564–569.

Carmichael, J.W., Joanne Bauer, John Sevenair, Jacqueline Hunter et al. 1986. "Predictors of first-year chemistry grades for black Americans." Journal of Chemical Education 63(4):33

Carmichael, J.W. 1976. "General chemistry by PSI at a minority institution." Journal of Chemical Education 53(12):91–792.

Carmichael, J.W., Joanne Bauer, Jacqueline Hunter, Diedre Labat, et al. 1988. "An assessment of a premedical program in terms of its ability to serve black Americans." Journal of National Medical Association 80(10):1094–1104.

Carmichael, J.W., Joanne Bauer, Jacqueline Hunter, Diedre Labat et al. 1987. "Predictors of MCAT scores for black Americans." Journal of National Medical Association 79(6):637–647.

Carmichael, J.W. and John Sevenair. 1991. "Preparing Minorities for science careers." Issues in Science and Technology: 55–60.

Carnevale, Anthony, Nicole Smith, and Michelle Melton. (2011). STEM. Center on Education and the Workplace. Georgetown University.

Carnevale, Anthony, Tamara Jayasundera, and Ban Cheah. 2012. The College Advantage: Weathering the economic storm. Center on Education and the Workplace. Georgetown University.

Castellanos, Jeanette, and Alberta Gloria. 2007. "Research considerations and theoretical application for best practices in higher education: Latina/os achieving success." Journal of Hispanic Higher Education 6(4):378–396.

Census Bureau. 2010. Current Population Reports. Series P25–1104. Population Projections of the United States by Age, Sex, Race, and Hispanic Origin 1993 to 2050. (www.census.gov/population/pop-profile/natproj.huml: downloaded August 9, 2010).

Chatterji, Madhabi and Radhika Iyengar. 2009. Profiles of 2007–2008 Entering kindergartners on comprehensive indicators of school readiness: A baseline study of the Chemung County School Readiness project. Assessment and Evaluation Research Initiative (AERI). New York: Teachers College, Columbia University.

Chemers, Martin, Li-tze Hu, and Ben Garcia. 2001. "Academic self-efficacy and first-year college student performance and adjustment." Journal of Educational Psychology 93(1):55–64.

Chi, Winny, Rita Cepeda, Melissa McLain, and Linda Hagedorn. 2007. "An investigation of critical mass: The role of Latino representation in the success of urban community college students." Research in Higher Education, 48(1):73–91.

Chickering, Arthur, and Linda Reisser. 1993. Education and identity. San Francisco: Jossey-Bass.

Chronicle of higher education. 2007. What research says about race-linked barriers to achievement. 53(39):a26–a27.

Chubin, Daryl, and Wanda Ward. 2009. Building on the BEST Principles and Evidence: A Framework for Broadening Participation. In Broadening Participation in Undergraduate Research: Fostering Excellence and Enhancing the Impact, edited by M. Boyd and J. Wesemann, 21–20. Washington, DC: Council for Undergraduate Research.

Clark, Kenneth. 1965. Dark ghetto: Dilemmas of social power. New York, NY: Harper & Row.

Clayton, Mark. 2003, November 10. College Presidents seek to close minority gap. The Christian Science Monitor, retrieved April 1, 2004, from www.csmonitor.com.

Clewell, Beatriz, Clemencia de Cohen, Nicole Deterding, and Lisa Tsui. 2006. Revitalizing the Nation's Talent Pool in STEM. Washington, DC.: Urban Institute.

Cochran-Smith, Marilyn. 1991. "Learning to teach against the grain." Harvard Educational Review 61(3):279–310.

Cochran-Smith, Marilyn, and Susan Lytle. 1999a. Relationships of knowledge and practice: Teacher learning in communities. In Review of Research in Education 24, edited by A. Iran-Nejad and C. Pearson, 251–307. Washington, DC: American Educational Research Association.

Cohen, Jordan, Barbara Gabriel, and Charles Terrell. 2002. "The case for diversity in the health care workforce." Health Affairs 21(5):90–102.

Cohen, Geoffrey, Claude Steele, and Lee Ross. 1999. "The mentor's dilemma: Providing critical feedback across the racial divide." Personality and Social Psychology Bulletin 25:1302–1318.

Cole, Stephen, and Elinor Barber. 2003. Increasing faculty diversity: The occupational choices of high-achieving students. Cambridge, MA: Oxford University Press.

Coleman, James. 1988. "Social capital in the creation of human capital." American Journal of Sociology 94:s95–s120.

Coleman, James. 1990. Equality and achievement in education. Boulder: Westview Press.

College Board, The. 1999. Reaching the top: A report of the national task force on minority achievement. New York: The College Board.

College Board, The. 2009. Coming to Our Senses: Education and the American Future. New York, New York: The College Board.

Collins, James. 2001. Good to Great. New York: HarperCollins.

Cooke, Richard, Bridgette Bewick, Michael Barkham, Margaret Bradley, et al. 2004. "Measuring, monitoring and managing the psychological well-being of first year university students." British Journal of Guidance Counselling 34(4):505–517.

Cooper, Richard. 2003. "Medical School and their applicants: An analysis." Health Affairs 22(4): 71–84.

Cooper, Laura. 2007. Why closing the research-practice gap is critical to closing student achievement gaps. Theory into Practice, 46(4):317–324.

Corbin, Juliet and Anselm Strauss. 2008. Basics of qualitative research: Techniques and procedures for developing grounded theory. Thousand Oaks CA: Sage.

Correll, Shelley. 2001. "Gender and the career choice process: The role of biased self-assessments." American Journal of Sociology 106(6):1691–1730.

Correll, Shelley. 2004. "Constraints into preferences: Gender, status, and emerging career aspirations." American Sociological Review 69(1):93–113.

Cota-Robles, Eugene. 2003. Scholarly requirements, pool size and faculty appointments in the life sciences. Lake Tahoe CA. June 16: NIH/MORE Lecture.

Council of Graduate Schools. 2009. Broadening Participation in Graduate Education.

Cousins, J. Bradley, and Lorna Earl. 1995. Participatory evaluation in education. Bristol PA. Falmer Press.

Creswell, John, and Dana Miller. 2000. "Determining validity in qualitative inquiry." Theory Into Practice 39(3):124–130.

Creswell, John, and Vicki Plano Clark. 2007. Designing and Conducting Mixed Methods Research. Thousand Oaks CA: Sage Publications.

Currie, Janet. 2005. "Health disparities and gaps in school readiness." The Future of Children 15(1):117–138.

Daempfle, Peter. 2004. "An analysis of the high attrition rates among first year college science, math and engineering majors." Journal of College Student Retention: Research, Theory and Practice 5 (1):37–52.

Darling-Hammond, Linda, and John Bransford. 2005. Preparing teachers for a changing world: What teachers should learn and be able to do. San Francisco, CA: Jossey-Bass.

Davidson, Martin, and Lynn Foster-Johnson. 2001. "Mentoring in the preparation of graduate researchers of color." Review of Educational Research 71(4): 549-574.

Dawson, George. 2005. Xavier University premedicine program's prescription for success: an interview with JW Carmichael Jr., MS, PhD. Journal of the National Medical Association 97:1294–1300.

Donato , Richard . 2004 . "Aspects of collaboration in pedagogical discourse ." Annual Review of Applied Linguistics 24:284–302 .

Donovan, M. Suzanne, John Bransford, and James Pellegrino. 1999. How people learn: Bridging research and practice. Committee on Learning Research and Educational Practice. Commission on Behavioral and Social Sciences and Education. National Research Council. Washington, DC: National Academy Press..

Dowd, Alicia, and Tarek Coury. 2004. The effect of loans on the persistence and attainment of Community College students. New York: Springer Netherlands.

Duckworth, Angela, and Martin Seligman. 2006. "Self-discipline gives girls the edge: Gender in self-discipline, grades, and achievement test scores." Journal of Educational Psychology 98(1):198–208.

Duffy, Elizabeth, and Idana Goldberg. 1998. Crafting a Class: College Admissions and Financial Aid, 1955–94. Princeton: Princeton University Press.

Dweck, Carol. 2006. Is math a gift? Beliefs that put females at risk. In Why aren't more women in science? Top researchers debate the evidence, edited by Steve Ceci and Wendy Williams, 47–55. Washington, DC: American Psychological Association.

Dweck, Carol. 2008. Mindsets and math/science achievement. New York: Carnegie Corporation of New York. Institute for Advanced Study. Commission on Mathematics and Science Education.

Educational Testing Service. 2008. Factors that can influence performance on the GRE general test 2005–2006. Princeton: Educational Testing Service.

Edwards, Thea, Barbara Smith, Danielle Watts, Charlotte Germain-Aubrey et al. 2011. Group-Advantaged Training of Research (GATOR): A Metamorphosis of Mentorship. BioScience 61(4):301–312.

Espenshade , Thomas, and Alexandria Radford. 2009 . No longer separate , not yet equal : Race and class in elite college admission and campus life . Princeton University Press.

Espinoza-Herold, Mariela, and Virginia Gonzalez. 2007. "The voices of senior scholars on mentoring graduate students and junior scholars." Hispanic Journal of Behavioral Sciences 29: 313–335.

Erikson, Erik. 1968. Identity, Youth and Crises. New York: W.W. Norton.

Falchikov, Nancy. 2001. Learning together: peer tutoring in higher education. London: Routledge- Falmer.

Falchikov, Nancy, and Margo Blythman. 2001. Learning together: Peer tutoring in higher education. Taylor & Francis: Routledge Falmer.

Feiman-Nemser, Sharon. 2001b. "Helping novices learn to teach: lessons from an exemplary support teacher." Journal of Teacher Education 52(1):17–30.

Feldman, Robert. 2005. Improving the first year of college: Research and Practice. Mahwah: Lawrence Erlbaum Associates.

Feldman, Kenneth, and Theodore Newcomb. 1973. The impact of college on students. Jossey-Bass: London.

Field, Kellyn. 2009. Obama's Pell Grant Proposal Would Make 260,000 More Students Eligible. NewsBlog: Chronicle for Higher Education. Available at chronicle.com/article/Obama-s-Pell-Grant-Proposal/42637.

Fitzpatrick, Jody, James Sanders, and Blaine Worthen. 2004. Program evaluation: Alternative approaches and practical guidelines. 3rd Edition. Boston: Pearson Education, Inc.

Fleming, Jacqueline. 2012. Enhancing Minority Student Retention and Academic Performance: What We Can Learn from Program Evaluations. Jossey-Bass Higher and Adult Education.

Finn, Michael. 2010. Stay rates of foreign doctorate recipients from U.S. Universities. Oak Ridge, TN: Oak Ridge Institute for Science and Education. orise.orau.gov/sep/files/stay-rates-foreign- doctorate-recipients-2007.pdf.

Fischer, Mary. 2007. "Settling into campus life: Differences by race/ethnicity in college involvement and outcomes." Journal of Higher Education 78(2):125–161.

Flavell, John. 1979. "Metacognition and cognitive monitoring: A new area of cognitive-developmental inquiry." American Psychologist 34(10):906–911.

Flowers, Lamont. 2004. "Retaining African-American students in higher education: An integrative review." Journal of College Student Retention Research Theory and Practice 6:23–35.

Flowers, Lamont, and Ernest Pascarella. 2003. "Cognitive effects of college: Differences between African American and Caucasian students." Research in Higher Education 44(1):21–49.

Freeman, Richard. 2008. Labor Market Imbalances: Shortages, Surpluses or What? In Global Imbalances and the Evolving World Economy, edited by Jane Sneddon Little, 152–182. Boston: Federal Reserve Bank of Boston.

Frehill, Lisa, Nicole DiFabio, and Susan Hill. 2008. Confronting the "New" American dilemma – Underrepresented Minorities in Engineering: A Data-Based Look at Diversity. Washington, DC: National Action Council for Minorities in Engineering.

Friedman, Thomas. 2006. The World is Flat: A Brief History of the Twenty-First Century. 2nd Edition. Farrar, Straus & Giroux.

Friedman, Milton. 1962. Capitalism and Freedom. Chicago: Chicago University Press.

Fries-Britt, Sharon. 1998. "Moving beyond Black achiever isolation: Experiences of gifted Black collegians." Journal of Higher Education 69(5):556–576.

Fries-Britt, Sharon. 2000. "Identity development of high-ability Black collegians." New Directions for Teaching and Learning 82:55–65.

Fries-Britt, Sharon, and B. Turner. 2002. "Uneven stories: Successful Black collegians at a Black and a White campus." Review of Higher Education 25(3):315–330.

Gandara, Patricia, and Juliw Maxwell-Jolly. 1999. Priming the pump: strategies for increasing the achievement of underrepresented minority undergraduates. New York: The College Board.

Gándara, Patricia. 2002. Meeting common goals: Linking K–12 and college interventions. In Increasing access to college: Extending possibilities for all students, 81–103, edited by W Tierney and L Hagedorn. Albany: State University of New York Press.

Gansemer-Topf, Ann, and John Schuh. 2005. "Institutional grants: Investing in student retention and graduation." Journal of Student Financial Aid 35(3):5–20.

Garcia, Ben, and Li-tze Hu. 2001. "Academic self efficacy and first-year college student performance and adjustment." Journal of Educational Psychology 93(1):55–64.

García Coll, Cynthia, and Lee Pachter. 2002. Ethnic and minority parenting. In Handbook of Parenting, Volume 4: Social Conditions and Applied Parenting, edited by M. Bornstein. Mahwah: Lawrence Erlbaum Publishers.

Gardner, Howard. 1991. The unschooled mind: How children think and how schools should teach. Basic Books: Perseus Book Group.

Gay, Geneva. 2002. Culturally responsive teaching: Theory, research & practice. New York: Teachers College Press.

Gee, J. 1990. Social linguistics and literacies: Ideology in discourses. N.Y.:Falmer.

Gee, James, Glynda Hull, and Colin Lankshear. 1996. The new work order: Behind the language of the new capitalism. New South Wales, Australia: Allen & Unwin.

Ginther, Donna, and Shulamit Kahn. 2006. Does Science Promote Women? Evidence from Academia 1973-2001. NBER Working Paper No. w12691. Gladieux, Lawrence, and Watson Swail. 2000. "Beyond access: Improving the odds of college success." Phi Delta Kappan 8(9):688–692.

Glennen, Robert, D. Baxley, and P. Farren. 1985. "Impact of intrusive advising on minority student retention." College Student Journal 35(4):335–339.

Goetz, Judith, and Margaret LeCompte. 1984. Ethnography and qualitative design in education research. Orlando, FL: Academic Press.

Goldin, Claudia, and Lawrence Katz. 2008. The Race between Education and Technology. Harvard University Press.

Goldman, Alvin. 1994. Argument and social epistemology. Journal of Philosophy 91:27–49.

Goldrick-Rab, Sara, Douglas Harris, and Philip Trostel. 2009. Why money matters (or doesn't) for college success: An interdisciplinary approach. In Higher Education: Handbook of Theory and Research, edited by J. Smart, 24:1–45.

Good, Catherine, Joshua Aronson, and Jayne Harder. 2008. "Problems in the pipeline: Stereotype threat and women's achievement in high-level math courses." Journal of Applied Developmental Psychology 29(1):17–28.

Good, Jennifer, Glenelle Halpin, and Gerald Halpin. 2002. "Retaining Black students in engineering: do minority programs have a longitudinal impact?" Journal of College Student Retention: Research, Theory and Practice 3(4):351–364.

Good, Catherine, Aneeta Rattan, and Carol Dweck. 2009. Why do women opt out? Sense of belonging and women's representation in mathematics. Unpublished paper. Baruch College.

Graham, Sandra. 1997. "Using attribution theory to understand the social and academic motivation in African American youth." Educational Psychologist 32:21–34.

Granger, Robert. 2010. Improving practice at scale. New York: William T. Grant Foundation.

Granger, Robert, Rebecca Maynard, Ed Seidman, Vivian Tseng et al. 2007. Why try to understand and improve social settings? New York: William T. Grant Foundation.

Greenberg, Mark, Roger Weissberg, Mary O'Brien, Joseph Zins et al. 2003. "Enhancing school-based prevention and youth development through coordinated social, emotional, and academic learning." American Psychologist 58(6–7):466–474.

Greeno, James. 1991. "Number sense of situated knowing in a conceptual domain." Journal for Research in Mathematics Education 22 (3):170–218.

Greeno, James. 2003. A situative perspective on cognition and learning interaction. Paper presented at Theorizing learning practices workshop. University of Illinois Urbana-Champagne.

Gross, Jacob, Don Hossler, and Mary Ziskin. 2007. Institutional Aid and Student Persistence: An Analysis of the Effects of Institutional Financial Aid at Public Four-Year Institutions. NASFAA Journal of Student Financial Aid 37(1):28–39.

Grossman, Pamela, Peter Smagorinsky, and Sheila Valencia. 1999. "Appropriating tools for teaching English: A theoretical framework for research on learning to teach." America Journal of Education 108(1):1–29.

Guba, Egon, and Yvonna Lincoln. 1981. Effective evaluation: Improving the usefulness of evaluation results through responsive and naturalistic approaches. San Francisco: Jossey-Bass.

Gurin Patricia. 1999. The compelling need for diversity in higher education: Expert testimony in Gratz, et al. v. Bollinger, et al. Michigan Journal of Race & Law 5:363–425.

Gurin, Patricia, Eric Dey, Sylvia Hurtado, and Gerald Gurin. 2002. "Diversity and higher education: Theory and impact on educational outcomes." Harvard Educational Review 72(3): 330–367.

Gutiérrez, Kris. 2005, April. Intersubjectivity and grammar in the Third Space. Scribner Award Talk. American Educational Research Association. Montreal, Canada.

Gutiérrez, Kris. 2008, April/May/June. "Developing a sociocritical literacy in the third space." Reading Research Quarterly 43(2):148–164.

Habermas, Jürgen 1990. Moral consciousness and communicative action. Cambridge: MIT Press.

Halsey, A.H., Phillip Brown, and Amy Wells. 1997. Education, culture, economy and society. Oxford University Press.

Hammerness, Karen, and Darling-Hammond, Linda. 2002. Meeting old challenges and new demands: The redesign of the Stanford Teacher Education Program.

Hammerness, K., L. Darling-Hammond, et al. (2002). "Toward expert thinking: How curriculum case writing prompts the development of theory-based professional knowledge in student teachers." Teaching Education 13(2):219–243.

Hanushek, Eric, and Ludger Woessmann. 2008. "The role of cognitive skills in economic development." Journal of Economic Literature 46(3):607–668.

Harris, Shanette, and Michael Nettles. 1996. Ensuring campus climates that embrace diversity. In Educating a new majority: Transforming America's educational system for diversity, edited by L Rendon and Richard Hope. San Francisco: Jossey-Bass.

Heiman, Tali. 2006. "Social support networks, stress, sense of coherence and academic success of university students with learning disabilities." Social Psychology of Education 9(4):461–478.

Hermanowicz, Joseph. 2004. "The college departure process among the academic elite." Education & Urban Society 37(1):74–93.

Higher Education Opportunity Program Annual Report. 2003. New York State Education Department.

Higher Education Opportunity Program Annual Report. 2007. New York State Education Department.

Hill, Catherine, Christianne Corbett, and Andresse St. Rose. 2010. Why so few? Women in Science, Technology, Engineering and Mathematics. Washington DC: AAUW.

Hilliard,Asa, and Nana Amankwatia. 2003. No mystery: Closing the achievement gap between Africans and excellence. In Young, gifted, and Black: Promoting high achievement among African-American students, edited by Theresa Perry, Claude Steele, and Asa Hilliard, 131–165. Boston: Beacon Press.

Hirsh, E.D. 1987. Cultural Literacy: What Every American Needs to Know. Boston: Houghton Mifflin.

Hirschman, Charles, and Morrison Wong. 1984. "Socioeconomic Gains of Asian Americans, Blacks, and Hispanics: 1960-1976." American Journal of Sociology 90:584–607.

Hoffman, Marybeth, Jayne Richmond, Jennifer Morrow, and Kandice Salomone. 2002–2003. "Investigating sense of belonging in first-year college students." Journal of College Student Retention: Research, Theory & Practice 4:227–256.

Hogan, Kathleen, and Michael Pressley. 1997. Scaffolding student instruction. Cambridge MA: Brookline Books.

Holmes, Mary, and Suzanne O'Connell. 2003. Where are the women geoscience professors? Paper presented at the National Science Foundation, Association for Women Geoscientists, and Association for Women Geoscientists Foundation-sponsored workshop. Washington, DC.

Hopwood v. Texas, 78 F.3d 932, 944, 948. 5th Cir. 1996.

Horn, Laura. 1998. Undergraduates who work: A Postsecondary Education Data Analysis Report using data from the National Postsecondary Student Aid Study (NPSAS:96). Washington DC: National Center for Education Statistics, U.S. Department of Education.

Hrabowski, Freeman. 1999. "Embracing excellence and diversity." The School Administrator 56(11):38–39. www.aasa.org/publications/sa/1999_12/hrabowski.htm

Hrabowski, Freeman. 2002. "Postsecondary minority student achievement: How to raise performance and close the achievement gap." College Board Review 195:40–48.

Hrabowski, Freeman. 2004. "University outreach and engagement: Responding to a changing world." Journal of Higher Education Outreach and Engagement 10(1):15–28.

Hrabowski, Freeman. 2006. Moral leadership: Promoting high achievement among minority students in science. In University Presidents As Moral Leaders, edited by D. Brown, 135–142. Praeger Press.

Hrabowski, Freeman, and Willie Pearson. 1993. "Recruiting and retaining talented african american males in college science and engineering." Journal of College Science Teaching 22(4):234–238.

Hrabowski, Freeman, and Kenneth Maton. 1995. "Enhancing the success of African-American students in the sciences: Freshman year outcomes." School Science and Mathematics 95(1):19–27.

Hrabowski, Freeman, Kenneth Maton, and Geoffrey Grief. 1998. Beating the odds: Raising academically successful African-American males. New York: Oxford University Press.

Hrabowski, Freeman. 2002. "Postsecondary minority student achievement: How to raise performance and close the achievement gap." College Board Review 195:40–48.

Hrabowski, Freeman, Kenneth Maton, G Grief, and Monica Greene. 2002. Overcoming the odds: Parenting successful African-American females. New York: Oxford University Press.

Hunter, Anne-Barrie, Sandra Laursen, and Elaine Seymour. 2007. "Becoming a scientist: The role of undergraduate research in students' cognitive, personal, and professional development." Science Education 91:36–74.

Hurtado, Sylvia, Jeffrey Milem, Alma Clayton-Pederson, and Walter Allen. 1998. "Enhancing campus climates for racial/ethnic diversity: Educational policy and practice." The Review of Higher Education 21(3):279–302.

Hurtado, Sylvia, Jeffrey Milem, Alma Clayton-Pederson, and Walter Allen. 1999. "Enacting diverse learning environments: Improving the climate for racial/ethnic diversity in higher education." Jossey-Bass. ASHE Higher Education Report Series.

Hurtado, Sylvia, Eric Dey, Patricia Gurin, and Gerald Gurin. 2003. College environments, diversity, and student learning. In Higher education: Handbook of theory and research, xviii, edited by J. Smart, 145–189. Dordrecht Netherlands: Kluwer.

Hurtado, Sylvia, M. Eagan, N. Cabrera, M. Lin, J. Park and M. Lopez. 2008. "Training future scientists: Predicting first-year minority student participation in health science research." Research in Higher Education 49 (2):126–152.

Hurtado, Sylvia, Nolan Cabrera, Monica Lin, Lucy Arellano et al. 2009. "Diversifying science: Underrepresented student experiences in structured research programs." Research in Higher Education 50 (2):189–214.

Hutchison, Mica, Deborah Follman, Melissa Sumpter, and George Bodnar. 2006. "Factors influencing the self-efficacy beliefs of first-year engineering students." Journal of engineering education.

Institute of Medicine. 2004. In the Nation's Compelling Interest: Ensuring Diversity in the Health Care Workforce. Washington DC: Institute of Medicine.

Irvine, Jacqueline, and Michèle Foster. 1996. Growing up African American in Catholic schools. New York: Teachers College Press.

Jackson, Shirley. 2003. The quiet crisis: Falling short in producing American scientific and technical talent. San Diego: BEST.

Johnson-Bailey, Juanita. 2004. "Hitting and climbing the proverbial wall: Participation and retention issues for black graduate women." Race Ethnicity and Education 7(4):331–349.

Jussim, Lee. 1986. "Self-fulfilling prophecies: A theoretical and integrative review." Psychological Review 93:429–445.

Just, Helen. 1999. Minority retention in predominantly white universities and colleges: The importance of creating a good "fit." Eric Document 439641.

Katz, Irwin, S. Oliver Roberts, and James Robinson. 1965. "Effects of task difficulty, race of administrator, and instructions on digit-symbol performance of Negroes." Journal of Personality and Social Psychology 2:53–59.

Kennedy, Mary. 1999. The role of preservice teacher education. In Teaching as the learning profession: Handbook of policy and practice, edited by Linda Darling-Hammond and Gary Sykes 54–85. San Francisco: Jossey-Bass.

Kennedy, Peter, and Barry Sheckley. 2000. The dynamic nature of student persistence: Influence of interactions between student attachment, academic adaptation, and social adaptation. Paper prepared for the annual meeting of the Association for International Research. May 21–24. Cincinnati OH. (ERIC Document 445632).

Kemple, James, and Jason Snipes. 2000. Career Academies: Impacts on students' engagement and performance in high school. New York: Manpower Demonstration Research Corporation.

Keup, Jennifer, and Betsy Barefoot. 2005. "Learning how to be a successful student: Exploring the impact of first-year seminars on student outcomes." Journal of the First-Year Experience & Students in Transition 17(1):11–47.

Killenbeck, Mark. 2004. Affirmative Action and Diversity: The Beginning of the End? Or the End of the Beginning? Princeton: ETS Policy Report.

Kirsch, Irwin, Henry Braun, Kentaro Yamamoto, and Andrew Sum. 2007. America's perfect storm: Three forces changing our nation's future. Princeton: ETS.

Krovetz, Martin. 1999. Fostering resiliency. Expecting all students to use their minds and hearts well. Thousand Oaks, CA: Corwin Press.

Kuglemass, Heather, and Ready, Douglas. 2011. "Racial/Ethnic disparities in collegiate cognitive gains: A multilevel analysis of institutional influences on learning and its equitable distribution." Research in Higher Education 52:323–348.

Kuh, George. 2003. "What we're learning about student engagement from NSSE." Change 35(2):24–32.

Kuh, George, and Paul Umbach. 2005. Experiencing diversity: What can we learn from liberal arts colleges? Liberal Education. Winter.

Kuh, George, Jillian Kinzie, John Schuh, Elizabeth Whitt et al. 2010. Student success in college: Creating conditions that matter. San Francisco: Jossey-Bass.

Kuh, George, Jillian Schuh, Elizabeth Whit et al. 1991. Involving colleges: Successful approaches to fostering student learning and development outside the classroom. San Francisco: Jossey-Bass.

Kuhn, Deanna. 1991. The skills of argument. England: Cambridge University Press.

Kulis, Stephen, Diane Sicotte, and Shawn Collins. 2002. "More than a pipeline problem: Labor supply constraints and gender stratifcation across academic science disciplines." Research in Higher Education 43(6):657–91.

Labaree, David. 1997. "Public goods, Private goods: The American struggle over educational goals." American Educational Research Journal 34(1):39–81.

Ladson-Billing, Gloria. 1994. The dreamkeepers: Successful teachers of African American children. San Francisco: Jossey-Bass.

Lampert, Magdalene, and Deborah Ball. 1998. Teaching, multimedia, and mathematics: Investigations of real practice. New York: Teachers College Press.

Lantieri, Linda. 2001. Schools with spirit: Nurturing the inner lives of children and teachers. Boston: Beacon Press.

Lave, Jean, and Etienne Wegner. 1991. Situated learning: Legitimate peripheral participation. New York: Cambridge University Press.

Layden, Susan, Ann Knickerbocker, and Monica Minor. 2004. Bridging the gap between achievement and excellence: The Skidmore College Summer Academic Institute and the Skidmore College Opportunity Programs. www.skidmore.edu/opportunity_program/upload/Bridge_Chapter1.doc.

Lee, Jaekyung. 2002. "Racial and ethnic achievement gap trends: Reversing the progress toward equity?" Educational Researcher 31(1):3–12.

Leggon, Cheryl. 2006. "Women in science: Racial and ethnic differences and the differences they make." Journal of Technology Transfer 31:325–333.

Lenning, Oscar, and Larry Ebbers. 1999. The powerful potential of learning communities: Improving education for the future. ASHE-ERIC Higher Education Report 26(6).

Lent, Robert, Steven Brown, Janet Schmidt, Bradley Brenner et al. 2003. "Relation of contextual supports and barriers to choice behavior in engineering majors: Test of alternative social cognitive models." Journal of Counseling Psychology 50(4):458–465.

Levin, Henry, and Clive Belfield. 2003. "The marketplace in education." Review of Research in Education 27:183–219.

Levine, Arthur, and Jana Nidiffer. 1996. Beating the odds: How the poor get to college. San Francisco: Jossey-Bass.

Light, Richard. 2001. Making the Most of College: Students Speak Their Minds. Cambridge, MA: Harvard University Press.

Lin, Nan. 2001. Social capital: A theory of social structure and action. New York: Cambridge University Press.

Lincoln, Yvonna, and Egon Guba. 1985. Naturalistic inquiry. Beverly Hills: Sage.

Lochhead, Jack, and Arthur Whimbey. 1987. "Teaching analytical reasoning through thinking aloud pair problem solving." New Directions for Teaching and Learning (Developing Critical Thinking and Problem-Solving Abilities) 30:73–92.

Lorge, Irving. 1945. Schooling makes a difference. Teachers College Record 46:483–492.

Lortie, Dan. 1975. School teacher: A sociological study. Chicago: University of Chicago Press.

Lowell, B. Lindsey, and Harold Salzman. 2007. Into the Eye of the Storm: Assessing the Evidence on Science and Engineering Education, Quality, and Workforce Demand. Madison, WI: Association for Public Policy Analysis and Management.

Lotkowski, Veronica, Steven Robbins, and Richard Noeth. 2004. The role of academic and non-academic factors in improving college retention. Washington DC: ACT policy report. Eric Document 485476.

Lundberg Carol, and Laurie Schreiner. 2004. "Quality and Frequency of Faculty-Student Interaction as predictors of Learning: An analysis by student race/ethnicity." Project Muse September/October 45(5):549–565.

Maldonado, David, Robert Rhoads, and Tracy Buenavista. 2005. "The student-initiated retention project: Theoretical contributions and the role of self-empowerment." American Educational Research Journal 42(4): 605–638.

Marcia, James. 1966. "Development and validation of ego-identity status." Journal of Personality and Social Psychology 3: 551–558.

Marcia, James. 1980. Identity in adolescence. In Handbook of adolescent psychology, 159–187, edited by Joseph Adelson. New York: Wiley.

Marin, B, and R Diaz. 2002. "Collaborative HIV prevention research in minority communities program: A model for developing investigators of color." Public Health Reports 117:218–230.

Marks, Helen. 2000. "Student engagement in instructional activity: Patterns in the elementary, middle and high school years." American Educational Research Journal 37(1):153–184.

Markus, Hazel, and Paula Nurius. 1986. Possible selves. American Psychologist 41:954–969.

Martinez, Michael. 2000. The cultivation of Intelligence. Mawah: Lawrence Erlbaum Associates.

Marshall, Catherine, and Gretchen Rossman. 1999. Designing qualitative research. Thousand Oaks CA: Sage.

Martinez, Monica, and Shayna Klopott. 2005. The Link between High School Reform and College Access and Success for Low-Income and Minority. Washington DC: American Youth Policy Forum and Pathways to College Network.

Massachusetts Institute of Technology. School of Science. Committee on Women Faculty. 1999. A study of the status of women faculty in science at MIT. Cambridge, MA.

Massey, Douglas, and Mary Fischer. 2005. Stereotype threat and academic performance: New data from the National Longitudinal Survey of Freshman. The DuBois Review: Social Science Research on Race 2:45–68.

Massey, Douglas, Camille Charles, Garvey Lundy, and Mary Fischer. 2003. The source of the river: The social origins of freshmen at America's selective colleges and universities. Princeton: Princeton University Press.

Maton, Kenneth, and Freeman Hrabowski. 2004. "Increasing the number of african american phDs in the sciences and engineering: A strengths-based approach." American Psychologist 59:547–556.

Maton, Kenneth. 2005. The social transformation of environments and the promotion of resilience in children. In Resilience in children, families and communities: Linking context to intervention and policy, edited by R Peters, B Leadbeater and R McMahon, 119–135. New York: Kluwer.

Maton, Kenneth. 2008. "Empowering community settings: Agents of individual development, community betterment and positive social change." American Journal of Community Psychology, 41:4–21.

Maton, Kenneth, Freeman Hrabowski, and Shauna Pollard. 2011. African American Males in the Meyerhoff Scholars Program: Outcomes and Processes. In Beyond Stock Stories and Folktales: African Americans' Paths to STEM Fields. Diversity in Higher Education 11, edited by Henry T. Frierson and William F. Tate, 47–70. Emerald Group Publishing Limited.

Maton, Kenneth, Freeman Hrabowski, and Carol Schmitt. 2000. "African American college students excelling in the sciences: College and postcollege outcomes in the Meyerhoff Scholars Program." Journal of Research in Science Teaching 37(7):629–654.

Maton, Kenneth, Freeman Hrabowski, Metin Ozdemir, and Harriette Wimms. 2008. Enhancing representation, retention, and achievement of minority students in higher education: A social transformation theory of change. In Toward Positive Youth Development: Transforming Schools and Community Programs, edited by M. Shinn and H. Yoshikawa, 115–132. New York: Oxford University Press.

Maxwell, Joseph. 1998. Designing a qualitative study. In Handbook of applied social research methods, edited by L. Bickman and D. Rog, 69–100. Thousand Oaks CA: Sage.

McDonald, Joseph. 1992. Teaching: Making sense of an uncertain craft. New York: Teachers College Press.

McKinney, Kathleen. 2002. "Engagement in community service among college students: Is it affected by significant attachment relationships?" Journal of Adolescence 25(2):139–155.

McKinsey & Company Social Sector Office. 2009. The economic impact of the achievement gap in America's schools.

McLaughlin , Milbrey. and Joan Talbert. 1993. Contexts that matter for teaching and learning. Stanford: Stanford University.

Mehan, Hugh. 1996. Constructing school success: The consequences of untracking low-achieving students. New York: Cambridge University Press.

Merisotis, James. 2009. It's the learning, stupid. Lumina Foundation for Education. The Howard R. Bowen Lecture, Claremont Graduate University. Claremont CA. October 14.

Merriam, Sharan. 1998. Qualitative research and case study applications in education. San Francisco: Jossey-Bass.

Merton, Robert. 1948. "The self-fulfilling prophecy." The Antioch Review 8:193–210.

Metcalf, Linda. 1995. "Great expectations: How changing your thinking can change your students." Learning 23(5):93–95.

Miles, Matthew, and A. Michael Huberman. 1994. Qualitative data analysis. Thousand Oaks CA: Sage.

Miller, L .Scott. 1995. An American imperative: Accelerating minority educational advancement. New Haven: Yale University Press.

Miller, L. Scott. 1999. Promoting high academic achievement among non-Asian minorities. In Promise and Dilemma: Perspectives on Racial Diversity and Higher Education, edited by E. Lowe, 47–91. Princeton: Princeton University Press.

Miller, L.Scott, Mehmet Oztuk, and Lisa Chavez. 2005. Increasing African American, Latino, and Native American Representation among High Achieving Undergraduates At Selective Colleges and Universities. University of California, Berkeley, CA: Institute for the Study of Social Change.

Miller, L.Scott, and Eugene Garcia. 2008. A reading-focused early childhood education research and strategy development agenda for African Americans and Hispanics at all social class levels who are English speakers or English language learners. Office of the Vice President for Education Partnerships. Arizona State University.

Milner, H. Richard. 2002. "Affective and social issues among high achieving african american students: Recommendations for teachers and teacher education." Action in Teacher Education 24(1):81.

Moore, James. 2006. "A qualitative investigation of African American males' trajectory in engineering: Implications for teachers, school counselors, and parents." Teachers College Record 108(2):246–266.

Moore, James, Octavia Madison-Colmore, and Dionne Smith. 2003. "The prove-them-wrong syndrome: Voices from unheard African-American males in engineering disciplines." The Journal of Men's Studies 12:61–73.

Moretti, Enrico. 2002. Estimating the Social Return to Higher Education: Evidence From Longitudinal and Repeated Cross-Sectional Data, NBER Working Paper No.9108, and Journal of Econometrics 121:2004.

Moretti. Enico. 2007. Crime and the costs of criminal justice in The Price We Pay: Economic and Social Consequences of Inadequate Education, edited by Clive Belfield and Henry Levin. Brookings Institution Press.

Mortenson, Thomas. 1999. "Refocusing student financial aid: From grants to loans, from need to merit, from poor to affluent." Postsecondary Education Opportunity 82:1–4.

Munby, Hugh, Tom Russell, and Andrea Martin. 2001. Teachers' knowledge and how it develops. In Handbook of research on teaching, edited by V. Richardson, 877–904. Washington D.C.: American Educational Research Association.

Myers, David, and Allen Schirm. 1999. The impacts of Upward Bound: Final report for Phase I of the national evaluation. Washington DC: U.S. Department of Education. Office of the Under Secretary.

Nagda, B., S. Gregerman, J. Jonides, W. von Hippel et al. 1998. "Undergraduate student-faculty research partnerships affect student retention." The Review of Higher Education 22(1):55–72.

National Academy of Sciences, Committee on Prospering in the Global Economy of the 21st Century. 2007. Rising Above the Gathering Storm: Energizing and Employing America for a Brighter Economic Future. Washington, DC: National Academies Press.

National Center for Education Statistics. 2008. Characteristics of Minority-Serving Institutions and Minority Undergraduates Enrolled in These Institutions. Washington DC: U.S. Department of Education.

National Educational Research Policy and Priorities Board. 1999. Investing in Learning: A Policy Statement with Recommendations on Research in Education by the National Educational Research Policy and Priorities Board. United States Department of Education.

National Research Council. 2010. Expanding Minority Participation: America's Science and Technology Talent at the Crossroads. Committee on Underrepresented Groups and the Expansion of the Science and Engineering Workforce Pipeline. Washington DC: National Academies Press.

Neidert. L., and R. Farley. 1985. "Assimilation in the United States: An analysis of ethnic and generation differences in status and achievement." American Sociological Review 50:840–850.

Nettles, Michael. 1988. Toward Black undergraduate student equality in American higher education. New York: Greenwood Press.

Newstead, S, and J Evans. 1995. Perspectives on thinking and reasoning: Essays in honour of Peter Wason. Hillsdale NJ: Erlbaum.

Nieto, Sonia. 1999. The light in their eyes: Creating multicultural learning communities. New York: Teachers College Press.

Ogbu, John. 2003. Black American students in an affluent suburb: A study of academic disengagement. Mahwah: Erlbaum.

Orfield, Gary and Susan Eaton. 1996. Dismantling Desegregation: The Quiet Reversal of *Brown v. Board of Education*. New York: New Press.

Orfield, Gary, and Erica Frankenberg. 2007. Lessons In Integration: Realizing the Promise of Racial Diversity in America's Public Schools. University of Virginia Press.

Oyserman,   Daphna,   and   Janet Swim. 2001. "Stigma: An insider's view." Journal of Social Issue 57:1–14.

Pascarella, E, and P Terenzini. 1991. How college affects students: Findings and insights from twenty years of research. San Francisco: Jossey-Bass.

Parsons, Talcott. 1959. "The school class as a social system: Some of its functions in American society." Harvard Educational Review 29:297–318.

Pascarella, Ernest. 1985. College environmental influences on learning and cognitive development: A critical review and synthesis. In Higher education: Handbook of theory and research 1, edited by J. Smart, 1–64. New York: Agathon.

Pascarella, Ernest, and Patrick Terenzini. 2005. How college affects students: A third decade of research. San Francisco: Jossey-Bass.

Patton, Michael. 1997. Utilization-focused evaluation. Thousand Oaks, CA: Sage.

Patterson, Orlando. 1980. "Language, ethnicity and change." Journal of Basic Writing 3(1):62–73.

Planty, Michael, Grace Kena, and Gretchen Hannes. 2009. The Condition of Education 2009 in Brief. NCES 2009-082. Institute of Education Sciences, National Center for Education Statistics. Washington, DC: U.S. Department of Education.

Plato. The Allegory of the Cave . Book. VII of The Republic.

Prawat, Richard, Janine Remillard, Ralph Putnam, and Ruth Heaton. 1992. "Teaching mathematics for understanding: Case study for four fifth-grade teachers." Elementary School Journal 93:145–152.

Prawat, Richard. 1989. "Promoting access to knowledge, strategy and disposition in students." Review of Educational Research 59:1–42.

Provasnik, Stephen, and Michael Planty. 2008. Community colleges: Special supplement to the condition of education 2008 (NCES 2008-033). Institute of Education Sciences. National Center for Education Statistics. Washington DC: U.S. Department of Education.

Rascoe, Barbara, and Mary Atwater. 2005. "Black males' self-perceptions of academic ability and gifted potential in advanced science classes." Journal of Research in Science Teaching 42(8): 888–911.

Rhatigan, James, and John Schuh. 2003. "Small wins." About Campus 8 (1):17–22.

Redden, Charlotte. 2002. Social Alienation of African American College Students: Implications for Social Support Systems. Paper presented at the National Convention of the Association for Counselor Education and Supervision. Park City UT. October 17–20. Eric Document 470257.

Resnick, Lauren. 2000. From aptitude to effort: A new foundation for our schools. In Taking sides: Clashing views on controversial issues in educational psychology, edited by L Abbeduto, 206-210. Guilford: Dushkin/McGrawHill.

Richards, Philip. 2002, September 13. "Prestigious colleges ignore the inadequate intellectual achievement of black students." Chronicle of Higher Education 49(3).

Richardson, V, and P Placier. 2001. Teacher change. In Handbook of research on teaching, edited by V. Richardson, 905–947. Washington DC: American Educational Research Association.

Rizvi, Fazal, and Bob Lingard. 2009. Globalizing education policy. London: Routledge.

Roberts, Amy. 2007. "Global dimensions of schooling: Implications for internationalizing teacher education." Teacher Education Quarterly 34(1):9–26.

Ryan, Mary, Donal Robinson, and J.W. Carmichael. 1980. "A Piagetian-based general chemistry laboratory program for science majors." Journal of Chemical Education 57(9):642–645.

Sandefur, Gary, and Anup Pahari. 1989. Racial and ethnic inequality in earnings and educational attainment. Social Service Review:199–221.

Schmidt, Peter. 1998, March 20. "A clash of values at CUNY over remedial education." The Chronicle of Higher Education 44(28):A33–A34.

Schmidt, Peter. 2008, July 4. "Three new studies question the value of remedial college courses." The Chronicle of Higher Education 54(43):A18.

Schoenfeld, Alan. 2010. How we think: A theory of goal-oriented decision making and its educational applications. New York: Routledge.

Schon, Donald. 1983. The reflective practitioner: How professionals think in action. New York: Basic Books.

Schultz, P. Wesley, Paul Hernandez, Anna Woodcock, Mica Estrada et al. 2011. "Patching the pipeline: reducing educational disparities in the sciences through minority training programs." Educational Evaluation & Policy Analysis 33(1):95–114.

Schunk, Dale, and Peg Ertmer. 2000. Self-efficacy and academic learning: Self-efficacy enhancing interventions. In Handbook of self-regulation, edited by M Boekaerts, P Pintrich, and M Zeidner, 631–650. San Diego: Academic Press.

Schunk, Dale. 1995. "Self-efficacy, motivation, and performance." Journal of Applied Sport Psychology 7(2):112–137.

Schunk, Dale. 2001. Social cognitive theory and self-regulated learning. In Self-regulated learning and academic achievement: Theoretical perspectives, edited by Barry Zimmerman and D Schunk, 125–152. Mahwah: Erlbaum.

Schunk, Dale, and Barry Zimmerman. 1994. Self-regulation of learning and performance: Issues and educational applications. Hillsdale: Erlbaum.

Sedlacek, William. 2004. "Why we should use noncognitive variables with graduate and professional students." The Journal of the National Association of Advisors for the Health Professions 24(2):32–39.

Seider, S. 2007. Catalyzing a commitment to community service in emerging adults. Journal of Adolescent Research 22(6):612–639.

Seidman, Alan. 2005. College student retention: Formula for student success. Westport: ACE/Praeger.

Seymour , Elaine, and Nancy Hewitt . 1997 . Talking about leaving: Why undergraduates leave the sciences. Boulder CO: Westview Press.

Shapiro, Harold. 2005. A Larger Sense of Purpose: Higher Education and Society. The 2003 Clark Kerr Lectures. Princeton: Princeton University Press.

Shapiro, Nancy, and Jodi Levine. 1999. Creating learning communities: A practical guide to winning support, organizing for change, and implementing programs. San Francisco: Jossey-Bass.

Shireman, Robert. 2003, August 15. "10 questions college officials should ask about diversity." Chronicle of Higher Education 49(49).

Shulman, Lee, and Judith Shulman. 2004. "How and what teachers learn: A shifting perspective." Journal of Curriculum Studies 36(2):257–271.

Sizer, Theodore. 1992. Horace's School: Redesigning the American high school. Boston: Houghton Mifflin.

Smedley, Brian, Adrienne Stith, and Alan Nelson. 2003. Unequal Treatment: Confronting racial and ethnic disparities in health care. Institute of Medicine Committee on Understanding and Eliminating Racial and Ethnic Disparities in Health Care. Washington, DC: National Academic Press.

Smith, Rachel, and Brittany Peterson. 2007. "Psst... What do you think?" The relationship between advice prestige, type of advice, and academic performance." Communication Education 56(3):278–291.

Smith, Mara. 1998. The college access, retention, and employment (CARE) program model. Miami-Dade, FL: Miami-Dade Community College, Florida, North Campus. Eric Document 418751.

Smith, Barbara, Jean MacGregor, Roberta Matthews, and Faith Gabelnick. 2004. Learning communities: Reforming undergraduate education. Jossey-Bass.

Solarzano, Daniel, Mighel Ceja, and Tara Yosso. 2000. "Critical race theory, racial microaggressions, and campus racial climate: The experience of African American college students." Journal of Negro Education. Winter.

Springer, Leonard, Mary Stanne, and Samuel Donovan. 1999. "Effects of small-group learning on undergraduates in science, mathematics, engineering, and technology: A meta-analysis." Review of Educational Research 69(1):21–51.

Stake, Robert. 1994. Case studies. In Handbook of qualitative research, 236–247, edited by N Denzin and Y Lincoln. Thousand Oaks CA: Sage.

Stake, Robert 1967. "The countenance of educational evaluation." Teachers College Record 68: 523–540.

Stall, Bill, and Dan Morain. 1996. Prop. 209 Wins, Bars Affirmative Action. L.A. TIMES. Nov. 6. A1.

Steele, Claude. 1997. "A threat in the air: How stereotypes shape intellectual identity and performance." American Psychologist 52:613–629.

Steele , Claude . 1999 , August. "Thin Ice: "Stereotype Threat" and Black College Students. The Atlantic Monthly, 44-47, 50–54.

Steele, Claude, and Joshua Aronson. 1995. "Stereotype threat and the intellectual test performance of African-Americans." Journal of Personality and Social Psychology 69(5):797–811.

Steele, Claude, Steven Spencer, and Joshua Aronson. 2002. Contending with group image: The psychology of stereotype and social identity threat. In Advances in experimental social psychology 34, edited by M Zanna, 379-440. San Diego: Academic Press.

Sternberg, Robert. 2003. Wisdom, intelligence, and creativity synthesized. Cambridge University Press.

Strauss, Anselm, and Juliet Corbin. 1998. Basics of qualitative research: Techniques and procedures for developing grounded theory. Thousand Oaks CA: Sage.

Strayhorn, Terell. 2011. "Bridging the pipeline: Increasing underrepresented students' preparation for college through a summer bridge program." American Behavioral Scientist 55 (2): 2142–2159.

St. John, Edward. 2000. "The impact of student aid on recruitment and retention: What the research indicates." New Directions for Student Services 89:61–76.

Sue, Derald, Annie Lin, Kevin Nadal, and Gina Torino. 2007. "Racial microaggressions and the Asian American experience." Cultural Diversity and Ethnic Minority Psychology 1310:72–81.

Sullivan Commission on Diversity in the Health Workforce. 2004. Missing persons: Minorities in the health professions. Washington, DC: Sullivan Commission on Diversity in the Health Workforce.

Summers, Michael, and Freeman Hrabowski. 2006. "Preparing minority scientists and engineers." Science 311.

Swail, Watson. 2000. Preparing America's disadvantaged for college: Programs that increase college opportunity. In Understanding the college choice of disadvantaged students. New Directions for Institutional Research 107, edited by Cabrera and S La Nasa. San Francisco: Jossey-Bass.

Swail, Watson. 2002. "Higher education and the new demographics: Questions for policy." Change 4:15–23.

Swail, Watson, Kenneth Redd, and Laura Perna. 2003. Retaining minority students in higher education: A framework for success. San Francisco: Jossey-Bass.

Tatum, Beverly. 1997). Why Are All the Black Kids Sitting Together in the Cafeteria and other Conversations About Race. New York: Basic Books.

Teitelbaum, Michael. 2003. "Do we need more scientists?" The Public Interest. Fall:40–53.

Thayer, Paul. 2000. "Retaining first-generation and low-income students." Opportunity Outlook: 2–8.

Thelin, John. 2004. A history of American higher education. Baltimore: The Johns Hopkins University Press.

Tierney, William. 2002. Reflective evaluation: Improving practice in college preparation programs. In Increasing access to college: Extending possibilities for all students, edited by W. Tierney and L. Hagedorn, 217–230. Albany: State University of New York Press.

Tierney, William, and Linda Hagedorn. 2002. Increasing access to college: Extending possibilities for all students. Albany: State University of New York Press.

Ting, Sui-man, and Tracy Robinson. 1998. "First-year academic success: A prediction combining cognitive and psychosocial variables for Caucasian and African American students." Journal of College Student Development 39(6):599–610.

Tinto, Vincent. 1993. Leaving college: Rethinking the causes and cures of student attrition. Chicago: University of Chicago Press.

Torres, Carlos. 1998. Democracy, education and multiculturalism: Dilemma of citizenship in a global world. Lanham, M.D.: Rowman & Littlefield Publisher.

Treisman, Phillip. 1990. A study of the mathematics performance of Black students at the University of California, Berkeley. In Mathematicians and education reform: Proceedings of the July 6–8 1988 workshop Issues in Mathematics Education. Conference Board of Mathematical Sciences, edited by H. Keynes, N. Fisher, and P. Wagreich, 33–56. Providence RI: American Mathematical Society with the Mathematical Association of America.

Treisman, Phillip. 1992. "Studying students studying calculus: A look at the lives of minority mathematics students in college." College Mathematics Journal 23(5):362–372.

Treisman, Phillip, and Rose Asera. 1995. Routes to Mathematics for African-American, Latino and Native American Students in the 1990s: The Educational Trajectories of Summer Mathematics Institute Participants. In Changing the Culture: Mathematics in the Research Community. Issues in Mathematics Education, Conference Board of Mathematical Sciences, edited by N. Fisher, K. Fisher, and P. Wagreich. American Mathematical Society with the Mathematical Association of America.

Tseng, Vivian. 2010. Learning about the use of research to inform evidence-based policy and practice: Early lessons and future Directions. New York: William T. Grant Foundation.

Tseng, Vivian, and Edward Seidman. 2007. "A systems framework for understanding social settings." American Journal of Community Psychology 39:217–228.

Turner, Ralph. 1960. "Sponsored and contested mobility and the school system." American Sociological Review 25(6):855–867.

Villalpando, Octavio, and Daniel Solórzano. 2005. The role of culture in college preparation programs: A review of the research literature. In Preparing for college: Nine elements of effective outreach, edited by W. Tierney, Z. Corwin, and J. Colyar, 13–28. Albany: State University of New York Press.

Villegas, Ann Marie. 2007. "Dispositions in teacher education: A look at social justice." Journal of Teacher Education 58(5):370–380.

Umbach, Paul, and George Kuh. 2006. "Student experiences with diversity at liberal arts colleges: another claim for distinctiveness." The Journal Higher Education 77(1):169–192.

U.S. Department of Education (2006). A Test of Leadership: Charting the Future of U.S. Higher Education. A Report of the Commission Appointed by Secretary of Education Margaret Spellings.

United States Commission on Civil Rights. 2010. The educational effectiveness of historically Black colleges and universities: Briefing Report. USCCR: Washington, DC.

Vye, Nancy, Daniel Schwartz, John Bransford, Brigid Barron et al. 1998. SMART environments that support monitoring, reflection, and revision. In Metacognition in educational theory and practice, edited by D. Hacker, J. Dunlosky, and A. Graessner. Mahwah: Erlbaum.

Vygotsky, Lev. 1934/1986. Thought and language. Cambridge MA: The MIT Press.

Vygotsky, Lev. 1978. Mind in Society: The Development of Higher Psychological Processes. edited by M. Cole, V. John-Steiner, S. Scribner and E. Souberman. Cambridge: Harvard University Press.

Wallace, Dawn, Ron Abel, and Becky Ropers-Huilman. 2000. "Clearing a path for success: Deconstructing borders through undergraduate mentoring." The Review of Higher Education 24(1):87–102.

Warburton, Edward, Rosio Bugarin, and Anne-marie Nunez. 2001. Bridging the gap: Academic preparation and postsecondary success of first-generation students.

Weidman, John. 1989. Undergraduate socialization: A conceptual approach. In Higher education: Handbook of theory and research 5, edited by J. Smart, 289–322. New York: Agathon.

Welch, Olga, and Carolyn Hodges. 1997. Standing outside on the inside: Black adolescents and the construction of academic identity. Albany: SUNY.

Whimbey, Arthur. 1985. "Reading, writing, reasoning linked in testing and training." Journal of Reading 29(2):118–123.

Whimbey, Arthur, J.W. Carmichael, Lester Jones, Jacqueline Hunter et al. 1980. "Teaching Critical Reading and Analytical Reasoning in Project SOAR." Journal of Reading 24(1):5–10.

Whimbey, Arthur, and Jack Lochhead. 1979. Problem solving and comprehension: A short course in analytic reasoning. Philadelphia: Franklin Institute Press.

Whitehead, Alfred. 1929. The Aims of Education. The Free Press.

Wirt, John, Patrick Rooney, Susan Choy et al. 2004. The Condition of Education 2004, NCES 2004–077. Washington, DC: National Center for Education Statistics, Institute of Education Sciences.

Yin, Robert. 2003. Case study research: Design and methods. Thousand Oaks, CA: Sage.

Zimmerman, Barry. 2002. Becoming a self-regulated learner: An overview. Theory Into Practice 41(2).

Zimmerman, Barry, and Anastasia Kitsantas. 2005. "Students' perceived responsibility and completion of homework: The role of self-regulatory beliefs and processes." Contemporary Educational Psychology: 397-417.

Zimmerman, Marc. 2000. Empowerment theory: Psychological, organizational and community levels of analysis. In Handbook of community psychology, edited by J. Rappaport and Edward Seidman, 43–63. New York: Plenum.

Zumwalt, Karen. 1989. Beginning professional teachers: The need for a curricular vision of teaching. In Knowledge base for the beginning teacher, edited by M. Reynolds, 173–184. Oxford: Pergamon Press.

Index

About the Authors/Contributors

Beatrice L. Bridglall, a Fulbright Specialist in Higher Education with the Council of International Exhange of Scholars, currently teaches at Montclair State University in Montclair, New Jersey. She has taught, as assistant professor of education, at Queens College, City University of New York. She was research scientist in the Institute for Urban and Minority Education at Teachers College, Columbia University and adjunct assistant professor in the Department of Health and Behavioral Studies at Teachers College, Columbia University. Her research areas include higher, international and comparative education; student development, engagement and persistence in K–12 and higher education; school reform; and program research and evaluation. She has co-edited several books, including *Supplementary Education: The Hidden Curriculum of High Academic Achievement* (Rowman & Littlefield, 2005), which makes the conceptual argument that high academic achievement is closely associated with exposure to family and community-based activities and learning experiences that occur outside of school in support of academic learning. The second, *Affirmative Development: Cultivating Academic Ability* (Rowman & Littlefield, 2008), argues that academic abilities are not simply inherited aptitudes but rather can be developed through pedagogical and social interventions. A recent co-authored publication, "Assessing School Supports for ELL students using the ECLS-K" (*Early Childhood Research Quarterly 24*), examined the association between the school resources available to English language learners and their trajectories from kindergarten to fifth grade. Dr. Bridglall obtained her doctorate in education from Teachers College, Columbia University.

    Freeman A. Hrabowski III, has served as President of UMBC (University of Maryland, Baltimore County) since May, 1992. His research and publications focus on science and math education, with special emphasis on minority participation and performance. He chaired the National Academies' committee that produced the 2010 report, "Expanding Underrepresented Minority Participation: America's Science and Technology Talent at the Crossroads." In 2008, he was named one of *America's Best Leaders* by *U.S. News & World Report*, which in 2009 and 2010 ranked UMBC the nation's #1 "Up and Coming" university and among the top institutions in the nation for commitment to undergraduate teaching. In 2009, *Time* magazine named him one of America's *10 Best College Presidents*. He serves as a consultant to the National Science Foundation, National Institutes of Health, and universities and school systems nationally; sits on several foundation and corporate boards, e.g., Alfred P. Sloan Foundation, Marguerite Casey Foundation (Chair), The Urban Institute; and holds numerous honorary degrees, including Harvard, Princeton, Duke, Haverford College, the University of Michigan, Georgetown University, and Harvey Mudd College. Other recent honors include election to the American Academy of Arts & Sciences and the American Philosophical Society; receiving the *McGraw Prize in Education* and the U.S. *Presidential Award for Excellence in Science, Mathematics, and Engineering Mentoring*; being named a Fellow of the American Association for the Advancement of Science and *Marylander of the Year* by the editors of the *Baltimore Sun*; and being listed among *Fast Company* magazine's first *Fast 50 Champions of Innovation* in business and technology. With philanthropist Robert Meyerhoff, he co-founded the Meyerhoff Scholars Program in 1988. The program is open to all high-achieving students committed to pursuing advanced degrees and research careers in science and engineering, and advancing minorities in these fields. The program has become a national model, and based on program outcomes, Hrabowski has authored numerous articles and co-authored two books, *Beating the Odds* and *Overcoming the Odds* (Oxford University Press), on parenting and high-achieving African American males and females in science. A child-leader in the Civil Rights Movement, Hrabowski was prominently featured in Spike Lee's 1997 documentary, *Four Little Girls*, on the racially motivated bombing in 1963 of Birmingham, Alabama's Sixteenth Street Baptist Church. Born in 1950 in Birmingham, Hrabowski graduated at nineteen from Hampton Institute with highest honors in mathematics. At the University of Illinois at Urbana-Champaign, he received his MA (mathematics) and his PhD four years later (higher education administration/statistics) at age twenty-four.

Susan Layden is associate dean of student affairs at Skidmore College. Dr. Layden has spearheaded the Opportunity Programs at Skidmore College. In this capacity, she is interested in enabling the development of academic identities for first-year under-represented students and related pedagogy designed to enhance their success. She has examined the various components of the Opportunity Program in a paper with colleagues: *Bridging the gap between achievement and excellence: The Skidmore College Summer Academic*

Institute and the Skidmore College Opportunity Programs. Her doctoral dissertation examined the identities of first-year poor, working-class and minority students' literate identities during the transition to college.

She is also in the midst of writing a paper with a colleague entitled: *Teachers' assessments of their students' literacy development in a high-stakes setting.*

Kenneth Maton is professor of psychology and director of the Community and Applied Social Psychology PhD Program in Human Services Psychology at University of Maryland Baltimore County (UMBC). He received his PhD degree in Clinical-Community Psychology from the University of Illinois, Champaign-Urbana. His research focuses on minority youth achievement, and includes the longitudinal evaluation of UMBC's Meyerhoff Scholarship Program. Books include: *Empowering Settings and Voices for Social Change (edited volume; Oxford University Press); Investing in Children, Youth, Families and Communities: Strengths-Based Research and Policy* (edited volume; American Psychological Association) and *Beating the Odds: Raising Academically Successful African American Males* (co-author; Oxford University Press). Dr. Maton is past-president of the Society for Community Research and Action (SCRA; APA Division 27), and the 2006 winner of SCRA's Distinguished Contribution to Theory and Research Award. He serves on the editorial boards of *American Journal of Community Psychology* and *Journal of Community Psychology.*

Sheldon Solomon is professor of psychology at Skidmore College. As an experimental social psychologist, his interests include the nature of self, consciousness, and social behavior. His work exploring the effects of the uniquely human awareness of death on individual and social behavior has been supported by the National Science Foundation and Ernest Becker Foundation and was featured in the award winning documentary film *Flight from Death: The Quest for Immortality*; he is co-author *In the Wake of 9/11: The Psychology of Terror* (2003, American Psychological Association Books) and co-founder of *The World Leaders Project.* Dr. Solomon is a Fellow in the American Psychological Society and the Society for Experimental Social Psychology, a 2007 recipient of an American Psychological Association Presidential Citation, and 2009 recipient of a Lifetime Career Award by The International Society for Self and Identity.